HARVEY MILK

Harvey Milk

His Lives and Death

LILLIAN FADERMAN

Yale

UNIVERSITY

PRESS

New Haven and London

To Phyllis—again and always

CONTENTS

CONTENTS

HARVEY MILK

Introduction

HARVEY MILK—charismatic, eloquent, a wit and a smart aleck—was one of the first openly gay men to be elected to any political office anywhere. On November 18, 1977, soon after he won a seat on the San Francisco Board of Supervisors, he made three tape recordings that he distributed to close friends. "To be played only in the event of my death by assassination," he instructed at the beginning of each tape, though he did not keep it a secret from associates that he had made the tapes. When his irreverent young City Hall intern, Cleve Jones, learned of them, he teased Harvey: "Hey, you're not Martin Luther King. You're not important enough."[1]

Harvey was shot to death one year and nine days later by Dan White, a fellow supervisor who had complained that San Francisco was being turned into Sodom by men who would not hide their homosexuality, and that Harvey Milk was in the forefront of the city's abhorrent transformation. The words Harvey

dictated into his tape recorder in 1977 would have sounded fool-
ishly melodramatic had he died a natural death; but with his
murder they took on the weight of prophecy. "If a bullet should
enter my brain," he had said on the tape he made for his friend
Frank Robinson, "let that bullet destroy every closet door."

During Harvey's lifetime (1930–78) most straight Americans could still entertain the fiction that they personally knew
no one who was gay. He prodded his gay audiences to "come
out"—to parents, friends, neighbors, fellow workers, even to
"the people who work where you eat and shop."[2] Coming out,
he exhorted in his dynamic speeches, would be the most effective way to break down the toxic lies about homosexuals that
characterized them as criminals, crazies, sinners, and subver-
sives. As he understood, once gay people came out in great
numbers they could no longer be seen as grotesque strangers
skulking in the shadows and ready to pounce on innocent children; they would be sons, daughters, brothers, sisters, neighbors, and friends who, most Americans would have to agree,
deserved first-class citizenship.

Harvey Milk's martyrdom and the outpouring of gay anger
and sorrow that followed helped trigger what has become a
steady exodus from closets everywhere. These days a majority
of Americans—75 percent—say they have relatives or friends
who are gay or lesbian.[3] As Harvey prophesied, the demolition
of closet doors has been the single most important factor in
changing America's hearts and minds and laws about gay people.

Harvey Milk has been dead for four decades; but his story
continues to capture the popular imagination. He has been
honored far beyond any other single gay figure. Tributes that
would have been inconceivable during his lifetime, because
they do not hide that he was a homosexual, have been heaped
upon him. In 1999 *Time* magazine published a list of "the 100
Most Influential Individuals of the 20th Century." Harvey Milk,
the only openly gay person on the list, was included in a section

called "Heroes and Icons," along with Anne Frank, Che Guevara, Charles Lindbergh, the Kennedys, and Mother Teresa. The 1984 documentary *The Times of Harvey Milk* and the 2008 movie *Milk*, which was based on his life, won Academy Awards. In 2009 President Obama awarded him a posthumous Medal of Freedom. That same year an annual Harvey Milk Day was proclaimed by the governor of California. In 2014 the U.S. Postal Service issued a stamp with his image. In 2016 the secretary of the navy announced that a combat logistics ship would be named after Harvey, who had served in the navy, and that "his example will live on in the steel of that ship and in all those who will serve aboard her."[4] People who know of no other gay historical figure know of Harvey Milk. He has gone from being a gay martyr to an American icon.

* * *

Harvey Milk was a complex man. There were seemingly many Harveys as he drifted for years through various stages, fumbling to find the niche from which he could fulfill the high, vague aspirations of his childhood. There was Harvey the supermacho college jock and navy deep-sea diver. Harvey the high school math teacher and earnest mentor to young people. Harvey the buttoned-down Wall Street securities research analyst and cheerleader for the protolibertarian presidential candidate and darling of the right wing Barry Goldwater. Harvey the longhaired, bead-wearing hippie. Harvey the actor, associate producer, and gofer to a Broadway celebrity. Harvey the businessman and leader of a business community. Harvey the progressive politician and gay icon. Each earlier "life" represented some genuine (if contradictory) aspect of Harvey Milk—and in each transformation he thought for a while that he had found himself. But it was only in his final life, as an openly gay politician, that he discovered who he had wanted to be all along. In the five years he had left to live, as he grew into becoming that person, he made a coherent whole out of the many parts of himself.

3

Harvey is a study in opposites too. He was a cutup and a clown, but he was dead serious in battling the enemies of his causes. He was driven by genuine passion for justice but also by a lifelong love of the limelight. He fought fervently for "the oppressed" as a group, but he could be outrageously insensitive to individuals. He was a joyful participant in a wildly sexual gay culture, but he was capable of extraordinary emotional faithfulness, and he longed to make a permanent home with a partner. He was a chameleon who could change his style in an eye blink, but in his deepest principles he was steadfast.

* * *

In his Jewish identity also he was complex. He claimed he was "not theologically oriented," but in one of his taped wills he clearly avowed his belief in God.[5] He sometimes called himself an atheist, but even more often he called himself a New York Jew. When he moved to Dallas, Texas, in the 1950s he worried because he was advised by a well-meaning businessman that if he hoped to find a job he had better change his name "to something like Miller or go to work for a Jewish firm."[6] But he never kept it a secret that Mausche Milch, his immigrant grandfather, had been a Yiddish-speaking peddler from Lithuania; or that Mausche had founded Sons of Israel, the first synagogue in Woodmere, Long Island, the town where Harvey was born.

Like many American Jews, Harvey did not see his strong Jewish identity as having anything to do with being religiously observant.[7] It was the Jewish culture he had been steeped in from childhood and the destruction of European Jewry he had heard about all through his adolescence that kept an unshakable grip on him as an adult. When in the company of his Jewish friends, Harvey relished talk of *Yiddishkayt* or of the joys of pastrami on rye and chopped liver with coleslaw. Using his mother's recipes, he cooked matzo brei and matzo meal pancakes for his gentile lovers' breakfasts. He told Jewish jokes, inflecting them with his grandfather's accent. He peppered his conversations with the Yiddish phrases he had heard all his growing-up years on Long Island. He even hung his bar mitzvah picture on the wall of his camera store in San Francisco's gay Castro District, not to confirm that he had been pledged to the faith but as a memento of his boyhood in a 1940s Jewish community.[8]

Yet his Jewish identification went much deeper than sentimentality. To exhort gays to be vigilant and battle-ready, he kept returning to cautionary stories of the Jews and the Nazis. The Holocaust became a major metaphor in the speeches he gave and the editorials he wrote. As a Jew and a homosexual, he felt himself to be doubly an outsider; and even when he was invited inside through his election to political office, he clung to his sympathies for the outsider, which he extended far beyond his own tribe. "Jews know they can't allow other groups to suffer discrimination," he wryly observed, "if for no other reason than we might be on that list someday."[9]

He was very aware of himself as part of an ultraliberal Jewish tradition that fought for the oppressed of all stripes. His oratorical style, fiery and blunt in his demands for social justice, recalled the soapbox speakers of Delancey Street in the early decades of the twentieth century. He championed workers, women, racial minorities, the disabled, senior citizens—all who suffered at the hands of the fat-cat insiders. He fought hard for San Francisco's strong gay rights ordinance; and he fought equally hard for rent control and the city's divestment from apartheid South Africa. Harvey Milk's politics were strongly influenced by his gay identity. But just as deep an influence was his Jewish identity, and especially the values that liberal Judaism holds dear.

1

The Milchs

HARVEY'S GRANDFATHER Mausche Milch was the Milk family patriarch in America. Born in 1864 in Joniskis, a Lithuanian shtetl near the Latvian border, Mausche eked out a living as a dairy farmer. In 1889 he married Hinde Ruchel Miller, who bore him four children in quick succession and in 1896 became pregnant again. The baby, who would become the father of Harvey Milk, was born in February 1897. Mausche, as poor as Sholem Aleichem's Tevye the Dairyman, had seven mouths to feed. But no shtetl dweller of the time could be ignorant of the fabulous stories of impoverished fellow Jews who had gone off to America and made fortunes. Mausche decided to join the great migration.[1]

An older stepbrother, Manuel Hurwitz, a merchant in Kansas City, agreed to be his sponsor and bring him to Kansas, but Hinde and the children had to be left behind in the shtetl until Mausche could earn enough money to send for them. Jews had tried to farm on the Great Plains before. A few years earlier Jewish philanthropists had even established seven agricultural colonies in Kansas so that Russian Jewish immigrants could earn their livelihood on the land instead of flocking to crowded cities where they were exploited in sweatshops. But by the time Mausche arrived, in July 1897, every one of the experimental Jewish colonies had failed. To purchase good dairy-farming land by himself would have been impossible. He moved in with his stepbrother, the stepbrother's Missouri-born wife, and their two young children and worked for him as a dry goods salesman.

Mausche, tall and handsome, with striking light eyes and an upright bearing, quickly shed his dairyman look, changed his first name to Morris, and learned English. He was ambitious, but his stepbrother paid him so little that after three years he was no closer to being able to send for Hinde and his five children than he had been when he arrived. And he hated Kansas City and was nauseated by the stench emanating from the stockyards and slaughterhouses. He decided to try his luck in New York City.

By then there were almost a half million Jews in the city, most of them squeezed into the Lower East Side, and their numbers were escalating with the arrival of every boat from Europe. But Morris escaped the hordes when an aunt living in the village of Lynbrook on Long Island agreed that he could stay with her until he got a job. With a peddler's pack over his shoulder, he boarded a train to Long Island's less-teeming shores.

Eventually he found a place to live in Woodmere, a little fishing village about twenty miles from Manhattan, and he peddled his wares to fishermen and potato farmers all over the neighboring towns and their outskirts. He was the only Jew in sight and decided to anglicize his last name to Milk. By 1903 he made enough money to open a store, Milk's Dry Goods.[2] He had been sending some of his earnings back to his understandably impatient wife and five children in Joniskis, though it had been six years since he last saw them. That summer he finally brought them to America.

When Mausche Milch left Joniskis, his oldest child, a daughter, Itka (Edith), was seven. The youngest was six months old. It must have been as hard for Morris to adjust to living with a wife and brood again as it was for them to adjust to having a husband and father around. Hieke, the baby of the family—who would be called William in America—was six years old when he and his mother and siblings got through immigration procedures at Ellis Island and finally saw Morris, a tall American stranger, waiting for them. William had no memories of a time when he'd had to share his mother's attention with her husband. For him it was a shock to suddenly have a father in his life. His misery was exacerbated when his mother's belly soon grew big. In 1904, a year after they arrived in America, William was cast out of the role of the baby of the family, replaced by Albert, a squalling new brother who would be called Babe even into adulthood.

William became the most rebellious and headstrong of the children, trying Morris's temper and often getting himself spanked. In 1913 his mother died at the age of forty-eight. William was sixteen. He had lost her first when he was six, then again when he was seven, and now forever to death. Life with his father got even grimmer for him. He was put to work in Morris's store alongside his older siblings, and he was not happy about it. His relationship with Morris was often explosive. When Morris could not control him there were skirmishes between them.[3]

They were polar opposites. As Morris became a successful businessman he began to value gentility and elegance in demeanor and dress. The more refined and dandified he was, the more his son Bill (as he now wanted to be called) strove to look like a prizefighter. In 1916 Bill, nineteen years old, quit the store and did the most virile, outlandish, non-Jewish thing he could imagine. He went to Texas to be a cowboy.

Morris remarried in 1918. Fannie Assenburg, twelve years younger than Morris, was beloved by his older children, who understood that Babe had been motherless since he was nine and needed a mother. But Bill, supplanted as the youngest in the family by the perennial "Babe," was enraged all over again that now his mother was supplanted by Fannie. He would not go back to Woodmere. He enlisted in the navy and went off to fight in the Great War. He became a chronically angry person, even after his own sons, Robert and Harvey, were born.[4]

* * *

Morris's family life may have been difficult, but his business life was a triumph of the American Dream. He seemed to know instinctively how to promote and advertise his wares. Milk's Dry Goods soon morphed into Milk's Department Store, which he located on Broadway, Woodmere's busiest street. Though modest by the standards of Macy's or Gimbels, it was the first store on Long Island where you could get overalls, cashmere sweaters, toys, and dress patterns all in one place. Milk's Department Store became one of the most flourishing retail establishments in town.

Eventually Morris Milk also invested in Long Island real estate, did very well, and became a prominent philanthropist in Long Island's expanding Jewish community.[5] Mausche Milch the dairy farmer and peddler long gone, Morris cultivated the look of a gentleman. His thick shock of hair turned silvery white prematurely, as did his well-trimmed mustache and goatee. He wore dapper three-piece suits and carried a walking stick, and his bearing remained erect even into old age. Had he gone back to visit Joniskis, he might easily have been taken for a nobleman. His grandson Harvey would inherit not only his determination to do well and do good but also his volatile nature and theatrical flare.

* * *

At the end of the Great War, Bill showed up again in Woodmere, now sporting a tattoo he had gotten as a sailor. That was
not what Jews did in the early decades of the twentieth century,
and it was as upsetting to his father as a slap in the face. But as
difficult as the relationship with Bill was, Morris was concerned
about his son. Bill was clearly at loose ends. With only a sixth-
grade education and having no career training of any kind, what
would he do with the rest of his life? Morris put him to work
again in Milk's Department Store, where he would remain for
the next quarter century, a gruff, stern, taciturn man with a frequent scowl on his face and a big cigar clamped always between
his teeth; a man who wore loud ties and prized virility.

Despite his discontent, Bill mostly toed the line. His one
further rebellion, when he was twenty-eight years old, was to
marry Minerva Karns—"Minnie," a dark-eyed and zaftig Brooklyn girl with a quirky sense of humor. Everyone agreed she was
a real character. (Harvey later described his mother as a hippie and "the real freak of the family.")[6] She had been an early
and ardent feminist. When the Yeomanettes, the first women's
branch of the navy, was formed during the Great War, Minnie
was one of the first to enlist. She remained in the services until
the Yeomanettes was disbanded, a couple of years after the war.[7]
She then found a job as a stenographer but was almost fired because at a time when most females still wore their hair long, she
bobbed hers.

In another era Minnie would surely have been a career
woman; but in hers, the choices for women—even offbeat, rebellious ones—were limited. She did wait until she was twenty-
five to get married, in a decade when women were typically
married before they were twenty-one. But once married she
quit her job and became a Woodmere housewife. Her first son,
Robert, was born in 1926. Four years later, on May 22, 1930, her
second son, Harvey Bernard Milk, was born.

Though Minnie kept a kosher house, as did most of the wives who were Sons of Israel congregants, she was not ortho-dox. She was, however, devoted to good causes and was a busy practitioner of *tikkun olam*, the Jewish obligation to help repair the world. A big woman who put on weight over the years, she would die of a heart attack in 1962 after carrying a twenty-four-pound turkey to a Lower East Side settlement house for a Thanksgiving dinner for the poor.[8] Her passion for social justice would be her eventual legacy to Harvey.

Harvey the child was stubborn, determined, and angered by injustice, especially when Bill would ignore him one minute and explode the next (as Morris had done with Bill). Minnie shielded her sons from her husband's temper by jollying them and mollifying him. But it left an indelible mark on Harvey, who as an adult—up until his last days—kept re-creating the father-son relationship in his intimate life, trying to make it right. The thorny relationship he had with Bill, who seemed never to approve of his younger son, also explains perhaps why Harvey had such difficulty figuring out who he was and wanted to become.

When Harvey was eight and nine years old he spent the pennies of his weekly allowance on Saturday movie matinees. He admitted to his brother, Robert, that what excited him about the Woodmere Theater was not the Hopalong Cassidy or Three Stooges movies that were shown there but the raffles the the-ater manager held before the movies started. That was because if he had a winning ticket he got to run up on stage and ham it up, bowing extravagantly to audience applause before he col-lected his prize of a Buck Rogers toy pistol or a Hopalong wrist-watch. If a camera was focused on Harvey, he was enchanted. In 1941, at a *pidyon haben* celebration for a firstborn male cousin, the eleven-year-old Harvey can be seen on a remarkable home video posed on a staircase, one hand raised to caress his hair, diva style, utterly luxuriating in the momentary attention.[9]

Years later, when Harvey announced to the family that he was running for public office, his brother was not surprised. Robert had known nothing about Harvey's passion for politics, but he remembered the kid who had lusted for the spotlight: "That's Harvey being Harvey again," Robert thought.[10]

Morris had been the only Jew in Woodmere when he settled there around 1900. But Jews who were advancing out of the sweatshop and pushcart trades soon began leaving the Lower East Side for more refined places to live. The Jewish population of Woodmere and neighboring Long Island towns burgeoned. Like the socially ambitious all over America, some transplants hoped to become members of a "country club," which since the 1880s had been a mark of having arrived. There was such a club near Woodmere, the Rockaway Hunt Club. It featured fox hunting, polo, steeplechase riding, and, like many country clubs of the era, a no-Jews-allowed policy. Morris, by now a prominent Jewish leader, helped establish the Woodmere Country Club, where Jews could play golf and tennis and make business connections in an atmosphere free of anti-Semitism.

But the restricted policy of the Rockaway Hunt Club was the genteel tip of anti-Semitism on Long Island. In Gibson, a town just two miles away from Woodmere, there was a very visible Ku Klux Klan chapter. Crosses blazed in the night at Klan rallies outside many Long Island villages. In 1923, on a rolling meadow in East Islip, about thirty miles from Woodmere, twenty-five thousand white-robed Klansmen, Klanswomen, and their children, too, listened raptly as their leaders harangued them, saying that Jews and foreigners were "the greatest threat to the American way of life."[11] That same year the *New York Times* reported that in the town of Bay Shore (where Harvey Milk eventually went to high school) a parade of hooded Klansmen stretched for an entire mile.[12] In 1924 the Klan attracted thirty thousand spectators when it marched through the village of Freeport, only eight miles from Wood-

mere. The Freeport chief of police was at the head of the procession.[13]

In that hostile atmosphere the Jews of the area drew closer
together. In 1922 a synagogue was built in Cedarhurst, a couple
of miles from Woodmere. Morris, who, together with Fannie,
his second wife, had become a very observant Jew, would not
ride in any sort of conveyance on the Sabbath; so to attend services he had to walk four miles round trip, often in rain and
snow. In 1928 he helped form a Woodmere minyan, which
founded Congregation Sons of Israel. Morris became its first
vice president. Fifteen years later the thirteen-year-old Harvey
Milk became a bar mitzvah there.

In the 1930s new pockets of anti-Semitism opened up on
Long Island, and American Nazi strongholds flourished there.
In the local newspapers the Milks would have learned of Camp
Siegfried, which had been established in Yaphank by a Nazi
front organization, the German-American Bund. On weekends in 1937 and 1938 trains from Penn Station carried flocks of
Bund members to Yaphank, and shuttle buses deposited them
in front of Camp Siegfried's clubhouse, next to the flagpole
that displayed a gigantic Nazi flag. Men in Nazi uniforms and
women in dirndls sieg-heiled as they listened to fevered tirades
about Jewish treachery.[14] Harvey was seven or eight, old enough
to understand when his parents worried aloud about what was
going on right there on Long Island. He must have understood,
too, when his parents talked about the refusal of the Woodmere
school board to hire a music teacher because she was Jewish.
Bill, who had not before been very political, even joined other
Woodmere Jews to force the board to reconsider.[15]

By the time of the war Harvey could not have failed to understand the danger that Jews across the ocean were in and the
magnitude of the hatred against people like him. The Milks
and all their Jewish Long Island neighbors were glued to their
radios for reports about those trapped in Hitler's Europe. On

May 16, 1943, only days before Harvey's bar mitzvah, he heard that the Jews of the Warsaw ghetto, after fighting for months, had been surrounded by Nazi troops intent on their annihilation. The Jews fought to the end, the adults in his family said, not because they believed they could win but because "when something that evil descends on the world, you have to fight, even when it's hopeless."[16] Harvey remembered his whole life that moment when he learned of the tragedy in Warsaw. Because anti-Semitism was rampant on Long Island, to the thirteen-year-old it seemed that the horrors of the Warsaw ghetto were not so far away, that it could happen in Woodmere. He imagined himself as a resistance fighter, battling to the death though besieged. That too marked him. When he became a politician, the trope he used over and over again in his speeches—to warn gay people about what could happen if they did not defeat their enemies—was the Holocaust.

* * *

Harvey was steeped in Jewishness as a child. His grandfather Morris was a pillar of Sons of Israel, the synagogue he had helped found. In his old age Morris was honored in a proclamation declaring that "his appearance on the *bimah* has graced our worship every Sabbath" and thanking him for guiding the congregants "to maintain our tradition."[17] Harvey loved his grandfather—who may not have been loving to all his children but doted on his grandchildren—and he wanted to please him. Harvey's father and uncles, who worked for Morris, strove to please him too, all of them keeping kosher homes, observing religious rituals, and maintaining their membership in Congregation Sons of Israel without fail. So there was no question that Harvey would go to cheder and be a bar mitzvah.

But his heart was not in it. He later claimed that he rejected religion because when he was twelve years old he "found out that religion was phony or hypocritical."[18] He was turned off to religion not only because he suspected that if he were truly known he would be an outcast to the Sons of Israel but also because he never took well to authoritarian types. It could not have been easy for the adolescent Harvey to abide Congregation Sons of Israel's rigid rabbi. "Please do not talk flippantly of sacred Jewish traditions in the hearing of your child," he scolded parents. "Have decent regard for the Sabbath and other holy days and a sense of responsibility for the Synagogue and its services," he lectured them in the synagogue's newsletter. "You must know more than your child does. Do you? Jewish magazines, Jewish books, are on the bookshelves of the library. Exert yourselves."[19]

Such patronizing orders from the rabbi were abhorrent to Harvey, who had been ordered around and disciplined by Bill and who would always relish the vision of himself as a warrior against authority, a rebel. When he sought a moral compass, he believed he found it in his grandfather, whom he saw not as a disciplinarian but as philanthropic, community-minded, even broadminded. "Don't hide your green hair," Harvey liked to remember Morris saying; "people will see it anyway."[20]

Though Harvey rejected Judaism, he made it a point throughout his life to proclaim his Jewishness, even during the 1940s when anti-Semitism was rampant. He called himself not Jewish but a Jew, a much more in-your-face appellation. Being a Jew was as central to his sense of who he was as being a gay. The intersections of his identities as a Jew and a gay reinforced his awareness of the injustices suffered by all who were other.

For many years, he believed he must not talk about being gay to nongays—but he always talked about being a Jew, to anyone and everyone. Even as a young man he announced that he was a Jew lightly, often humorously, and in every situation possible. To his classmates at Bay Shore High School he let it be known that his real family name was not the anglicized Milk but its Yiddish meaning, Milch. When he came back to Long Island during winter break from college in Albany, he visited a high school friend, Artie Schiller, who was Catholic. The Schillers were hanging outdoor Christmas lights, and Harvey volunteered to help. But lest anyone forget who he was, he fashioned the section of lights he had been given into a twinkling Star of David.[21]

2

Deep, Dark Secrets

HARVEY WAS ELEVEN years old when he discovered that Metropolitan Opera performances could be heard on the radio. He began spending Saturday afternoons sprawled in an armchair beside the big Philco in the living room, listening. He was totally ignorant of the French, Italian, and German in which the operas were usually sung, but he was enthralled by the grandeur and high drama that could be communicated by the human voice. Finally, when he was fourteen he convinced his mother he was old enough to take the train into the city on Saturday afternoons to see the opera live. Minnie, pleased at her younger boy's cultural precociousness, always gave him the money to buy a standing-room ticket at the Met; but she was a little concerned about him wandering around New York all by himself. She cautioned that there were homosexuals who liked to prey on young boys. Harvey must have been horrified. She had touched on his biggest secret.

His exuberance for what was on stage at the Metropolitan Opera House was genuine. (Years later he would describe his ecstasy in listening to a recording of *Der Rosenkavalier*, which, he said, transported him "like an amyl nitrate high.") But his enchantment with what was going on around him in the standing-room section was just as potent. He had made the discovery by sheer chance: among the opera enthusiasts who were packed four deep in the corridor along the back of the darkened auditorium were many gay men—opera queens, they called themselves in campy self-mockery. They sometimes turned their attention from the stage to one another. They cruised, and, if the object of their gaze responded, they sometimes groped. Harvey was quick to see what was happening and knew right away that he wanted to be part of it. He had his first sexual experiences in the standing-room section of the Met.[1]

Harvey always maintained about those early sexual contacts that he had not been molested, because they were exactly what he had been anxiously looking and hoping for. He had had homosexual feelings ever since he could remember, long before he found his way to the Met. Based on what he knew of his own history, Harvey was certain that nobody chose to be homosexual: he or she was born that way.

Years later, when he became a gay rights activist, his insight into himself made him vehement in attacking antigay Christian fundamentalists like the pop singer Anita Bryant, who led a national charge to repeal all gay rights ordinances by arguing that homosexuals were bent on seducing kids and convincing them to follow a homosexual lifestyle. "Imagine a young girl or boy brought up by heterosexual parents in a fiercely heterosexual society [which] considers homosexuals the lowest form of life, suitable fodder for queer-baiting, rape, murder," Harvey declared angrily in 1978. "Now try to imagine this impressionable adolescent, who wants nothing more than to be part of his or her own peer group, somehow deciding [after being seduced] that homosexuality is the best of all possible worlds." It was Bryant who was perverse, Harvey said, when she railed that homosexuality was not inborn but a choice made only after being introduced to homosexual practices.[2]

His anger in that 1978 speech hints at recollections of his own agony as a boy when he realized that he was very different from his brother and the other kids he knew. The fourteen-year-old Harvey already understood that to everyone—even his offbeat mother—homosexuals were criminals, loonies, and a danger to society; and that he had better keep his secret hidden away in a deep, dark closet. Though he continued to live with his family until he went off to college, after he became sexually active he felt that his parents' house "was never 'home' again to me," because there he had to pretend to be someone he was not.[3] He was sure that if his mother and father discovered who he really was, the knowledge would kill them—or, at the least, they would stop loving him. He had to protect them and himself.

His self-imposed secrecy took a toll. He had had experiences that were marvelous revelations to him; but if those he loved knew about them, they would be horrified. He was perplexed and distraught. He needed to find someone to trust, a sounding board who could tell him if he was wrong to feel that what he had done was right for him.

Surprisingly, he chose a rabbi. What Harvey actually said to the man will never be known; but what the rabbi said to him, or what he heard in what the rabbi said, he cherished his entire life: "You shouldn't be concerned about how you live your life, as long as you feel you're living it right" were the rabbi's words as Harvey recalled them. "People spend more time legislating about morality and telling others how to spend their lives than about how to make life more enjoyable. Most legislators think they're godlike. That's wrong. But," the rabbi said—empowering the teenager with the sort of Jewish values he could find meaningful—"you should have *rachmones* for [such benighted people], have sorrow and pity and love and compassion." Years later, when Harvey told the story, he declared that that very enlightened rabbi "almost brought me back into religion, but," he added, "I found out he was a rare bird."[4]

In any case, the rabbi's wondrous tolerance about homosexuality did not make Harvey rush to tell his parents his secret. Minnie died in 1962, when Harvey was thirty-two years old; he had never had a conversation with her about his homosexuality. Bill lived until 1976. By then Harvey had run for political office three times, and newspapers were often referring to him as "the homosexual politician." But he knew he would not be outed to his father through the newspapers. Bill's eyesight had failed years before, and he was not reading anymore.[5]

* * *

In 1944 Milk's Department Store burned almost to the ground. Arson was suspected. The store was rebuilt, but Bill Milk decided that after twenty-five not very happy years it was time to make a break from the business his father had started. Most of his working life had been in retail, so he decided he would go into the fur business, which was largely a Jewish industry in New York. The next year Bill moved his family to Bay Shore, about twenty-five miles from Woodmere, and with money from the fire insurance, he opened Bay Shore Furriers. Harvey, who was fifteen years old, enrolled at Bay Shore High School.

Harvey's best friends in high school were Roman Catholic. In fact, there were few Jews in Bay Shore in 1945, and there were still traces of anti-Semitism in town, left over from the days when the Klan had a chapter there. The in-crowd at the high school excluded Jews, and Harvey's stereotypical Jewishness was obvious to them, as one girl of the in-crowd observed of him: "He ha[s] the largest nose of anybody I've ever seen in my life."[6] But Harvey was as upfront about being Jewish in that uncomfortable atmosphere as he would always be. When he declared to his classmates that his real name was Milch, they nicknamed him Glimpy Milch after the character Glimpy Mc-Clusky in the *East Side Kids* movies that were hugely popular in the early 1940s. What Harvey shared with Glimpy, played by the actor Huntz Hall, was a substantial nose, soulful eyes, and a tough-sounding New York accent.

Harvey cultivated a tough image. It was a good disguise. In secret he could be an opera queen; but for the world he would be a man's man, as much as he could. He played varsity football and basketball in high school. He ran track. He wrestled for the school team. His hypermasculine enthusiasm for sports was surely a way of placating Bill, who would not have been tolerant of effeminacy in his son. But Harvey also felt compelled to "butch it up" because he saw what his fate could be at Bay Shore High School if he did not. One of his classmates, the local paint store owner's effeminate son, who was miserably inept at passing a basketball, had been teased and bullied until he broke down in tears.[7] Harvey resolved that this would never happen to him.

To further prove his manly bona fides and heterosexual appeal he dated girls. He was slim and muscled, with dark brown hair and an engaging smile. Some of the prettiest girls, who were not in the in-crowd and were not prejudiced against Semitic features, found him good-looking.[8] To confirm his interest in heterosexual activities, he even got himself on to the junior prom committee. He kept mum about his passion for opera, of course. And for good measure he cultivated a persona as the class clown, always ready with a wisecrack—lest anyone think he was not talkative because he had something to hide.

His parents' new home was on the direct road to the ferries that went to Fire Island, a premier gay haunt. During the warm months there was a nonstop procession of gay men rushing to catch a ferry or returning home from the sorts of good times for which Harvey yearned. To observe them was both scary and thrilling. He went on double dates with his brother, Robert, to make sure his family did not suspect his fantasies.[9]

In June 1947 Harvey graduated from Bay Shore High School. He had not been a stellar student and was not sure what he wanted to do next. But his parents let him know that drifting was not an option. Though neither Bill nor Minnie had gone to college, they urged him to apply to New York State College for Teachers at Albany. He could be a teacher. That was a good, steady profession. There was a lot to recommend the place too: Georgian-style red-brick buildings with classical white columns and verdant lawns that made it look like an expensive private liberal arts college; a student population of only fifteen hundred, which promised small classes and personal attention from professors. And best of all, since Bay Shore Furriers was only two years old and still getting a foothold, tuition was totally free.[10]

Harvey was determined to have fun that last summer before he had to knuckle down and prepare for the rest of his life. Having fun meant going to the city as often as possible and cruising in the gay area he had discovered in Central Park. One broiling day in August he took his shirt off in the park—because of the heat but also to show off his muscled torso. Vice squad officers spotted him, ordered him into a paddy wagon with the other gay men they had collected in the cruising area, and deposited them all at the police station. Years later, when Harvey became political, he would wage energetic campaigns against such harassment of gay men, whose alleged crimes were victimless. But now he only swore when questioned that he was just trying to get a suntan, that he was a high school kid who was completely innocent. Though he was released without being booked, he was shaken. How calamitous it would have been had the police notified his parents that their seventeen-year-old son had been arrested in Central Park while trying to pick up homosexuals.

* * *

In September, Harvey headed for Albany and the start of his new life outside his parents' house. His first disappointment at the New York State College for Teachers was the discovery that the student body was mostly female. The college had been a two-year normal school when it was created in 1844. About the time of the Civil War, women students, who had few choices other than teaching if they wanted a profession, began to out-number the men. At the end of the century it became a four-year institution, and more male students enrolled as the public school population grew and teaching jobs grew too. By the 1930s men made up one-third of the student body. But that came to an abrupt end with World War II, when all able-bodied college-age men were drafted. In 1944 and 1945 only one-twelfth of the students at the New York State College for Teachers were male. The fraternities had to close down. When Harvey ar-rived on campus, only two years after the end of the war, there were almost no men in the junior and senior classes. The inter-collegiate athletics program was nil. A woman was the student body president. A woman was the head of Myskania, the pres-tigious senior student council. A woman was even the head of the college newspaper. The seventeen-year-old Harvey, enam-ored of masculinity and totally lacking the feminist principles he developed later, was not happy.

He struggled to find his footing: hard for most college fresh-men but excruciating for those who were homosexual in such hostile times. He knew very well, as did all homosexual students in those days, that if he wanted to survive in college it was im-perative for him to keep that essential part of himself hidden. But at least he could look for a friendly home where another big part of who he was would be welcome. He applied to and was accepted by Kappa Beta, a Jewish fraternity that had been established at New York State College for Teachers in 1936, when Jews were routinely excluded from other fraternities.

The fifteen students who started Kappa Beta had declared that their purpose was to live in a house where they could "keep kosher and maintain their Jewish identity." They called themselves Kappa Beta because it was an inversion in Greek letters of what they considered their real name, B'nai Chaim, which they loosely translated as Brothers for Life.[11] Kappa Beta had to close down in 1942, when all the brothers went off to war; but in 1946 it started up again. By then, keeping kosher was not high on the list of priorities for the new Jewish students, and Kappa Beta refocused itself as a nonsectarian fraternity with a Jewish history. When the brothers invited a rabbi to address them, it was not for religious purposes but to speak on subjects such as "A Bird's-Eye View of Jewish Philosophy and Ethics."[12] That was a comfortable enough fit for Harvey.

With his Kappa Beta brothers he also attended the campus Hillel. Away from home for the first time, he must have found comfort in Hillel events: Shabbat dinners, Chanukah parties, Passover seders.[13] He also went to meetings of the newly formed Intercollegiate Zionist Federation of America—which surely pleased his parents, who, like most American Jews in the 1940s, were Zionists and prayed for Israel's statehood. The Intercollegiate Zionist Federation on campus held "Palestinian" folk dance evenings and showed wrenching films like *Home Are the Hunted*, about survivors of the Holocaust who found a safe harbor in the land of "Palestine" that would become "Israel."[14] Those were things Harvey could share with Bill and Minnie in his letters home, to make up for what he felt he could not share.

* * *

He tried hard to get his fellow students to see him as he wanted to be seen, to make a name for himself, to grab a bit of limelight at the college. His ambitions were often frustrated. In his freshman year he ran for class president, but he came in fourth in a field of five.[15] He ran for Athletic Association treasurer and lost again. But he would not be daunted. If he could not win an election, he would do other things that announced that Harvey Milk was on campus. He cultivated his high school Glimpy role, a cutup with a tough-guy accent. He played intramural football, soccer, volleyball, and basketball. He competed in wrestling and track. He polished his image as a man's man. In those days when male students wore sharply creased slacks, high-polished loafers, and button-down shirts under V-neck sweaters, Harvey's usual outfit to class, a gray sweat suit and sneakers, heralded him as a serious jock.[16] In his sophomore year he began writing a sports column for *State College News*, which he would continue almost until graduation. He ran for president of the Athletic Association as a junior, but yet again he lost.

He also put his name up for the prestigious Myskania—the organization for seniors who were deemed the "intellectual, moral, and civic leaders" of the campus. His hopes were high after a columnist for the college paper predicted he would be among the elected that year.[17] In his candidate's statement for Myskania he put forth all the qualifications he had accumulated over the previous three years: columnist for the *State College News*, member of the college's Constitutional Committee, assistant director of Frosh Camp as a junior, member of the publicity committee for the junior prom, manager of intramural football. Maybe hoping to get the Jewish vote—or maybe just being as upfront as he always was about being a Jew—he even included among his qualifications that he was a member of Hillel.[18]

Students elected to Myskania were informed of their good fortune by a long-standing tradition called the tapping ceremony. The ceremony was held during a student body assembly at which all the students were decked out in academic gowns. As the audience grew hushed in suspense, a pair of outgoing officers of Myskania circled the auditorium, halted at the aisle where a chosen one sat, and then approached and tapped him or her on the shoulder as a speaker on stage broadcast the person's name over the microphone. The officers then escorted the honored student up to the stage and returned to the auditorium to repeat the process, until all the new Myskanians were assembled in a row. The outgoing president then chanted an incantation and solemnly pinned each of the lucky ones with a purple and gold tassel. Harvey would have loved both the campiness and the honor of it.

But he sat and waited and never received the tap. He masked his disappointment with a childish prank. When a student sitting in front of him got the coveted tap and tried to rise, he found he couldn't move. Harvey had grabbed hold of his academic gown.[19]

* * *

It is tempting to wonder whether Harvey's repeated failures to get elected to student office had to do with his secret being surmised despite his best macho efforts to hide it. Had he been spotted perhaps on the trails of Pine Bush or Thatcher Park, where gay men went to cruise? Or maybe he made a move on a fellow student who blabbed? In the fall of his senior year a couple of wiseacre student columnists, writing for the college paper about the forthcoming election of homecoming queen, declared, "We're really going out on a limb, but here goes [our prediction] for Campus Queen . . . : Queen Harriet Milk."[20] Four other male students were given female first names and dubbed Queen Harriet's princesses. Whether those words were written in innocent jest or malice, to read them must have been heart-stopping for Harvey, who had done everything in his power not to be seen as a "queen." If his secret were guessed it could even have meant expulsion. Just a few years earlier there had been witch hunts to expunge all homosexual students and faculty from the University of Texas and the University of Missouri. Similar witch hunts would soon begin at colleges all over the country.[21] The column surely caused him sleepless nights.

But maybe Harvey never won a college election for other

reasons. Aside from his sexuality, he had yet to figure out who he really was or wanted to become, and it would be a long time until he did. He hadn't a clue about how to win friends and influence people, as a popular book of the era said one must do to be a success. As one classmate described him, he was abrasive, opinionated. He was always demanding attention, "thrusting himself into the forefront."[22] He was still the kid who was mindlessly ambitious to win the raffle at the Woodmere movie theater just so he could run up onstage and make exaggerated bows.

He lacked subtlety and nuance in the columns and letters to the editor he wrote for the college paper too. He was a badger one week, a charging bull the next. He harangued his schoolmates about their lack of school spirit, grousing that their "attendance at the basketball games wouldn't have done justice to a small high school."[23] He seemed to lay the blame for the college's indifference to sports on its overwhelming number of women students, who, in the sexist language of the era, didn't care to "worry their little heads" about it.[24] In a column at the start of a school year he observed (in all seriousness), "Those booklines in front of the co-op look like a Salvation Army soupline. If we could only get that many people up to see today's game! Around here students will wait three hours in a bookline but can't give up two or three precious hours to watch a soccer game!"[25] About his fellow athletes he griped, "The difference between a winning and a losing team is an overt team spirit. At State it is totally lacking."[26]

After reading Harvey's hectoring columns, one student wrote, "I feel a little curious as to whether there is anything in State College outside of basketball, [athletic clubs], and he-men, of which Mr. Milk approves."[27]

* * *

But in his last semester, glimmers suddenly emerged of the man who eventually became the iconic Harvey Milk. During the 1950–51 Christmas break he went to Cuba. At the time, the island was a fabulous gay playground where Harvey could let loose without having to worry that his classmates might somehow discover his secret. But that was not all that impressed him in Cuba. That visit—or Harvey's companions on that visit, whoever they may have been—awakened a new awareness in him. The dictator Fulgencio Batista had not yet overthrown Cuba's duly elected president, Carlos Prío; and Batista's overthrow by Fidel Castro was still eight years away. The country seemed so politically free and civil. The twenty-year-old Harvey, though not very sophisticated in his political understanding, nevertheless found it obvious that Cubans were better off than Americans, who were being subjected to the underhanded tactics and witch-hunting horrors of McCarthyism.

When Harvey returned to campus after Christmas break, he abruptly quit writing his sports column, and he started writing opinion pieces that could not have been predicted from his previous persona as the single-minded jock. "One of the interesting things I noticed on my trip to Cuba," he declared in his new column, "was that every session of their legislature is broadcast. Our government would probably be more efficient if we did the same."[28] When the college launched an ROTC program for the increasingly male student body, Harvey penned another one of his usual red-blooded macho rants about how such a program might raise "the caliber of the men [so] that they won't be bookworms but somewhat more of a healthy specimen of a male." But, he added more thoughtfully if somewhat contradictorily, New York State College for Teachers is "preparing teachers of our children. Can we tell our children not to fight one another and then send them to classes on correct battle tactics? Can we tell them how war is bad and then teach them from a militaristic point of view?"[29]

His opinions on integration in another column foretold the fierce champion of minorities that Harvey would eventually become. Blacks had been students at New York State College for Teachers since the nineteenth century, but the school's fraternities and sororities followed the lead of the National Interfraternity Council, which affirmed in the 1950s that "[the] choosing of one's friends is a social right that cannot be confused with civil rights."[30] Blacks were kept out of State College Greek life. Harvey loathed the narrow-mindedness, which included restrictions against Jews too, of course. In 1951, when the campus Phi Delt sorority threw out the restriction clause in their constitution and welcomed black members, he wrote a column titled "In the Right Direction," declaring heartily, "Congrats to you girls!"[31] In other columns he rebuked a senator who had been an inquisitor in the McCarthy hearings for "outshouting his witnesses so they couldn't answer him," and he mocked McCarthyites for persecuting people because they had belonged to the Communist Party five or ten years in the past.[32]

But Harvey's newly awakened interest in ideas, which, had it come earlier, might have made him pay more attention to his studies, emerged too late to save his mediocre academic record. He had thought when he first came to State College that he might major in languages, since he loved the French and German of his favorite operas. But in his freshman year he flunked French. In his second year he got a D in German. In his third year he flunked German, though he managed Bs and Cs in his other classes. Though in his fourth year he got a D in statistics, he had passed enough units for a math minor; but he had to find another major. He had done well enough in history classes, and in summer school before his senior year he took Origins of the First World War; the First World War and the Peace; America's Foreign Relations; and the Civil War and the New Nationalism. He came out clutching two As and two Bs, and he declared himself a history major.[33] But his far from impressive overall record did not put him in the best position to get a teaching job; and he had never been sure anyway that he wanted to teach. He had no idea what he would do with the rest of his life.

In Korea there was a war going on. The United States had entered it the year before. Despite his declarations in his *State College News* column against a "militaristic point of view," Harvey joined the navy.

3

Drifting

Harvey, who opposed the war in Vietnam in the sixties and seventies, claimed with some embarrassment that he had enlisted in the navy in 1951, when America was at war in Korea, because "it was then patriotic to fight for your country."[1] Patriotism may have been one factor that led him to the enlistment office, but there were other reasons too. Bill and Minnie, upset that after four years of college their younger son still did not know what he wanted to do, must have nudged him toward the navy. It was what they had both done when they were young and drifting. Their nudging must have made sense to Harvey. At State College he had seen for himself the male students who came back from World War II and seemed so much more mature and clearer than he and his cohorts about what they wanted in life.

The navy was also appealing because, as Harvey would have learned through the gay grapevine, with just a little bit of discretion navy life could be terrific for gays. It was true that after World War II the military conducted homosexual witch hunts. But when America entered the Korean War, the need for personnel again meant that all military branches would turn a blind eye to homosexuality, just as they largely had during World War II.[2] Photographs of Harvey in the navy capture him looking handsome and in his element. He is camping it up with other buff young men sporting butch navy haircuts.

As a college graduate, Harvey qualified for Officer Candidate School and was sent to the naval station in Newport, Rhode Island. There, he demonstrated his keen athletic bent and was trained as a deep-sea diver. In 1952 he became chief petty officer on a submarine rescue ship that was stationed in Korea. His ship patrolled the North Korean coastline, though he never saw combat. The next year, commissioned as an ensign, he was sent to the naval base in San Diego. It was a plum assignment for a young gay man. As in other port cities, the gay scene in San Diego had mushroomed during World War II, when gay people who had been isolated in towns all over America were suddenly brought together through the military. They created enough of a critical mass so that gay businesses could be established. In San Diego's downtown Gaslamp District, bars such as Blue Jacket and Bradley's and other friendly dives and cruising places flourished. Gay sailors could easily find companionship to suit all tastes, from drag queens to rough trade.[3]

They did not have to worry that the Shore Patrol would spot them, either, because there were "locker clubs" in the Gaslamp—such as the 7 Seas Locker Club and Jack's Steam and Locker Club—which for a fee provided a sailor not only with a place to take a bath but also to stash his uniform and get into civvies before heading over to off-limits joints. Locker clubs also served heterosexual sailors who wanted a night on the town in civvies, but among gay men these establishments had a reputation for being such bountiful hunting grounds that those who were not in the military wanted in too.[4]

By the time Harvey arrived in San Diego, gay life was so lively that the authors of a sensationalistic book in 1952, *U.S.A. Confidential*, claimed, in language calculated to shock, that the "fairy fleet has landed and taken over the nation's most important naval base" and that the "fairy dives" were packed with "prancing misfits in peekaboo blouses, with marcelled hair and rouged faces."[5] The authors' titillating intent aside, it was true that gay servicemen were plentiful in San Diego. And Harvey was in a good position to enjoy that plentitude because officers were allowed to keep an apartment off base. He had the privacy to party with gay sailor friends or tryst with civilians whom he picked up.[6] During his navy years he learned that he had no problem raising desire in other men. Decked out in his navy uniform, he looked mature and manly, his virility underscored by his brass belt buckle with its navy diver's insignia. He wore it for years after he left the navy.

* * *

Harvey had signed up for a four-year stint, and it came to an end in 1955. He had been promoted to lieutenant junior grade and had racked up an array of medals: the Korean Service Medal, the National Defense Service Medal, the Navy Good Conduct Medal. On February 7, 1955, he was given an honorable discharge; and then he was suddenly a civilian again.

At a loss for what to do or where to go, he traveled a hundred miles north, settled in Los Angeles, and explored the gay scene there. Mike Sather, a gay man he met in L.A., introduced him to a bright and pretty sixteen-year-old Jewish girl, Susan Davis. In the gay vernacular of the 1950s, Susan was a "fag hag," a straight female who enjoys the company of gay men. She and Harvey immediately clicked. She was a good listener, and he was an avid talker. Susan would go on to become a student at the University of Illinois and then to have a brief career in television and film—but Harvey's conversations with her centered on his gay world, which fascinated her. She was charmed by the lively, funny ex-sailor who was nine years her senior but seemed to value her take on things. For the next seven years she was one of Harvey's main correspondents and his confidante.[7]

Susan introduced him to another gay man in her circle of friends, John Harvey, who would become Harvey Milk's first serious affair and whom he described in a letter to Susan—in the ultraromantic language he would fall into whenever he was enamored—as "a god, whom I was very much in love with."[8] That fall and winter the two men lived together in Los Angeles; then in early spring 1956 they moved to Miami. But it did not work out. As Harvey Milk later wrote to Susan, he had "a blind love" for John Harvey but John never made him believe it was returned.[9]

Feeling cut loose from John, Harvey sometimes went cruising on Powder Puff Lane, so called in camp talk because many of Miami's gay hangouts were located there. It was not a safe place to be. Since the start of the 1950s the Miami Police Department had been cracking down on the city's expanding gay population, and Powder Puff Lane was the prime target. To entrap gay men, the police sent handsome young vice squad officers, muscles bulging in civilian attire, onto the streets or into the bars of Powder Puff Lane. Their job was to flirt with homosexuals and arrest them if they responded. The police also raided the bars; or sometimes, just to harass, they parked their marked cars in front of a gay bar, red and blue emergency lights whirling, and shone high beams at the entrance. The *Miami Herald*, as hostile to homosexuals as most newspapers were in the 1950s, blared front-page headlines such as "5,000 Perverts Here, Police Say" and "Pervert Clean-Up Starts Tonight."[10]

But gay men, including Harvey, frequented the gay hangouts anyway; there were not many other places they had to congregate in 1956.

Harvey was arrested in one of the Miami Police Department's "pervert clean-ups" and charged under a "Vagrant-Pervert" law. Because such arrests were intended mostly to shame and intimidate, he was released without being sentenced.[11] It was sheer harassment, but young Harvey, like most gays, chalked it up to the price of being gay.

* * *

That May he turned twenty-six and, totally without financial resources, moved back to his parents' home on Long Island. It must have been painful after years of freedom; and he knew that his critical father saw him as a failure because Harvey still had no idea what he wanted to do in life. Since he had gotten a degree in teaching, he decided he would use it. He signed a contract to teach tenth- and eleventh-grade math and history and coach basketball in the fall. George W. Hewlett High School, in an upscale Jewish neighborhood in Hewlett Harbor, was only two or three miles away from Woodmere, where Harvey had been born. After four years in college, four years in the navy, a year knocking around L.A. and Miami, he had ended up almost exactly where he began.

He told himself that even though he was going to be a teacher at Hewlett High, he did not have to be trapped on Long Island. With the promise of a steady paycheck starting in the fall, he left his parents' home at the beginning of the summer and rented an apartment in the Rego Park neighborhood of Queens. As he hopped from bar to bar in the city that summer, he met a young man he really liked, Joe Campbell—nineteen, good-looking, with dark eyes and hair and a firm, compact body. Joe was bright (Harvey would say he had "a wonderful mind") and funny too;[12] but he dropped out of school at sixteen and worked as a gay hustler, a Western Union delivery boy, and a Good Humor Ice Cream man. His father had died when he was only a year old, and his mother had five kids to raise. Joe looked for older lovers who would be a father to him.

Before he met Harvey he had been the kept boy of a well-off bar owner.[13]

Harvey was eager for the relationship. After years of one-night stands and short affairs, he was craving family life. "I guess I ran around a lot," he wrote Susan Davis, "and now want to be settled down to someone, and since I found Joe—I've got that someone."[14] For a good while it seemed to Harvey he had found a perfect fit. He fell right into the role Joe required of him: the mature one, paternal, loving and demonstrative as Bill, his own stern father, had never been to him. Consciously or not, he strove to heal his boyhood wounds by being himself everything he had sorely missed in his father. In every one of his serious relationships, for as long as he lived, the dynamic that Harvey tried to establish with Joe Campbell became the pattern he was destined to repeat. He would be the caretaker of a troubled youth who desperately needed taking care of. He would be his protector. He would be there for him 100 percent. He would educate the young man too. They would go to operas, museums, do all the cultural things Harvey was able to afford once the money started coming in.

* * *

Much as Harvey resented having to return five days a week to where he had not very happily grown up, the students at Hewlett High adored him. He could still be Harvey the Clown, and it played well among tenth and eleventh graders. And he genuinely liked them. To make extra money, he tutored. He enjoyed difficult cases, such as the fifteen-year-old whose parents hired Harvey to come sit in their well-appointed living room and help their son with math. The Greenbaums had been sending the boy, Robert, to a psychologist twice a week after he announced that he hated school and was flunking algebra. Robert resented going to the psychologist because it interfered with baseball practice. As an alternative to shrink visits, he agreed to be tutored.

Robert was just Harvey's kind of kid, difficult and resistant like Harvey had been as an adolescent and sports-minded too. Harvey humored the boy out of his grumpiness; he talked sports and souped-up cars with him; he told corny jokes and clowned. And then he taught the now-willing adolescent some algebra so he could pass the class, to the Greenbaums' gratitude.[15] Harvey was gifted with young people, there was no doubt. But he stopped teaching after just one year.

He knew that if you were a teacher, homosexuality was sure grounds for dismissal. Anticipating the worst—because the worst often did happen to gay people in the 1950s—he decided that rather than be fired he would quit. Teaching was not what he really wanted to do, anyway. What about the dreams he had since he was a little kid at the Woodmere movie theater: audiences cheering him? And what about the exhilarating sense of risk and adventure he had felt wandering around New York City by himself when he was a teen? The life of a high school teacher was the antithesis of those heady delights.

But he had not yet figured out who he really wanted to be. Family lore said that when Bill Milk was a young man he went to look for himself out west. Following in his father's footsteps, Harvey pulled up stakes at the end of the school year, and, with Joe in tow, he bought a secondhand Plymouth and drove the fifteen hundred miles to Dallas.[16]

* * *

Joe was the first to find employment in Dallas. He had discovered he was skilled in painting antique reproductions and furniture; and when Harvey could not find a job, their roles were oddly reversed. Joe kept them afloat. After almost half a year in Texas, Harvey was still at loose ends. "Things have been no good—there are no good jobs, and no job pays near New York wages," he lamented in a letter to Susan, whom he now called "one of the few pleasures in my life."[17] He blamed his troubles on bigotry. One businessman told him that in Dallas "a Baptist wouldn't even hire a Methodist," so how could a Jew hope to be hired?

He finally found a job as an assistant credit manager in a store owned by Jews. But he lost it when the owner replaced him with his son, who had just graduated from college. Harvey did find another job fairly quickly, this time selling sewing machines to poor people on credit. That was "the only job they'll let a Jew have in Dallas," he complained to Joe, but he took it.[18] He did not last long. When he learned that many of his customers could not make their monthly payments and that the machines he sold them had been repossessed by the company, he quit. He hated not only the job situation but everything about Dallas. "The people are not the type we like, and the city really isn't much," he wrote Susan.[19] After eight months, it was definitely time to go back to New York.

But he and Joe had no place to live there and no job prospects, and though they were practically broke, moving back to his parents' house was not an option. His mother might have been happy to have him and Joe there, but his father would never understand why this young, uneducated guy was trailing his son. Desperate, Harvey wrote to his cousin Shirley, the daughter of one of Bill's sisters. She had married a wealthy Manhattan businessman, Meyer Salem, who sold high-end stockings to customers like Greta Garbo, Lillian Gish, and Marilyn Monroe and who billed himself as Hosier to the Stars. The Salems were living in Kew Gardens, an upscale neighborhood of Queens, in a lavish house that had belonged to the actor Will Rogers. Harvey heard from his mother that Shirley was redecorating, so he touted Joe's talents: Joe had experience painting gold leaf on ceilings to make them mansion-worthy. For a small fee, Harvey said, he and Joe would be willing to live in the Salem house while Joe did his magic on the ceilings. As soon as Shirley accepted the offer, Harvey and Joe packed up the Plymouth and put Dallas behind them.[20]

* * *

Eventually, Harvey found a job as an actuary, calculating insurance risks and premiums for the Great American Insurance Company. To earn extra money he worked in the little store his father, Bill, unsuccessful in the furrier business, had opened in New York City. From five o'clock to seven every weekday evening and on Saturdays from twelve thirty to four thirty Harvey sold men's work clothes.[21]

Harvey and Joe rented an apartment, bought furniture, and settled in. Joe worked hard for their joint benefit too. In the daytime he painted and did electrical work and various other handyman chores at Casa Cugat, a new nightclub on East Forty-Eighth Street owned by Xavier Cugat, the Latin bandleader who popularized the cha-cha. In the evenings Joe donned a pageboy uniform like Johnny in the Philip Morris commercial and welcomed Casa Cugat patrons at the door or ran around the restaurant selling them cigarettes and matches.[22] When Casa Cugat went out of business after a year, Joe started selling tropical plants that he grew in the apartment where he and Harvey lived. A bamboo tree grew to seven feet in their living room.[23] By that time they had been together for four years.

Harvey called his relationship with Joe a marriage, but he was beset by uncertainties. He even fantasized on occasion about what it would be like to be heterosexual. When Susan Davis moved to Chicago to go to college he wrote her a flirtatious letter, calling her "the most beautiful girl in Chicago" and declaring that if he were straight he "would fly to Chicago to sweep you off of your feet & rush you to the nearest justice of the peace—and I would not hear a word that you or your parents would say untill [sic] I heard you utter, speak, shout, project & so forth—the message 'I do. . . .' Really, Sue," he went on, elaborating on his fantasy, "I wish I could sweep you right on down to the marriage window at city hall." However, he had to admit, there were a few things preventing it—like he "wasn't straight (& so forth)."[24]

Yet he was painfully ambivalent in his gay relationship. He longed to feel the delirium of passion, and he had stopped feeling it with Joe. But he also wanted a home and a stable life, and Joe, who turned out to be so dependable, did give him that. In July 1960 Harvey confided his confusion to Susan. He still felt love for Joe, he wrote, "but not a very strong driving love." He had never gotten over John Harvey, he confessed. He kept weighing the pros and cons of staying with Joe. "I am not too happy with my present relationship with Joe," he wrote in a state of deep bewilderment, "but at least we have each other & it is better to have someone you love some than no one."[25]

He operated on that principle all the next year, but it was not a happy time. His complaints to Susan continued: he and Joe just weren't getting along. They would fight, and Harvey would get increasingly angry, while Joe would pull inside himself. Harvey could not reach him. One night Joe went out and picked up a young sailor, and he began seeing him regularly. In July 1961 Joe announced that he was leaving.

Harvey was crushed. Now, suddenly, Joe was all he wanted. The threat of losing the relationship made him value it as he had not for years. He tormented himself that he had not been good to Joe. "I'm going to write a book on what to do and what not to do to keep a marriage strong," he told Susan.[26]

To Joe, he wrote heartbroken letters, begging him to reconsider. He despaired about the terrible ease with which gay relationships could end. If they had been man and wife, Harvey argued in one letter, they could not just quit each other, as Joe was doing. They would have to go before a judge, who would make them try everything "to save the marriage and all that had been wonderful." In page after pleading page Harvey refused to acknowledge that their relationship was over. "Why in gay life must two lovers break up without trying what man and wife do—get help, face their problems and not just give up?" He was bitter that a "marriage" between two men had less weight than one between a man and a woman—though it would not have occurred to him or anyone in 1961 to demand for same-sex partners the legal tie that made heterosexual marriage more stable.

He tried to cajole Joe into staying, admonishing him that if he left he would be setting a bad habit for the rest of his life. Once you give up on a relationship, Harvey wrote, "the next one will be just that much easier to give up & so on until it is no longer any lovers but just short affairs." In his panic over losing Joe he resumed his old role of parent and authority figure, haranguing the younger man about his immaturity, his emotional flimsiness. To be true to oneself is to find out what one wants in life, he lectured: "If one wants many loves, etc., he will not fight to keep a lover. However, if one wants a relationship with meaning & one to build upon & one to cherish, then to be true is to fight for that love & fight for oneself & not run when hurt but fight back until the one hurting loves instead."[27] It was sheer emotional bullying, but Harvey was desperate.

On top of the threat of losing Joe, he feared he was losing his dear confidante, or at least that she would not be as available to him as she had been for the past six years: in April 1961, Sue Davis, at twenty-two years old, married George Alch, a thirty-year-old San Franciscan. Feeling the panic of looming loneliness, Harvey thought maybe he should get married too—to a woman, a lesbian, as he wrote to Sue in mid-September. There were many benefits to a heterosexual marriage. If he married "one of the 'strange girls' I know," he said, "we would have companionship, a front, and each would not be in the way of the other."[28] The notion did not last long, but it was an indication of how deeply he felt that he could not be alone.

In late September Joe left to be with his new lover. But

Harvey refused to give up. In December he wrote to Joe with the tenderness of their first years: "I wish so much to hold you once again." He presented himself as the supplicant: "Forgive me for writing as I have, but I do feel like I have a truly broken heart—I miss you—I love you—I want you."[29] But nothing he said would change Joe's mind. The younger man left New York and moved to Tennessee with his sailor.[30]

* * *

One evening after Joe left, Harvey went cruising in Central Park West, where he picked up an intense young man, Craig Rodwell, who was just the physical type that attracted him most: dark-haired, dark-eyed, and about ten years younger than Harvey, with the muscles of a dancer. They spent the night together, and Harvey wanted to see him again. But he also let Craig know that he was still grieving the loss of Joe Campbell. As he tearfully confessed to Craig, on the morning that Joe removed all his possessions from their apartment Harvey stood at the window, several flights up, and "wanted to jump out the window and follow him."[31]

Yet, despite his genuine pining for the old relationship, Harvey was romantically chivalrous in his new one. He brought the young man flowers and cooked him meals. If they spent a night apart, Harvey called in the morning to wake him up with funny little jokes and good cheer. Craig Rodwell, who was raised by his mother, a divorced, low-paid secretary in Chicago, had never met a man so attentive and cultured. Craig was smitten.

But as much as Harvey liked Craig, he held back. Maybe it was because Craig was a radical gay militant—long before there was such a category—and that made Harvey nervous. Harvey had come of age in 1951, at the height of McCarthy-era homophobia, when all gay people understood that you had to keep your homosexuality quiet or you were likely to be thrown out of work and dwelling and family too. Craig Rodwell, who came of age a whole decade later, had no such understanding.

He had deep respect and admiration for black people's protests against racial injustice, and he thought that gays needed to take a page from the civil rights movement. He joined New York Mattachine, a small, quiet "homophile" group, which had started in Los Angeles in 1950. He tried to shake things up in the New York chapter because Mattachine had yet to accomplish anything significant to further the rights of homosexuals. So-called homophile organizations like Mattachine would not get braver, Craig was convinced, until all homosexuals joined the fight. But most homosexuals were unaware that such groups existed. They had never even dreamed of an organized fight for homosexual rights.

One night over dinner Craig boasted to Harvey about his efforts to spread the word about homosexual organizing. He and a friend had been scrutinizing Greenwich Village mailboxes and stuffing flyers into every one of them that displayed names of two inhabitants of the same sex. The flyers invited the presumed homosexuals to come hear a speaker at the homophile West Side Discussion Group.

Harvey was shocked at what Craig was telling him. "You shouldn't do that to people!" he lectured the younger man. "Getting those [flyers] in mailboxes will make people paranoid that everyone knows about them being gay!" It was an expression of Harvey's own fears. He worked for a corporation. He knew he had to be closeted if he wanted to keep his job. He was unaware that homosexuals had been organizing for more than a decade and that men such as Frank Kameny, who had started a Mattachine group in Washington, D.C., were even beginning to fight the federal government for civil rights. Harvey thought Craig Rodwell's notions—that homosexuals should *want* everyone to know they were gay, that homosexuals should come out to everyone—were ludicrous.

At another point in their relationship Craig disappeared for several days. He had been arrested at Riis Park Beach because he got into a fight with police officers who were harassing gays who wore skimpy bikinis. The judge sentenced him to three days in jail, where his hair was buzzed off. Craig's shaven head made him look like a jailbird to Harvey, who was dismayed that Craig had brought such an awful misadventure upon himself. Craig Rodwell's militancy, which Harvey considered naïve and silly, triggered the beginning of the end of the relationship. The morning phone calls dwindled and then disappeared. When Harvey began having gonorrhea symptoms, and Craig confessed that the bug had originated with him, their relationship was completely undone.

As an adolescent, Craig Rodwell had been despondent after police caught him with an adult male, who was sentenced to five years in prison because of him. Craig was given two years' probation and ordered to see a psychiatrist. He tried to commit suicide by downing a handful of aspirins with a Coke, which he had heard would be lethal. It wasn't. Now, after Harvey left him, he went into a tailspin again. He swallowed half a bottle of barbiturates but passed out before he could finish the whole bottle. His roommate, who came home early from a double feature, called an ambulance. Craig's stomach was pumped, and he was locked up in a psychiatric ward for a month.

But he recovered, and he never stopped being a gay radical. As the sixties progressed, a lot of other young gays joined him. In 1967 Craig opened the Oscar Wilde Memorial Bookshop in Greenwich Village, the first bookstore in America to stock exclusively lesbian and gay literature. He also coined the term "gay power," and during the Stonewall riots in 1969 he ran through the streets of the Village shouting out the phrase and leading others to shout it too. Later that year he was at the forefront of a battle to turn sedate homosexual-rights pickets at Philadelphia's Independence Hall—organized by Frank

Kameny and his small homophile group—into what eventually became huge gay pride rallies all over America and ultimately all over the world.[32]

Harvey could not tolerate Craig's gay activism when they were lovers. But in San Francisco in the 1970s he adopted Craig's views—the importance of coming out, of promoting gay power, of being militant—and he took them many steps further. He became a gay leader by figuring out how to make Craig Rodwell's groundbreaking ideas go well beyond an inchoate radical gay community.

* * *

Harvey was overwhelmed by all his failures in 1962. Not only did his boring job at Great American Insurance Company make a mockery of his youthful fantasies of spotlights and high adventure, but he had ruined his marriage, he had no one to love and come home to, and his brief relationships were disappointing. He was in his thirties already, and nothing in his life was as he had hoped it would be.

And then his mother, Minnie, doing a Thanksgiving mitzvah for the poor, had a heart attack. She died five days later, on November 27. After the death of Harvey's grandfather Morris, she had been the only family member to whom Harvey felt close. She never acknowledged in words that her son was a homosexual—and Harvey never dared to tell her that he was—yet she had intuited Joe's importance in her son's life, and she had treated him like Harvey's mate. She even knitted matching afghans and slippers for them.[33] Now he had lost not only Joe but his mother too.

In March 1963, Joe let Harvey know he was returning to New York. He was not coming back to their relationship, but he did want to be friends. Harvey told Joe that he was leaving for Puerto Rico. He could not bear to be in the same city with Joe, Harvey wrote, because of "that unfortunate too strong love for you."[34] He had gotten so used to romanticizing the relationship he had once described as "not a very strong driving love" that he surely believed what he wrote. It was at least partly true. But Joe's return was not the only reason Harvey was leaving for Puerto Rico. He had been frustrated in his hunt for a job that would be less boring than crunching numbers at an insurance company; and he imagined that in Puerto Rico he would have better luck. But he did not. "The only jobs that are to be had (if they are good ones)," he complained in a letter to Joe, "are for people who can speak English and Spanish." Harvey did not know a word of Spanish.[35]

Worried that his supervisor at Great American would not write a good letter of recommendation for him because he had quit, Harvey had resorted to a little larceny, which, as an outlaw already by society's standard, he would never be above if it accomplished something of importance. Before leaving the company he had filched a small stack of letterhead that bore the logo "Great American Insurance Company New York," so he could forge his own reference letters.[36] He also provided Joe with several pieces of the stationery. On job applications he listed Joe Campbell as a former employer and gave Joe's residence on Central Park West as 444 CPW, which might sound to non–New Yorkers more like a serious business address. From at least one firm, the Puerto Rican Industrial Development Company, Joe Campbell received a letter declaring, "Dear Sir, Mr. Harvey B. Milk has given your name as a former employer" and requesting information about Mr. Milk's capabilities and reliability.[37] But Joe's recommendation, if he wrote it, must not have been convincing. Having gotten no job offers at all in Puerto Rico, Harvey flew to Miami Beach to search for a job there.

That did not work out either. From Miami he sent Joe a telegram, fuming that jobs seemed to be open only to "non-Jewish individuals."[38] It was true that anti-Semitism had been rife in the Miami Beach of the 1940s, when owners of luxury apartment houses advertised their rentals with brochures that boasted, "Always a view, never a Jew."[39] By 1963, however, the Jewish population of Miami Beach was huge. That Harvey saw anti-Semitism even in Miami Beach was a sign of his despondency. In May, after two months in Miami, he returned to New York.

* * *

Summer 1963: three months in New York and Harvey still had not found a job he liked. His savings were depleted; he realized he had to be less picky and more realistic. In August he donned a suit and tie, summoned all his chutzpah, and went down to Wall Street. At one of the largest retail brokerage and investment firms in the United States he touted his mathematical talents and landed an entry-level job as a securities research analyst at Bache and Company. There, he could even stop worrying about anti-Semitism because the company had been founded in the nineteenth century by Jules S. Bache, a Jew, and it was still being run by his nephew Harold Bache. The job paid pretty well, too, so Harvey was able to rent a nice apartment on the Upper West Side, not far from Central Park. He could also afford to shop at Brooks Brothers, where he bought himself some well-tailored suits. And he could afford to go to the opera again—and sit in a good seat.

Being hired by Bache and Company may not have been the success he had dreamed about, but it was affirming. Wall Street did not hire slouches. In his first year he was promoted to supervisor of Bache's information center. He was also entrusted with issuing the daily investment reports that went out to Bache offices all across the country. And raises were generous and regular. He stayed with the company for more than five years.

Harvey's second year at Bache, 1964, was a presidential election year. The archconservative Republican Barry Goldwater— a fierce champion of laissez-faire economics and small government and zealous foe of labor unions and communists—was running against the Democratic incumbent, Lyndon B. Johnson, who had announced a War on Poverty. Harvey had no doubt about whom he would be supporting in the election. Not only was he steeped in the culture of Wall Street, but he was also genuinely excited about some of Goldwater's tenets—ideas that would later come to be called libertarian. As a homosexual, Harvey believed that government had no right to butt into people's private lives; and that's what Goldwater believed too. The Democrats certainly were not saying anything like that. Under Presidents Kennedy and Johnson government employees were investigated, and if they were found to be homosexual they were kicked out of their jobs.

That fall Harvey rose at the crack of dawn most mornings so that he could get to the subway station early and spend some time passing out Goldwater for President flyers to his fellow commuters on their way to work.

4

Will-o'-the-Wisps

HARVEY WAS PRETERNATURALLY outgoing and uncensored. Even as a teenager he was so talkative that in his Bay Shore High School yearbook classmates wrote beneath his picture, "And they say WOMEN are never at a loss for words." Harvey was also loquacious with his colleagues at Bache. Everyone in the office knew, for instance, that he got out of bed at six in the morning to hand out Goldwater flyers. But in that year, 1964, he understood that there was one thing he must not reveal: that he left sleeping in his bed seventeen-year-old Jack Galen McKinley, whom he had met that fall. Galen, as he was usually called, fit the mold of most of the young men who preceded him in Harvey's life: dark hair and eyes; compact and muscled; gifted but barely educated; and in dire need of a father figure. He had been born into a big working-class Christian fundamentalist family that took for granted that all homosexuals were doomed to hell. In 1963 he dropped out of high school in Hagerstown, Maryland, and hopped a bus to New York—to Greenwich Village, where young homosexuals had been heading for at least half a century. He knocked around the Village for a year or so, hustling, sleeping wherever he could, scrounging meals. His situation was not much improved when he hooked up with a forty-year-old hippie named Tom O'Horgan, who walked around with holes in the bottoms of his shoes, even in winter.[1] O'Horgan had been a nightclub harpist and standup comic and was now trying to get established as a director of off-off-Broadway experimental theater. Galen moved in with him.

For a while it seemed an okay arrangement. Galen loved theater, and O'Horgan promised to train him to work backstage. O'Horgan had recently signed on with La MaMa Experimental Theatre Club on Second Avenue, which had been formed three years earlier by Ellen Stewart, a black woman, "the mama" to edgy and unappreciated playwrights, directors, and actors. La MaMa encouraged them to do their own creative thing, the wilder the better. In 1964 O'Horgan was preparing to direct a production of Jean Genet's *The Maids*, using men in the women's roles (as Genet himself had intended); he was so consumed with staging this work that he was oblivious when a good-looking Wall Street type called Harvey Milk started pursuing Galen.

To Harvey it was obvious that after rough months of hustling to get by in New York, Galen was a jaded kid; yet he seemed hungry to learn everything Harvey could teach him. Harvey was as charmed by that as by the young man's physical appeal and sexual willingness. He wrote Galen sweet and playful love notes, took him to museums and operas and ballets, and made him feel like he was the only person in the world who mattered. It was not long before Galen announced to Tom O'Horgan that he was moving out. That was fine with O'Horgan. He had already guessed that Galen was looking for some kind of father figure, and unlike Harvey he had no time and no inclination to be that.[2]

Harvey found an apartment in Greenwich Village because that was where Galen wanted to live. Their household was rounded out by a dog and a cat whom they called Trick (gay slang for a one-night stand) and Trade (gay slang for a heterosexual who will have gay sex for money); and they settled in.

Harvey was in love, but he was nervous too. Galen, who had turned seventeen in October 1964, looked like a kid. And even though New York's age of consent was seventeen, "sodomy," which stood for any kind of homosexual behavior, was illegal at any age. Harvey could imagine how the relationship would appear to his coworkers at Bache. He knew he could not hide Galen from them indefinitely if he was going to squire the boy to cultural events all over town; so he told people that Galen McKinley was his ward.[3]

* * *

Tom O'Horgan held no grudge that Galen had gone off with Harvey, and he even kept a promise to teach Galen about props and sets. It was quickly clear that Galen was bright, meticulous, and a natural; and O'Horgan took him on as stage manager for his La MaMa productions. Galen's new life in the theater opened up a brand new life for Harvey too. Most evenings, after a day at Bache, Harvey showed up at La MaMa to watch Galen and the plays he was working on. After a while Harvey was buying burgers for Tom O'Horgan whenever he was broke and hungry, which was often.[4] The more the director got to know the loquacious, funny Wall Street man in the three-piece suits who had taken Galen off his hands, the more he liked him. Harvey, who had been enchanted by the stage since he was an eight-year-old running up to collect his raffle prizes at the Woodmere theater, offered himself to O'Horgan as an actor.

O'Horgan had written and was directing *Saint Siegfried, or How to Make a Hero*—an "Op-Ra," as he called it, and he cast Harvey in it. The theater bug bit hard, and Harvey felt that finally he had found who he wanted to be. In the daytime he had to show up at his Wall Street office decked out in Brooks Brothers–style clothing because he had rent to pay and two mouths to feed. But at night and on weekends he donned jeans and a T-shirt and went off to where he was becoming most comfortable, at rehearsals with bohemians and hippies in the La MaMa loft.

He decided he needed a stage name and chose the most Oscar Wildean one he could devise: Basil Farckwart. After the Op-Ra ran for a week, he went into rehearsal for another O'Horgan play at La MaMa, *And Now the Weather.* He worked backstage too, helping Galen with his stage manager duties. La MaMa was becoming his chief hangout, and when O'Horgan needed more money for the production Harvey was quick to reach into his pocket.

In 1966 O'Horgan introduced him to Robert Elias, who, like Harvey, was the grandson of Lithuanian Jews. Under the name Robert Downey Sr., Elias wrote, produced, and directed absurdist low-budget films that were shown mostly in tiny underground theaters. His wife, Elsie Downey, appeared in many of his films, as eventually did their son, Robert Downey Jr. Tom O'Horgan wrote the music for Elias's 1966 movie *Chafed Elbows*—a manic comedy in colossally bad taste, featuring sock-sniffers in church, a pregnant man who has a hysterectomy, and mother-son incest. Elias gave Harvey the bit part of an actor playing Reggie the Prisoner in a movie within the movie. Harvey got to wear zany goggle-like glasses and a prison uniform with horizontal stripes, and he camped it up as a voiceover shouted his lines in a Yiddish accent: "I didn't do it! I swear I didn't! Somebody help me! I vant justice! I vant recognition!" Harvey adored the idea of being a movie actor.

* * *

Life with Galen, however, was rocky from the start, and Harvey's hopes to be his protector and mentor were quickly dashed. Galen's talents made him desirable as a stage manager at La MaMa; but his emotional problems—the depression he'd had from the time he was a kid growing up in a Bible-thumping family, the manic behavior that Harvey initially mistook for a sparkling spirit—all got worse with the pot, LSD, speed, and alcohol that Galen could not stop abusing. He picked up men, too, and then tried to aggravate Harvey by describing his sex adventures in detail. And he was bent on self-destruction. Sitting alone one night in their apartment, Harvey heard an odd noise in the garage below. He ran down just in time to cut Galen loose from a noose he had fastened around his neck. Another night, as they walked along a Greenwich Village street arguing, Galen hurled himself into the path of a speeding taxi that screeched to a halt just in time.

Harvey decided that they had to get out of New York. Surely in a place where drugs and casual sex weren't so easy to find, and life wasn't so frenetic, Galen could cut down and calm down, and things would get better. Though Harvey was having a fine time moonlighting as an actor, he had to save Galen. The opportunity to leave arose when Harvey's boss announced that he had accepted a transfer to the Bache office in Dallas.[5] Harvey hated Dallas. It had been a disaster when he lived there with Joe. But now his young lover was in dire straits; and Harvey, determined to try to save him, asked his boss to arrange a transfer to the Dallas office for him too. By now Harvey loathed working in finance. Yet he was good at what he did, and the company did not want to lose him. In January 1967 he and Galen packed up their Greenwich Village apartment and their dog Trick and their cat Trade and moved to Dallas.

Galen despised Dallas right away. To him it was as dull and backward as Hagerstown, Maryland, and within two months he took Trick and went back to New York, leaving Harvey and Trade stuck in Texas.

* * *

Galen, still favored by Tom O'Horgan as his best stage manager, returned just in time to get in on the beginning of his former lover's meteoric rise. O'Horgan was directing a new play, *Futz!*, for which he had also written the music. *Futz!* was about Cyrus Futz, a simple farm boy who falls in love with and marries Amanda, who he thinks is beautiful—and who is a barnyard animal, a pig. The outraged villagers kill Cyrus for his unconventional choice of love object. Gay audiences flocked to see the play because to them it was obviously about society's cruelty to homosexuals. But straight audiences flocked to see it too. O'Horgan had created in *Futz!* a fresh, new kind of theatrical experience, as a *New York Times* critic wrote of the play when it moved up a notch from off-off-Broadway to the off-Broadway Theater de Lys.[6] Under O'Horgan's direction, the *Times* critic raved, the troupe of actors mugged and careened with limitless energy in wild and fevered Dionysian dances in a style such as had never before been seen on stage.

That was only the beginning of Tom O'Horgan's triumphs. Toward the end of that year he was hired to take over as director of a musical about the hippie counterculture that had been playing off-Broadway. The production, called *Hair*, was moving to a Broadway theater, and it needed work. Under O'Horgan's direction, *Hair* became a "tribal love-rock musical," Dionysian in the style of *Futz!*, about the flower children of "the Age of Aquarius," replete with nude bodies of all colors and genders.

When *Hair* opened at Broadway's Biltmore Theater in April 1968, audiences went wild, and O'Horgan became the first off-off-Broadway director ever to make it big on Broadway. *Hair* ran for 1,750 sold-out performances. A recording by the cast sold three million copies. Tom O'Horgan, critics declared, had brought "a high voltage fusion of new juices into the theater. . . . Things will never be the same [on Broadway] after this season."[7]

Galen, who had gone to Broadway to be stage manager for *Hair*, kept sending Harvey delirious accounts of Tom O'Horgan's conquest of the artistic world. It was the sort of success Harvey had dreamed about. He reminded himself that O'Horgan was forty-two already, four years older than he. Such triumph might yet happen for him in a few years. That Christmas, Harvey, alone in Dallas, wrote Joe Campbell, with whom he had remained close, that the Apollo 8 spacecraft, which had left Earth's orbit on December 21, was circling the moon. The astronauts' feat had given him hope about himself, he told Joe. "As for the future," he quipped, "well, with the stars now open, there is no limit to what I can do and where I can go."[8] But it was hard to imagine what he could accomplish that would make the *New York Times* say that "things will never be the same" because of Harvey Milk.

* * *

If anything great was going to happen for him, Harvey knew, it would not be in Dallas. He put in a request to be transferred back to the Bache office in New York. There, he resumed his life with Galen and hung around Tom O'Horgan, who had not forgotten his friends in the midst of his success. Harvey grew his hair longer and longer, sprouted a mustache as bushy as Tom O'Horgan's, and donned love beads after work, all of which reflected the new way of being that Harvey had discovered. His politics began shifting too. Though he still thought Goldwater was right about some issues, such as wanting government out of people's lives, it would have been humiliating if his *Hair* friends learned that he had handed out flyers for a right-winger. Harvey threw himself wholeheartedly into the new ethos. Republicans were reprehensible. The war in Vietnam was unconscionable.

When O'Horgan was invited to stage a production of *Hair*

in San Francisco to open in the summer of 1969, he asked Galen to be his special assistant. Harvey was welcome to come too, of course. Harvey had been at Bache for more than five years at this point, and all that time he had done an okay job of hiding the ways he did not fit in; but he was tired of concealing who he was. In September 1969 he quit Bache and moved to San Francisco.

Since there was no place for him on the *Hair* payroll in San Francisco, and he still had to earn a living, he shaved his mustache and clipped his hair and once again went to work in the investment business. This time it was with J. Barth and Company, a Jewish-owned brokerage on Montgomery Street in San Francisco's financial district. His job interview went well enough that he parlayed his five-plus years with Bache into a starting salary of $25,000 a year (about $170,000 in today's money).[9] Despite the generous salary, however, Harvey was not wild about the job. He had the skills to manipulate money well, but to work at Barth he had to assume a role he now loathed.

However, he adored San Francisco. The city still showed signs of the 1967 Summer of Love, when a hundred thousand hippie kids, all looking like they could be in the *Hair* cast, hitchhiked from everywhere in America to converge on Haight-Ashbury and start a psychedelic revolution of love and compassion. Harvey relished their flower power rhetoric and incorporated it into his own way of speaking.

He was keen, too, on the new in-your-face quality of the gay scene in San Francisco. A group of sexual revolutionaries had started giving theatrical performances the same fall that Harvey arrived in the city. The Cockettes was the provocative name they chose for themselves. Harvey had barely heard about the Stonewall uprising that took place the previous June, when he was still in New York, though it had triggered the start of a militant gay political movement; but the "hippie acid-freak drag queens," as the Cockettes were called by one reporter, represented to him a personal sort of gay liberation. He loved their sassiness, their chutzpah; the massive amount of glitter they wore, even on their exposed pubic hair; their costumes, which weren't just drag but wearable art. Most of all, he loved their unapologetic pride in being who they were. It was the city of San Francisco that made a phenomenon like the Cockettes possible, Harvey thought. The quirkiness and daring that seemed to be tolerated in the Bay City opened up new and exciting ways of being.

That November, when municipal elections were being held, Harvey—who had had no political ambitions whatever since he ran unsuccessfully for student government at the end of his junior year of college—suddenly announced to his friends, in all apparent seriousness, "I want to be mayor of San Francisco."[10] He had not been interested even in presidential candidates since Goldwater ran in 1964. But now he began paying attention to who got elected to the San Francisco Board of Supervisors and what they stood for. The top vote-getter in a field of sixteen was a thirty-six-year-old woman by the name of Dianne Feinstein. Harvey heard that she was "a lady in pearls" and that she had poured an unprecedented amount of money into her campaign—money from her wealthy father and wealthier husband, money from real estate developers and businessmen. He had not heard that she was one of the rare "gay friendly" candidates in 1969 and also one of the first politicians ever to seek an endorsement from a homophile organization, San Francisco's Society for Individual Rights. Feinstein was a Democrat, but Harvey's new radical values made him view her and her rich supporters as suspect. If he got into politics, he said, he would fight developers and businessmen, who didn't give a damn about people or about keeping the beautiful city livable.

Soon after the municipal elections, 250,000 demonstrators marched in San Francisco to protest the war in Vietnam. That was the kind of political statement that resonated with Harvey now. A few months later, after President Richard Nixon sent American troops to invade Cambodia, Harvey heard there would be a lunch-hour protest at the Pacific Stock Exchange. He was rankled already because after seven months at Barth he had been getting careless about the length of his hair, and just that morning his boss suggested to him that it was too long and that he would have to cut it. Wearing one of his old Brooks Brothers suits that he had put on to go to work that morning, Harvey showed up at the protest, stepped to the front, where he made a speech denouncing war profiteers, and cut up his BankAmericard for all to see. News of what he had done beat him back to the Barth office. He had already fallen out of his boss's good graces, and now he was unceremoniously fired.[11]

* * *

Harvey had made enough money to live for a while without a job, but that could not go on indefinitely. In December 1970, eight months after he was terminated by J. Barth, Tom O'Horgan came to his rescue. O'Horgan had composed the score for a Paul Mazursky film about moviemaking in Hollywood called *Alex in Wonderland* that starred Donald Sutherland, with a cameo appearance by the celebrated Italian director Federico Fellini. O'Horgan now hoped to transfer his talents to Hollywood. He hired Harvey to come along as an assistant; and while Harvey was there he could listen in on negotiations for a film O'Horgan hoped to direct. It would be about the standup comic and social satirist Lenny Bruce, whom O'Horgan had known in the days when he himself was a comic on the nightclub circuit.[12] Bruce had been convicted on obscenity charges in 1964 and died two years later. O'Horgan considered him a martyred hero who had fought for free speech by challenging the conventional notion of what was obscene.

Harvey was so excited about the movie project that he forgot about his vague mayoral ambitions and dreamed that this might be the start of a new career. A film about Lenny Bruce—

a man who was ostensibly straight but who had been harassed and persecuted by fascistic police, just as gay people were if they let their homosexuality show: to have even the most tangential role in such a project would be auspicious.

But *Alex in Wonderland* was a flop: one reviewer, comparing it to Fellini's film *8½*, quipped that it "could be called '2' or '2½.'"[13] Negotiations to make *Lenny* dragged on and on. O'Horgan lost faith and returned to New York. And once more Harvey followed.

* * *

Before Harvey left San Francisco, Galen tried to kill himself yet again. This time he had jumped off a pier at Fisherman's Wharf, landing in water that was just four feet deep. He came home dripping with mud, furious, and screaming at Harvey that he wanted to die because Harvey had been flirting with someone at a Cockettes show he and Harvey had gone to together. Though Galen now had a solid reputation for his backstage talents, he was just as emotionally unstable as he had been when Harvey tried to rescue him by carrying him off to Dallas. But he was no longer the kid that Harvey had once hoped to save; and Harvey finally had to admit that it was foolish to keep trying. They would never stop being friends, and they would continue to work on O'Horgan productions, but their life together was over.

Harvey was deeply upset that there had been so many suicide attempts by people he loved: Galen; Craig Rodwell, the young radical with whom he had had an affair; even Joe Campbell, with whom he had lived for five years, later tried to kill himself after a new lover left him. It was not easy for Harvey, who had so much vitality and optimism—even when it was not warranted—to understand why people simply could not stop being depressed, could not pull themselves out of the depths of despair. After Joe Campbell's suicide attempt, Harvey wrote him a scolding letter, saying, "Life is rotten—hard—bitter and so forth—but life is life and the best that we have"; and "people in worse situations than you have come back strong." He told Joe he must find it in himself to summon reasons for hope.[14] But he wondered if a lot of gays thought about killing themselves because homosexuals were so universally despised that it was hard for them to imagine a future when things might be better. One of the chief messages of his political career would become that young gay people must be given reasons to hope.[15]

* * *

By 1971 Tom O'Horgan was the most successful director on Broadway. With the twenty-five-year-old Marc Cohen, whom he met in Hollywood, he moved to a three-thousand-square-foot loft on Broadway and Thirteenth Street, its walls covered with rare and exotic instruments from around the globe. He threw parties at which celebrities like Norman Mailer, Neil Diamond, Susan Sarandon, and Beverly Sills mixed genially with O'Horgan's hippie entourage.[16] He had three hits going simultaneously: *Hair* was at the Biltmore Theater; *Lenny* was at the Brooks Atkinson Theater and would gain O'Horgan a Drama Desk Award for Outstanding Director; and *Jesus Christ Superstar*, playing at the Mark Hellinger Theater, had had the largest advance ticket sales in Broadway history. The October 25, 1971, issue of *Time* magazine announced on its cover, "Jesus Christ Superstar Rocks Broadway" and featured a picture of a bearded, long-haired Jesus in a sequined dress. O'Horgan's musical not only questioned Christ's sexuality but also dressed King Herod in drag and presented a black actor as Judas. Yes, *Jesus Christ Superstar* was outrageous, a *New York Times* reporter, John Gruen, observed, but "the production bristles with life."

Harvey, who was described in that same article as "a long-time friend of O'Horgan's and a general aide on all of his productions," lived in the shadow of his friend's glory. Harvey was forty-one now, "an aging hippie," as Gruen, the *Times* reporter, called him, "a sad-eyed man . . . with long, long hair, wearing faded jeans and pretty beads." Gruen presented Harvey as Tom O'Horgan's gofer, who "seemed to be instinctively attuned to all of O'Horgan's needs," even serving as his chauffeur. The reporter, who had interviewed O'Horgan in his Broadway loft, wrote that Harvey was there throughout the interview, "lying sleepily outstretched on an immense pillow." He hinted that Harvey was stoned.[17]

* * *

Harvey might have been feeling by now that for a man approaching middle age he had not accomplished much—except that on his forty-first birthday, the same week that *Lenny* opened, magic suddenly entered his life again. Walking down the stairs of the Christopher Street subway station, he spotted a young man who was walking up the stairs. Harvey reversed directions to cruise him. The young man's first impression of him was not good. "This guy's a hippie gay clown," Joseph Scott Smith thought. With his scraggly hair, coal-black mustache and beard, and his tragic-looking eyes, Harvey resembled an extra from *Jesus Christ Superstar.* But his patter was as nonstop as it was entertaining. He would not leave to catch his train until he had Scott Smith's phone number in his jacket pocket.

Scott was eighteen years younger than Harvey, a southern boy who had grown up in Jackson, Mississippi. He had been a student at Memphis State University for a couple of years before making his way to New York, with the hope of becoming an actor. His shoulder-length hair and mustache were blond: Harvey had always preferred dark types, but he thought Scott was beautiful. He called him the next day. "Would you like to go to the opening night party for *Lenny*?" he asked. Of course, the twenty-three-year-old with Broadway ambitions said yes.

Scott found the opening night party thrilling: the glamour of the most outrageous in-group on Broadway; being backstage in a Broadway theater for the first time; the smell of marijuana that was so overpowering that Marc Cohen, the stage manager, had to send smokers to the second-floor dressing room so as not to bring on a raid; the hint that Scott might actually be hired as an assistant stage manager—and, most of all, Harvey's amusing quips and lively energy and his knack for making anyone he was interested in feel that they were fascinating and the most important person he knew.[18] In this case, that would be true: the night of the backstage party was the start of the major love relationship of Harvey's life.

*   *   *

Once in a while Harvey did get billing that went beyond "Tom O'Horgan's general aide." Eve Merriam's *Inner City Mother Goose*, a book of shocking "nursery rhymes" about the grim realities of life in the inner city, was adapted to become a Broadway production, *Inner City: A Street Cantata*, and opened on Broadway in December 1971. Again, Tom O'Horgan was the director. When Harvey befriended a husband and wife who were heirs to a Ceylonese tea distributing fortune and convinced them to be the major backers, he was given the title associate producer.[19] Harvey loved the play's social message. He was also certain that finally his big break had come.

But the critics panned it, complaining that *Inner City* dwelt on the drugs, pain, and numbness of the ghetto "in deep and dreary mono-color."[20] With such dismal reviews, ticket sales were sluggish. Yet when a backstage notice was posted saying that the run would end the following week, Harvey tore it down, shouting, "No! It's not going to close!"[21] He begged the backers for a further infusion of money, just until sales picked up. But they refused to throw good money after bad. Desperate, he invented promotional schemes that were new to Broadway, such as two-for-one ticket sales; and he ordered flashy flyers to lure an audience in.[22] Nothing worked. *Inner City* lasted on Broadway for three months. Harvey was heartbroken when it closed.

He was in love with Scott Smith, but he felt disheartened about his professional prospects. He could probably be Tom

O'Horgan's hanger-on forever, but that was not who he wanted to be. He hated being in New York now. It was the scene of his failures, and he found it ugly and dirty. In March 1972 he decided he would return to San Francisco, where he had been happiest, where he could make a fresh start. As soon as he reached that decision, he begged Scott to go with him.

The younger man was not sure what to do. He had come to New York to try his luck on Broadway, and he had not given his acting career a chance. Yet he had never met anyone as loving and interesting as Harvey.

Then Galen, always unhappy with his own life and jealous of Harvey's new passion, took Scott to dinner and told him about all of Harvey's quirks and defects.[23] Scott decided he needed time to weigh what Galen said against how he felt. "Let's test the relationship to see if it can stand the separation," Scott told Harvey, who was unaware of Galen's mischief and hurt by Scott's indecision.

Harvey went to San Francisco by himself, and Scott agonized that he might have lost him. But from San Francisco, Harvey wrote to Scott almost every day, determined anew to win him over. He swore that if Scott would live with him, Harvey would run around with a smile on his face all day long. He promised Scott, "You'll have my love and my cheer, my laughter, my arms, my schmaltz, my joy, my warmth, my heart."[24] He was unrelenting, irresistible. One month after Harvey left, Scott flew to San Francisco to join him.

Part 2

"They Call Me the Mayor of Castro Street"

5

"Who Is This Mr. Yoyo?"

WHAT HARVEY KNEW for certain was that he wanted to be with Scott. What he did not know was what he would do with the rest of his life. He thought briefly of opening a Jewish delicatessen in San Francisco. Then he decided not to rush into anything. He had saved up a little money; and Scott had received a couple of income tax refund checks before he left New York. They would see California before they settled down.

Harvey bought a secondhand Dodge Charger with a beat-up black vinyl roof and tattered bucket seats. They named the car the Green Witch in memory of Greenwich Village. For three months they drove around the state. When funds got low, they camped in the Redwoods. They loafed under trees, spent days reading magazines and newspapers, and made love whenever they were sure no one was around. Harvey, the consummate urban Jew who had never been camping before, was enraptured by the novelty and romance of it. When they tired of a place, they packed up the Green Witch and moved on.[1] It seemed they could happily live that way forever. Scott would gladly have done that. He cared only about being with Harvey now. But Harvey, who had his forty-second birthday in May, could not quiet the voice within that kept telling him he had done little of value with his life thus far.

In the early summer they headed back to San Francisco, where they found a cheap apartment on Grant Avenue in Chinatown; but it did not feel like home. In a month or two they moved to another place, on Fillmore and Jackson; but the rent was too high. Finally, in September they settled into an apartment at 577 Castro.[2] The area, which was part of Eureka Valley, had once been a conservative district of working-class people who held jobs such as longshoremen, factory workers, clerks, and cab drivers. Many were Irish or Italian, and their Sundays were spent at the Most Holy Redeemer Catholic Church, two blocks from Castro Street. But the Castro area had been changing. The maritime jobs in which many of the Castro's straight working-class residents were employed had seriously dwindled; automation ate up a lot of their other blue-collar jobs; and local factories were moving across the Bay to Oakland, where it was cheaper to operate.[3] On top of the job losses, it seemed to many of the straight residents that the chain migration of homosexuals, begun at the end of the 1960s, was unstoppable. The gays were taking over the streets, and the Castro was no longer a good place for working-class heterosexuals to live and raise families. They started selling out cheaply to the invading homosexuals, and they fled.

By the time Scott and Harvey arrived that summer of 1972, the Castro was already a gay mecca. Those who were settling the Castro were like pioneers: everything was possible in this fresh "Boystown" that suddenly seemed to be populated and run by gay men. There was a twenty-four-hour gay diner called Andy's Donuts just down the block from 577 Castro. There were shops like Leather Forever and High Gear, which sold day-glo jock-straps. There were seven or eight gay bars in a two-block strip, including Toad Hall, Nothing Special, the Honey Bucket, the Men's Room, and, Scott's and (teetotaling) Harvey's favorite, the Midnight Sun. And nearby was the gay-friendly Bud's Ice Cream to satisfy Harvey's sweet tooth.

In the window of his and Scott's apartment, Harvey placed a plant that signified how he saw his life thus far: it was a lavender-leafed Wandering Jew—but now, it and Harvey had found a home.[4]

At the SPCA pound they got a puppy. The pets Harvey had had with Galen—Trick and Trade—were given names that con-noted outlaw sex. But this dog Harvey and Scott called The Kid, a droll indicator that they saw themselves as a family, replete with a four-legged child. Still, they were an almost-broke fam-ily. They applied for unemployment compensation and learned that they were each eligible to receive ninety-one dollars a week; and that is what they lived on while they tried to figure out what to do next. Harvey briefly thought of getting a job in the finance industry: but to end up there again, after his glorious freedom . . . that would be the worst thing that could happen to him, he decided.[5] Throughout the fall and into the winter, he and Scott were unemployed.

The following February Tom O'Horgan came through for Harvey again by offering him a minor role in a Hollywood film he would be directing based on Eugène Ionesco's *Rhinoceros*, an absurdist play that decried the tyranny of mob mentality. It was just O'Horgan's sort of thing, and Harvey's too. Gene Wilder, Zero Mostel, and Karen Black signed on for the major roles.

Harvey hurried back to Hollywood to be in the movies! He played a chef, a role in which he mostly stood around in an absurdly tall white hat and looked grumpy. When *Rhinoceros* was finally released, in 1974, it got reviews so devastating that he could only be relieved he had ended up as the face on the cutting-room floor. But by then he had concluded that his glory was not to be found in Tinseltown.

*   *   *

One day in the Castro Harvey took a roll of film he had shot, mostly pictures of Scott, to a nearby pharmacy. It came back ruined. After getting over their anger, Harvey and Scott decided that what the Castro lacked was a neighborhood store that would serve the photographic needs of the community with care and respect—and that is what they could do for a living. They would open a store that would offer a reliable developing service, and the gay clientele would not have to worry that the developer might disapprove of the subject of their photos. They could also sell rolls of film at discount prices. Maybe they could sell photograph paper and darkroom chemicals too. They would call the place Castro Camera, though they would not stock many cameras because that would require more financial investment than they could manage.

Harvey turned to Tom O'Horgan yet again, and O'Horgan lent them a thousand dollars to get started. Half the money went for rent on a twenty-five-hundred-square-foot space at 575 Castro Street, right next door to their apartment. (Eventually they would move to an apartment upstairs from Castro Camera.) The other half of O'Horgan's loan went for supplies and a flowery antique cash register. They signed a five-year lease, and on March 3, 1973, they opened the doors. In the window, they placed a placard that announced, "We are VERY open." But stock was so meager that only the front third of the store was used for business. A friend who was moving lent them a battered art deco maroon sofa—only until he was settled in his new place, he said; but he never reclaimed it. Harvey and Scott tacked plywood to the bottom to keep the springs from falling out. The springs bulged through the top instead, but the sofa sat in Castro Camera for as long as the place was open for business.[6] They also brought in an old barber's chair and a 1950s-era easy chair. That was where The Kid slept or kept watch. Behind a gray curtain that separated the store from the "office" was a modest refrigerator, a coffeepot that was often perking, and a beat-up wooden desk. A stereo was always on, and the recorded voices of Maria Callas, Magda Olivero, Jon Vickers, and Franco Corelli were heard in every corner of the store.[7]

They settled into being merchants, and at first Harvey was fine with that role. He remembered that his grandfather had once opened a store and that he had made a great success of it. Then several things happened to make Harvey dream that something grander might yet be possible. A few days before his forty-third birthday the televised Watergate hearings, about the break-in and illegal wiretapping at the Democratic National Committee headquarters, began. In his senior year at college he had written a column for the school paper saying that political proceedings in America ought to be broadcast. Now they were, and they were about Republican crooks, and he was going to watch every minute of them.

He turned the stereo off and lugged the TV down from his apartment, placed it on a chair behind the counter, and let Scott tend to business while he sat glued to the screen. Every once in a while he hurled curses at President Nixon's attorney general, John Mitchell; at the White House counsel John Dean; and especially at Richard Nixon, whom he loathed. Customers who came into the store would see scantily filled racks, a small TV set balanced on a chair, and a middle-aged man with long hair and dark circles under his eyes screaming at the TV set, "You two-faced son-of-a-bitch!" "You lying, fucking son-of-a bitch!"[8]

Harvey later claimed it was Watergate that truly politicized him and sent him on his way to his next step in life. He was spurred along also by a couple of other incidents that happened around the same time as the hearings. The first was an altercation with a Board of Equalization official who came to the store to tell Harvey he had to pay a one-hundred-dollar deposit for his business license. Immediately. Harvey did not have the money to spare on hand. "You mean to tell me that if I don't have one hundred dollars I can't open a business in free-enterprise America?" he screamed at the official. The man screamed back, and two customers scurried out. "I'm paying your fucking salary and you're running my customers away!" Harvey shrieked. He spent hours on the phone fighting with the Board of Equalization. Finally, he was able to negotiate the deposit amount down to thirty dollars. He regarded the episode as his "first political victory."[9]

The next incident happened soon after. An elementary school teacher came into the store wanting to rent a slide projector that she could use in her class the next day. Her school did have a couple of projectors, she told Harvey, but you could not get one unless you reserved it months in advance. "So the city has enough money to send out bureaucrats to bug people, but not enough to get a teacher a slide projector she could use for her kids!" he complained to Scott.[10]

These incidents brought Harvey to a thrilling realization. The stage he had sought his whole life could be the political arena. He could do something momentous after all, something worthy of his dreams. He could change the system. Municipal elections were coming up in November. He would start by getting himself elected to the Board of Supervisors, which had jurisdiction over all legislation for the city and county of San Francisco.

Harvey assumed that if he ran as an openly gay man he would easily get votes in the Castro. But San Francisco did not have district elections; supervisors had to run citywide. He would have to get votes in Pacific Heights and Visitacion Valley and everywhere else in San Francisco. A calmer mind would have found the prospect daunting, but in his zeal Harvey could not contemplate failure.

He must surely have known that in the whole history of America only three self-declared homosexuals had ever run for public office. More than a decade earlier, in 1961, José Sarria, a celebrity drag queen who entertained at San Francisco's notorious Black Cat Café, made a bid for the Board of Supervisors against thirty-three other candidates.[11] Five seats were open, and Sarria came in ninth. In 1971 Frank Kameny ran for a seat in the U.S. Congress. He came in fourth in a field of six. In 1972 Rick Stokes, an openly gay lawyer, was urged by San Francisco's gay establishment to run for a very modest office—trustee on the Community College Board. He too lost his bid. But once Harvey made up his mind, he would not be discouraged. He would run as an out homosexual.

Scott was perplexed. He had no particular interest in politics, but Harvey was throwing himself headlong into this new enthusiasm. He wrote Scott an excited "love note" in which he begged the younger man to help him realize his aspiration: "I hope to make many things out of my love for you—I hope to use it so that everyone can enjoy our love—We can bring joy not only to each other but to others as well—There is enough strength between us to help others."[12]

Scott would have preferred to go on with their old life, but when it was clear that Harvey's new passion was not going away, he pledged his help. They would run a campaign together, though neither he nor Harvey knew the first thing about how to do it. Harvey gave Scott, who was not Jewish, a gift of a little gold *chai*, two attached Hebrew letters, *chet* and *yod*, whose numerological significance symbolizes "life." Scott wore it for a while on a chain around his neck. It seemed to say that now they were truly one.[13]

With the help of Tom Randol, an artist friend of Scott's who had recently migrated to the Castro from New York, Harvey and Scott hung up clotheslines in the back of Castro Camera and dried silk-screened campaign posters on them. They wrote press releases. They plastered the windows of Castro Camera with handwritten signs that declared, "Put Milk on Your ~~Shopping~~ [*sic*] List!" and "Milk Needs HELP COLD CASH WARM BODIES WILLING HANDS COME IN AND TALK!" They hung a large placard that announced, "YOUR CANDIDATE FOR SUPERVISOR HARVEY MILK" over a photograph of Harvey sporting a big, black mustache, his hair tied back in a messy ponytail.[14]

Harvey sported the mustache and ponytail when he went out campaigning too; and he wore his usual laid-back uniform: sneakers, jeans, denim or Pendleton shirts with open collars exposing his abundant chest hair. His was the style of Tom O'Horgan and most New York theater people he knew; it was the style too of the antiwar protestors and practically every male on the Left. But even Harvey's friends thought he looked less like a bohemian or even a radical than a "freak," "like Rasputin, with eyes like drills," "like a wandering Jew looking for his tribe."[15] Yet to cut his hair, shave his mustache, don a suit and tie and leather shoes—it smacked too much of the bourgeois conformity to which he had put himself in opposition since his La MaMa days. He refused to look like a Wall Street cutout ever again.

His appearance and everything else about him was abhorrent to San Francisco's gay establishment. The leading power broker of that establishment was Jim Foster, a buttoned-down man in his late thirties who had been working in the homophile movement since he was witch-hunted and booted out of the army in 1961. In 1971 he helped found the Alice B. Toklas Memorial Democratic Club, a gay and lesbian group that supported liberal mainstream politicians who promised to oppose discrimination against homosexuals. The next year, 1972, Foster ran a successful campaign to get the presidential candidate George McGovern, who had made some gay-friendly remarks, listed at the top—the most advantageous spot—of the California ballot in the Democratic primaries. Foster's feat gave him prominence among gays and led to his being chosen to speak in a plenary session of the 1972 Democratic National Convention. Granted, he was not allowed to speak until five o'clock in the morning, and the gay rights plank he was promoting went down to resounding defeat—nevertheless, he was the first openly gay person in the history of American politics to have a few minutes at the microphone of a Democratic National Convention.[16] Foster's celebrity among gays gave him virtual carte blanche in spending the money the Alice Club raised in its Dollars for Democrats drives. The worthy recipients of that money, in Foster's estimation, were politicians like George Moscone, Willie Brown, and Dianne Feinstein, who were friendly to the kinds of gays who wouldn't embarrass them (and Alice Club members) by being swishy or shrill or otherwise outrageous.[17]

So when Harvey came to Jim Foster to say he was running for supervisor and he hoped the Alice Club would endorse him, Foster's first thought was, "Who is this Mr. Yoyo?"[18] Harvey's long hair and sloppy dress were a wild contrast to the conservative style of San Francisco's gay leaders. But it was not just his appearance that turned Foster off.[19] It was also the fact that here was this guy who had arrived in San Francisco a few months earlier, had no history of working for the gay community, and had the temerity to think that an uncloseted homosexual could get elected to the Board of Supervisors. If it were possible for someone who was openly gay to win an election, Jim Foster surely would have run himself. Now he relished being brutally blunt to the weirdo with the heavy New York accent who stood before him. "Well, there's an old saying in the Democratic Party," he told Harvey. "You don't get to dance unless you put up the chairs. I've never seen you putting up the chairs."[20] Harvey reiterated his intention to fight fiercely for gay rights once he got elected; but Foster was unimpressed. "We're like the Catholic Church," he sneered. "We take converts, but we don't make them pope the same day."[21]

* * *

Since Foster was not going to let him through the gate, Harvey had to figure out how to attract a constituency that was broader than the gay community. He would court the elderly, the poor, the young, the worker, all the racial minorities. They were outsiders too, and as a double outsider—a homosexual and a Jew—his deepest sentiments were always with outsiders. Asked to fill out a questionnaire for a group that was preparing a voter's pamphlet, Harvey wrote zealously about how government threw away taxpayers' money by hiring police to arrest people for victimless crimes instead of spending it where it ought to go—on expanding health care, especially for the elderly, "particularly dental care"; on expanding "Operation Bootstrap for black, Spanish, welfare [recipients], young" and helping them "go into business for themselves." Marijuana should be legalized, and "hard-drug addicts" should be helped, he declared. To a question about whether halfway houses and board and care homes should be placed in residential areas he replied, "If people who call themselves Christians are Christians then the only answer is 'of course.'" In answer to a question about civil rights he wrote,

> For all—esp. gay
> esp. black
> esp. Mexican
> esp. Oriental

The questionnaire also asked what the candidate's source of campaign financing would be. "Passing the hat for dollars and coins" was Harvey's plan.[22]

With little money to spend he had a hard time getting noticed by the media, though once in a while he got lucky. A writer for the gay biweekly *Kalendar Magazine* interviewed Harvey at home and gushed with enthusiasm, writing that Harvey's "ideas came racing out at me as I sipped my coffee. I could feel the excitement in him, the intensity, the idealism he had to build a better world."[23] It was exactly how Harvey wished to be perceived; it was exactly how he felt. But a glowing article like this was scarce.

For the most part the gay press was dubious about his candidacy, even hostile. In August, at the beginning of his campaign, Harvey wrote a long and very serious letter to the editor of the *Advocate*, America's largest national gay newspaper, whose circulation of tens of thousands was boosted by hookup ads and spreads of beautiful beefcakes. Harvey explained in the letter that he was running because he thought it was time for gay people to elect uncloseted gays to political office instead of relying on gay-friendly politicians who did no more than throw the community "a few crumbs." If a gay person got elected to the Board of Supervisors, Harvey wrote, there would be a gay voice that the other board members would have to listen to. An uncloseted gay on the board would even force the issue of decriminalizing homosexual acts, he argued, because the government would be embarrassed to call a political leader criminal. If a gay was elected, he declared optimistically, that person would fight for human rights, and the image of gays "would change overnight and bring respect to all of us."[24] The letter was an ingenuous and impassioned statement of his aspirations.

It was never published, and when the image-conscious *Advocate* finally printed an interview a month before the election, it was deflating. The *Advocate* virtually mocked him. He was "not exactly a glamour boy," the writer of the article observed. "Born in 1930, he looks a bit like a slightly overage hippie, with largish hair and mustache, and a bit like a neighborhood shopkeeper—which he is."[25]

On the rare occasions that he got mainstream papers to pay attention to him, the results were no more flattering. An article in the *San Francisco Examiner* featured a picture of him that made him look like a weird cross between a hippie and a Hasid, with long sideburns that could be mistaken for *peyas*. The reporter portrayed him as a curiosity, almost a crackpot, who bellyached about "lack of respect by 'our so-called leaders' because [I] represent no large voting block or monied group." Harvey did try hard to convey to the reporter who he was and whom he would champion, and he is quoted as saying, "I will strive to bring the government to the people, be they intellectuals or fellow homosexuals, be they blacks or fellow Jews, be they the tax-starved elderly or fellow small-shop owners." But in the context of the article it was hard to see him as anything but a flake.[26]

He fared no better in the *San Francisco Chronicle*, which ran a photo of him over the caption "A Gay Jewish Democrat" and exposed his failure to raise support from those who should have been his base. The president of the San Francisco Council of Democratic Clubs scoffed in the article, "This guy Milk couldn't even get the endorsement of his own people, the Alice B. Toklas Democratic Club, so how could he expect to get the Council's endorsement?"[27] The *Chronicle* columnist Herb Caen quipped that Harvey Milk was "running for Supervisor on the homo ticket, and I don't mean homogenized."[28]

Harvey pretended to be impervious to all the insults. "Sticks and stones may break my bones," he told Scott, "but spell my name right. And there's not too many ways to spell Milk."[29] He could not admit defeat. He had finally discovered—after a lifetime of searching—what he was meant to do; and now he would put everything into winning the right to do it.

Scott missed their old, laid-back life, but there was no going back. When he was not making campaign flyers or posters or writing press releases he faithfully minded the store while Harvey threw himself into campaigning. When Harvey had volunteered for Barry Goldwater, a lifetime ago, he would get up early and hurry to the subway with a fistful of Goldwater flyers to

hand out to people on their way to work. Now he took fistfuls
of Milk flyers to hand out to the early morning crowd at the
San Francisco bus stops. With a humorous allusion to Delancey
Street orators he printed the word SOAP on a wooden box,
and at a little plaza on Castro Street he mounted his soapbox,
shouted out that he was running for the San Francisco Board of
Supervisors, and schmoozed everyone who passed by until they
took a Milk flyer. The election was citywide, so he covered the
entire city. He handed out flyers in shopping centers and gay
bars and even at his old place of employment, the financial district. His energy had no limit.

Hungry for an audience who would listen to his platform,
he was eager to go anywhere he could squeeze out an invitation. But all the big gay organizations that held Candidates'
Nights, such as the Society for Individual Rights, followed the
lead of the Alice Club. They snubbed him, making no distinc-
tion between Harvey and another candidate for the Board of
Supervisors, Jesus Christ Satan, who described himself as being
androgynous and wore flowing robes and a gaudy flowered hat.[30]
Both were considered kook candidates and "bad for the gays."

* * *

When Harvey did manage to get an invitation to speak to
a group, he delivered his on-target message passionately, and he
knew how to connect with his audience. His years in the theater had not been wasted. In a speech to the newly established
San Francisco branch of the National Women's Political Caucus he emphasized that the city had to stop spending funds on
ugly freeways and convention halls and start putting money into
childcare centers and "poverty areas."[31] In a speech to the Joint
International Longshoremen and Warehousemen's Union he
blamed the present Board of Supervisors for caring only about
"bigness and wealth" and not about the welfare of the San Francisco workingman.[32] At a Candidates' Night for an environ-

mentalist group, San Francisco Tomorrow, he berated developers who were destroying neighborhoods and the whole city with their ugly high-rises. His presentation stole the show.[33]

But Harvey had not mastered the politic art of self-censorship—he never would. For instance, when a San Francisco Tomorrow member asked how he hoped to win the election without significant financial backing, Harvey joked that since he was openly gay some kid's father who was upset about the recently discovered Houston serial killer Dean Corll, who had raped, tortured, and murdered twenty-eight boys, would shoot Harvey—and then "I'll be lucky and survive and get lots of sympathy as well as the liberal and gay votes." His bizarre sense of humor totally canceled out his fine speech. Not surprisingly, San Francisco Tomorrow decided it would not endorse Harvey Milk.[34]

* * *

Harvey was sure that if only he had more money to put into the campaign, he could win, but donations barely trickled in. Desperation led him to call his brother, Robert, back east, to ask for help. Harvey's relationship with his brother had been cool since 1962, when their mother died. Jewish law forbids cremation, and Harvey knew that Robert was observant. Despite that, Harvey had Minnie cremated, as he wished to be himself someday. Robert was furious. And now, eleven years later, Harvey dared to call and ask Robert for money to run for some sort of office in San Francisco. As Harvey told friends, his brother bellowed, "Are you crazy? No way!" and hung up.[35]

Harvey did manage to raise about twenty-five hundred dollars from supporters. And he put another two thousand dollars of his own money into the campaign.[36] But the spending cap per Board of Supervisors candidate that year was almost a dozen times that, fifty-one thousand dollars.[37] Many of his competitors spent the limit. Realistically, Harvey did not have a chance.

In spite of the slim odds, his enemies in the gay establishment were not taking the chance that he might squeak through. There were five open spots on the Board of Supervisors; and they did everything to make sure Harvey would not win enough votes to get one of them. They took out a huge ad in *Kalendar*, San Francisco's biggest gay paper, reminding its readers that over the past few years the gay community "has developed a political strength unmatched by any other community in the city"; and in order to maintain that strength, the ad said, it was necessary to "insure Responsible [*sic*] representation"—this was patently aimed at Harvey, who was not, in the power brokers' eyes, "Responsible." They then presented their choices for the supervisor slots—politicians who had proven themselves to be gay friendly. Dianne Feinstein led the list.[38]

But Harvey had struck a chord with some San Franciscans. The young in particular loved his idealism and iconoclasm. With his long hair and jeans, he looked more like them than any politician they had ever seen. Three weeks before the election the University of San Francisco conducted a poll among its students asking who they intended to vote for in the Board of Supervisors race. Harvey came in first. Feinstein came in second.[39] Nevertheless, such enthusiasm was not widespread enough to get him one of the five seats. When the citywide election was held, Harvey came in tenth in a field of thirty-two candidates. Four incumbents who ran had been reelected. The only newly elected supervisor was the San Francisco–born Al Nelder, a longtime police officer who in 1970 had been appointed chief of police by Mayor Joseph Alioto.

Yet, despite Harvey's political enemies, despite his lack of money, despite the heavy odds against him, seventeen thousand people had been impressed enough by Harvey Milk to turn out and vote for him.

*   *   *

Across the San Francisco Bay, on the same day of the Board of Supervisors election, November 6, 1973, Marcus Foster, the black superintendent of the Oakland School District, was shot to death. He had been killed by eight hollow-point bullets filled with cyanide. His assassins were members of the Symbionese Liberation Army, a radical group that was angry with Foster for supporting a plan to force students to carry photo ID cards on campus to distinguish them from the drug dealers who were roaming the school halls. The head of the Symbionese Liberation Army, a black man called Cinque, had told his followers, "We are gonna off that nigger. We want to show the oppressed peoples there are black pigs just as there are white pigs."[40] Evidently it could be dangerous to be a public official in the Bay Area in the 1970s.

* * *

Harvey was disheartened by the election results. All that effort, and he had lost. Scott, ever solicitous of Harvey, suggested they needed a little vacation to regroup. He remembered the lovely time they had had when they first came to California, driving around in the Green Witch. Harvey agreed it would be good to get away. They locked up the store, packed the car, and again they drove. In a coastal city in Monterey County—Pacific Grove—they found a tacky motel they could afford and paid for three nights. They walked on the beach, ate picnic suppers while watching the sunset, and lolled about in bed. All the while Harvey kept telling himself and Scott too that he really had nothing to be down about. After all, he did not start campaigning until August. And all through the campaign he had gone around looking like a hippie. He realized that that was a big mistake. Still, seventeen thousand people had voted for him. Next time, he would do better.[41]

6

Learning to Put Up the Chairs

SINCE HE WAS a merchant now, Harvey would begin to raise his profile by becoming a leader of the gay business community. Two days before Christmas 1973 he walked into a meeting of the Eureka Valley Merchants Association with Scott by his side. The organization went back to the days when the Church of the Most Holy Redeemer was not only a place of worship but also a center of social activity for much of the conservative Eureka Valley business community, of which the Castro District was a part. Although the character of the Castro was already hugely changed by the gay invasion, the Eureka Valley Merchants Association remained intent on pushing back those changes. The merchants were searching for a way to block the granting of a business license to a gay couple who wanted to open yet another antique store in the neighborhood where there used to be family-oriented businesses such as baby furniture stores and women's dress shops.

At the December 23 meeting they had been augmenting Christmas cheer with spiked eggnog, but they sobered up quickly when they saw Harvey Milk—who had made himself notorious as a homosexual during his failed run for supervisor—walk through the door with his young lover. The merchants did not even bother pretending to be civil. Before Harvey could open his mouth someone called for adjournment, and the meeting came to an abrupt end.[1]

Fine, Harvey decided. His grandfather had once helped found a Jewish alternative to the Rockaway Hunt Club from which Jews had been banned. He would do the same: he would help found an organization for gay businessmen who were banned from the Eureka Valley Merchants Association—and if straights wanted to join, that was okay with him.

He discovered that two or three years earlier there had actually been a gay business organization in the Castro, the Castro Village Association. It was started by Ian Ingham, the owner of one of the antique shops, the Gilded Age. Ingham, an early blackball victim of the Eureka Valley Merchants Association, had concluded that gay businessmen needed to form their own group. But try as he might, he could not find enough members to keep it going, and the Castro Village Association quickly became defunct.[2]

Harvey figured out how to start a new Castro Village Association and make it work. When he was running for supervisor he had knocked on the door of every gay business in the Castro. The owners knew him because he had schmoozed them all, hoping for campaign donations. Now he went back to each gay-owned store, talked personally to the proprietors about the Eureka Valley Merchants Association's history of nastiness to gays, and then invited them to a confab. They came not only because they were convinced by his arguments about why a gay business organization was necessary but also because Harvey Milk was famous as the gay guy who had just won the votes of seventeen thousand San Franciscans. In the back room of the Sausage Factory, a Castro pizzeria owned by a gay-friendly Italian couple, the Castro Village Association was reborn. Harvey Milk was voted its president.[3]

Harvey put tremendous energy into making the association grow. He convinced a young heterosexual woman photographer, the co-owner with her husband of Cliff's Variety Store on Castro Street, not only to drop out of the hidebound Eureka Valley Merchants Association and join the Castro Village Association but also to go around with him to every business that was a member of the CVA and take photos of it. He included those photos in a brochure he and Scott put together that advertised neighborhood stores that the gay community ought to patronize. Then Harvey decided that if he could get the local Hibernia Bank to join the Castro Village Association, it would give the new organization more legitimacy. Hibernia's chief officer could not see any point in his bank signing on, until Harvey pointed out that most of the gay residents of the Castro kept their money at Hibernia—and that could be changed.

Once Hibernia joined, Harvey went to the Castro branch of the Bank of America and told its chief officer that "Hibernia Bank is now a member of the Castro Village Association." Bank of America joined too.[4] Before long the Castro Village Association represented ninety local businesses, including about two dozen gay-friendly, straight-owned establishments. The Eureka Valley Merchants Association disbanded, most members having sold their businesses—primarily to gays—and fled what they considered Sodom.

* * *

Harvey's major achievement as a leader of the Castro Village Association was to establish a yearly street fair that would draw San Franciscans to Castro businesses, just as the popular Polk Street Fair was doing for Polk Street businesses. The first Castro Street Fair, held on a gorgeous day on August 18,

1974, covered two long blocks between Market and Nineteenth Streets. It featured the artwork of the Castro's countless artists, food from every culture, clowns, jugglers, tightrope walkers, belly dancers, and drag queens. It had the verve and color of Tom O'Horgan's Broadway hit *Hair*, at which Harvey had been a mere hanger-on. Now *he* was the director.

More than five thousand people showed up at the first fair; and Harvey surpassed that success the following year, when he booked a personal friend, the flamboyant black entertainer Sylvester, for the second fair. A former Cockette whose records would eventually top the American pop charts and "go gold," the androgynous Sylvester sang in falsetto and was known as the Queen of Disco. His appearance at the Castro Street Fair was a coup that drew intrigued newspaper and TV reporters, who presented Harvey to the media as the fair's creator and spokesman.[5] Twenty-five thousand people attended that year's fair. Within a few years the Castro Street Fair would be attracting as many as one hundred thousand visitors and would be the largest of the San Francisco street fairs.[6] How's that for "putting up the chairs"? Harvey might well have asked Jim Foster.

From the very first fair, Harvey set up a voter registration booth directly in front of Castro Camera. He discovered that fewer than half the gay people in the Castro were registered to vote. After the fair wrapped, he started a registration drive inside Castro Camera. When customers came into the store he was less interested in selling them merchandise than in finding out whether they were registered voters—and if they were not, registering them.[7] In 1974 alone he personally talked 2,350 gay people into becoming voters. He had a game plan for his future and theirs that depended on their being able to vote.

* * *

As the leader of the Castro Village Association Harvey played a nominal role as a man of business, but it did not interest him much. Scott was beginning to feel overwhelmed and a bit resentful; nevertheless, he picked up the slack at the store while Harvey engaged in what did interest him: being the unofficial mayor of Castro Street. Castro Camera soon became less a business enterprise for Harvey than a community center where people knew they could go to ask about the best place to look for an apartment or a job or what agency to turn to if they had complaints about city government. Before the 1974 June primary and November general election, Harvey filled out sample ballots and posted them in the store window in case anyone wanted his advice on whom to vote into office or how to vote on the propositions.

Neighborhood gays started making Castro Camera a hangout. They would sprawl on the maroon couch or the old barber's chair or lean against the walls, listening to Harvey hold forth on everything—politics, opera, theater, relationships, sex. He also offered one-on-one personal advice to those who wanted it (he called it putting on his "shrink's robe"), like how to deal with a judgmental sibling's upcoming visit or what to do if your lover has an alcohol problem.[8] Harvey was in his element. He had a knack for making whomever he was talking with feel like they had 100 percent of his attention, that despite the recording of *Tosca* or *Der Rosenkavalier* that was loud enough to be heard in every corner of the store, whatever they had to say was the most interesting thing he could possibly be listening to.[9]

He also put himself forward as a mouthpiece for the gay world. In response to a rash of incidents of police harassment of Castro gays he wrote an open letter, nominally addressed to the City of San Francisco Hall of Justice, using the trope that would become recurrent in his future writings and speeches: it harked back to what he had learned as a child about the treatment of Jews at the hands of the Nazis. He argued that police brutality against gays was being ignored in San Francisco, just like Nazi brutality against Jews had been ignored in Germany—

and San Franciscans had better learn their history lesson: "The Germans who hated Jews and allowed the Jews to be beaten should have fought for Jewish freedom. For in fighting for the Jews they would have in reality been fighting for their own freedom!" Even those San Franciscans who disdained homosexuals, he warned, must side with them against police brutality because if they don't they will "one day find that they too are becoming victims of a police state."[10]

Harvey put himself forward physically too, jumping into the fray whenever he saw police harassing gays. One such incident happened on a hot Labor Day night in 1974, two weeks after the first fair. Many of the patrons who poured out of the gay bars at closing time, two in the morning, extended the evening by heading to the only Castro Street establishment that was still open, Andy's Donuts. They purchased their Boston Creams and Long Johns and then stood around in clusters in front of Andy's consuming what they bought, chatting with friends, cruising interesting prospects. Suddenly the police, intent on "cleaning the Castro Street sidewalks" because an election was coming up in November, swooped down on them. Dozens of gays were beaten, and a small riot ensued. Fourteen men were arrested—charged with public drunkenness, disturbing the peace, resisting arrest, and obstructing traffic. Harvey heard the commotion from his apartment across the street, and he came running. "What laws were being broken by these guys?" he demanded of the police. In the morning he informed the media that the "Castro 14," as he called the victims, had been picked on by the cops only because they were gay.

Charges against the Castro 14 were quickly dropped; but Harvey, determined to teach the police a lesson, encouraged the men to sue for $1.375 million. They hired the openly gay lawyer Rick Stokes to represent them, and Castro Camera became headquarters for the Castro 14 Defense Fund. Harvey got the police department worried enough to agree to send representatives to a Police Community Relations Seminar, where he presented his criticisms so forcefully that the San Francisco Police Department promised to make a training film that would defuse police prejudice in dealing with the gay community.[11] He also got himself elected to the board of Friends of San Francisco Deputies and Inmates, a nonprofit oversight group. It was Harvey's second election victory in less than a year.

* * *

In February 1974 he began writing a weekly column for a new San Francisco gay paper, the *Sentinel*, called "Waves from the Left." It was meant to appeal to a big segment of gay San Francisco—those nonestablishment gays who despised the moderate groups that had rejected Harvey, such as the Alice B. Toklas Memorial Democratic Club and the Society for Individual Rights. Yet very soon Harvey undercut his column's title, which had been his editor's idea, by flatly denouncing what he called the "extreme left."[12]

Harvey was not a radical. He had no interest in the revolution—throwing out the whole system, starting over—for which the Gay Liberation Front, born of the Stonewall riots, had called. "Sexual liberation for all people cannot come about unless existing social institutions are abolished," the GLF had said in their Statement of Purpose in 1969.[13] That was crazy, Harvey thought. He wanted a reformed society that would let gay people be first-class citizens with the right to participate fully in American life. One of his first columns for the *Sentinel* revealed his basic conviction: homosexuals would not be free, he wrote, until they could "join the police force or any government agency as an open homosexual. It's as simple as that."[14]

In his hippie years Harvey disavowed Barry Goldwater, who was associated with archconservatism; yet, in fact, he never stopped being attracted to certain Goldwater tenets, like those that were picked up by the Libertarian Party when it was founded in 1971. In a "Waves" column on March 28, 1974, for instance, Harvey rejected big government: "Let those on the Left stand up for big daddy doing it all," he proclaimed, echoing Goldwater. "When you allow the government to get too powerful there are always encroachments": he gave as examples the laws against sodomy and pot. He was an ardent believer in free enterprise and capitalism, and he saw himself as someone whose "thinking [was] based on business acumen," as he told Scott (who may have been wishing by now that Harvey would apply that acumen to Castro Camera, which was not a flourishing business).[15]

Yet Harvey would always spurn the orthodoxy of any party line. He was most comfortable in the role of maverick. Despite his nod to Goldwater and the Libertarians, he embraced the Left's perspective on the function of government. Where government money ought to go, he declared in his column, is into schools, hospitals, housing for the poor. "So where do I stand?" he asked his readers. "I stand about as far Left or as far Right as you see me, depending upon where you're standing."[16]

* * *

Many of Harvey's columns for the *Sentinel* and other gay publications such as the *Bay Area Reporter* and *Vector* were concerned with rousing apolitical gays to see themselves as belonging to a gay political community. The tone of these columns was reminiscent of the red-blooded, rah-rah sports pieces he wrote in college, in which he tried endlessly to stir a thirst for school spirit and victory in the apathetic student body. Now, though, the stakes had changed from winning a pennant to winning civil rights. Harvey aimed to galvanize in his gay readers an appetite for the fight by telling them that homosexuals have been "the longest and most deeply suppressed" minority; and that just as black people realized they would never gain freedom if their leaders were Uncle Toms, gays needed to realize they would never gain freedom if their leaders were Aunt Marys who asked for crumbs instead of first-class citizenship.

"To win our rights to self-respect and equality," he argued, gays had to band together and come out in full force, so that the straight world would see that homosexuals are legion and united, that they're in "respected and necessary positions," and that they mean business.[17]

Because he had spent years of his life on Wall Street, he believed he had the right to talk like someone who knew something about the power of money and how gay people could use it. In a piece he called "Gay Economic Power" he urged his readers to develop community spirit with their money. Just as they regularly traveled out of their neighborhood to visit a gay bar, they must go out of their way to shop at a gay store rather than at a convenient neighborhood store. As for gay merchants, they must take seriously their responsibilities to the gay community. They needed to support gay activities and gay organizations. Practices like that were "a step towards gay civil rights" because they promoted the cohesiveness of a community, which is the sine qua non in the fight for rights, Harvey wrote—remembering no doubt how he had lost the election because there had been no cohesive community behind him.[18] In another piece, "Buy Gay," he reminded his readers of the great success of the bus boycott in Montgomery, Alabama. "Gays can learn a lot from that," he declared, urging gays to unite in the same way blacks had and to use their economic clout to fight for gay civil rights.[19]

* * *

In the early 1960s Harvey had rejected the radical gay talk of his young lover Craig Rodwell. Neither had Harvey connected with the Marxist language of the Gay Liberation Front, which in 1969 had proclaimed the fight for gay freedom "a people's movement, a class struggle with the rights of every oppressed person linked to one another."[20] But now, in San Francisco, he mixed his libertarianism with ideas that were not very different from those of the gay radicals in New York. Gay people must build bridges with workers and racial minorities, he declared. Not only was it the morally right thing to do, but workers and racial minorities were "us"s with gays, he said, because they all had common enemies—the "them"s who wanted to keep the powerless in their place. Self-interest, too, was a big reason to build bridges, he proclaimed. If gay people fought for the rights of the others, the others would help gays fight for their own rights. Harvey soon had a chance to put his theories into play.

Allan Baird, who lived a couple of blocks from Castro Camera and had grown up in the area when it was an ethnic working-class enclave, was a beefy man with long sideburns and graying hair. For years he had been a truck driver for the *San Francisco Chronicle*. He was also president of the Joint Council of Teamsters, where he worked with the beer drivers on certain employment grievances. Baird was a tough bird, and homosexuals were not usually part of the crowd he hung out with. But Harvey's seventeen thousand votes the year before had made him one of the most famous gays in San Francisco. Baird paid him a visit at Castro Camera.[21]

A boycott against Coors Beer had started with Hispanics in the 1960s because less than 2 percent of Coors employees were Hispanic, and the few who were hired were stuck in the most menial jobs. The boycott expanded in the fall of 1973, when Coors and five other breweries tried to union-bust by refusing to hire any driver who was a union man. That was when Allan Baird became the Teamsters' boycott leader against the breweries. He had finally been able to persuade a small federation of grocery stores in San Francisco, mostly Arab- and Chinese-owned, to refuse deliveries by scab drivers; but by themselves the groceries were not plentiful enough to provide a knockout punch to the breweries. Then, in the summer of 1974, Baird had a brainstorm.

He came to Castro Camera to ask Harvey to organize in all

of San Francisco's gay bars a boycott of the six offending beer companies. "Absolutely!" Harvey exclaimed. The Coors Beer Company, owned by an ultraconservative family dynasty, was notorious among gays. Harvey had heard that prospective Coors employees had to take a polygraph test to make sure they did not lead an "immoral lifestyle," which usually meant a homosexual lifestyle.[22] But he also jumped at the chance a boycott would give him to demonstrate to gays that he was right when he said that if they banded together they would have substantial economic power, which they could use to promote gay power.

He had another idea too. "I've got one non-negotiable proviso before I'll help with the boycott," he told Baird: the Teamsters had to agree immediately to hire openly gay truck drivers. Baird was not sure how over-the-top-macho Teamsters would react to such a proposition, but he said he would give it his best shot.

Harvey was now writing a regular column for the *Bay Area Reporter*, "Milk Forum." To begin his part of the bargain with Allan Baird, he used his bully pulpit to announce in a headline, "Teamsters Seek Gay Help," and to reiterate what he had been saying all along: "If we in the gay community want others to help us in our fight to end discrimination, then we must help others in their fights."[23] Word went out that gays were boycotting the six beer companies. In case any of the one hundred or more San Francisco gay and lesbian bar owners did not get the word, Harvey and several of his Castro Camera buddies visited all of them; he made sure the press knew about it too. With news cameras clicking, gay-bar owners dramatically took the affronting bottles off the shelves and poured the contents down the drain. Beers on the blacklist simply stopped being available to the sizable beer-drinking San Francisco gay-bar crowd. The boycott was so effective that five of the breweries let no time lapse before they retracted their policy about not hiring union drivers.

To Harvey's satisfaction and almost everyone's astonishment, the Teamsters did become welcoming to openly gay truck drivers—beginning with Howard Wallace, a gay radical and union activist who had worked with Harvey on the boycott. Openly gay drivers were soon hired by Budweiser, Lucky Lager, Falstaff, and the other companies that had come back into the fold.[24] When Coors held out, Harvey reminded gays that the fight was not over: "I think Coors should be shown the strength of gay economic power," he wrote, adding the trope to which he often returned: "I do not think that any Jew would buy the greatest of products if Hitler was the salesman. I do not think any of us should buy one bottle of Coors beer." For four years a bottle of Coors was a rare to nonexistent sight in a gay bar, and sales of Coors in California fell by one-third. Coors finally relented.[25]

When that happened, Allan Baird gave Harvey something he figured every activist leader needed—a red and white bullhorn, battered by police batons, which Baird had used in rousing the masses to action.

* * *

By the end of 1974 Harvey had done everything he could think of to put himself in a good position for the 1975 Board of Supervisors race. He had put up every chair in sight. He had even cut his ponytail. Had he left out any detail? he wondered. Of course he had! He shaved off his mustache.

During his theater years, when jeans and love beads had been his sartorial preference, he emptied his closets of the Brooks Brothers suits he wore to work on Wall Street because they felt like a costume. Now he needed that costume back. He went shopping with Scott, and at a dry cleaner's he bought himself a secondhand suit that a customer had failed to pick up. At a charity thrift shop at Ninth and Castro he bought some laundered button-down shirts and conservative-looking ties and a pair of used wingtip shoes. Scott abhorred the new look. Where was *his* Harvey? But no one could say Harvey did not look like a San Francisco supervisor now. If he looked the role and acted the role, he could inhabit the role. For Harvey, being in politics was much like being in the theater. His old Broadway pal Tom O'Horgan understood that: "Harvey spent all his life looking for a stage," Tom would later say, "and when he moved to San Francisco, he found it."[26]

7

◆┃◆┃◆

Strike Two

In 1975, soon after the hugely successful second annual Castro Street Fair, Harvey informed the media that he had just filed his papers to run again for one of the six vacant seats on the Board of Supervisors. But the timing was not good. In September, Patty Hearst, a kidnapped heiress-turned-armed-soldier for the Symbionese Liberation Army, whose slogan was "Death to the fascist insect that preys upon the life of the people," was arrested in a San Francisco apartment. Four days later President Gerald Ford was almost assassinated outside the St. Francis Hotel in San Francisco. His would-be killer, Sara Jane Moore, was a middle-aged radical who made her living as a bookkeeper. She had been inspired by the newspaper photo of the machine-gun-toting Patty Hearst helping the SLA rob a bank. Those stories dominated the papers.

However, there were a few reporters who remembered Har-

vey's 1973 campaign and did pay attention to his announcement—
because they were astounded by the new Harvey Milk. He was
shorn, shaved smooth, and decked out in a conservative gray
suit and rep tie. Harvey the Hippie was apparently gone. A few
papers ran his handsome new publicity photo alongside their
stories. "I changed my image, but I haven't changed one word
of what I always said," he hastened to assure the radical newspapers that might have been confused.[1]

Harvey was determined to be even more focused than he
had been two years earlier. If they did it right, he told Scott,
they would have a real chance this time around. But he really
needed Scott's help. Scott resigned himself to the realization
that, though his love for Harvey was unchanged, their old life
together was gone forever.

He agreed to run the day-to-day management of the campaign. He would set up Harvey's speaking appearances and interviews. He would find volunteers to hand out campaign brochures. He would look for supporters to give money. He and
Harvey had little time for Castro Camera now. But how could
they give up the store? They were still dependent on it for their
livelihood; and it was more than a store—it was a vital gay community center. They had to find someone reliable to keep the
doors of Castro Camera open while they were off campaigning.

Danny Nicoletta was an aspiring photographer and filmmaker. The nineteen-year-old, who could have passed for fifteen, had been anxious to get as far away from Utica, New
York, as possible: he thought he might be gay, and Utica, where
he grew up, did not feel like a safe place. He moved first to
Kansas City to go to the Art Institute and then farther west, to
an art school in Oakland, California. One evening he crossed
the Bay to visit a friend who worked at the Castro Street Café.
"Just about everyone you see in here or on the streets is gay,"
the friend told Danny. Danny looked around and knew he'd

come home. A few days later he found a vacancy in an apartment house with six flats, all of them buzzing with recent arrivals to the Castro, young gays, mostly artistic types like him.

Danny's new apartment was a half block away from Castro Camera, where Harvey still loved to chat with the customers or anyone who happened to drop in. One day Danny came into Castro Camera with a couple of rolls of unexposed film, and Harvey invited the blond young man to take a seat near the counter, on the arm of the ratty, overstuffed chair in which The Kid always slept. They talked about art and movies and the classes Danny thought he might take at San Francisco State University. Harvey always liked to encourage gay kids to get an education and make something of themselves.

Danny started coming around often, even when he did not have film to be developed, just to hang out, like so many gays did. Harvey registered him to vote, telling him, "This is a very crucial thing to be doing, to bring about gay civil rights." Danny showed Harvey and Scott his photographs, and they deemed them very good. He told them he was having a hard time making ends meet. He had been a messenger for Gold Street Messenger Service, he had painted mushrooms on leather belts for a specialty company, he had done tedious clerical work.

The next time Danny passed Castro Camera, Harvey ran out to him. "Come in. We need to talk," he said. "Scott and I want you to come work for us." It could be a godsend for all of them because Harvey and Scott needed to devote themselves full-time to Harvey's campaign, and Danny needed a reliable paycheck. Danny took the job on the spot. He would keep the store open, deal with the customers, sell the film, answer the phone, which seemed always to be ringing off the hook, take the photographs at the next Castro Street Fair, and take many campaign pictures of Harvey Milk decked out in business suits, looking extremely supervisorial.[2]

* * *

For the 1973 campaign Harvey and Scott had raised twenty-five hundred dollars. In 1975 they raised three times that much, and Harvey also took twenty-five hundred dollars out of their business to run the campaign.[3] But that was nowhere near enough to buy TV ads or even billboard ads that could compete with the lavish spending of Harvey's opponents. A gay friend and neighbor, the artist Lee Mentley, had just returned from Hawaii, where signage was prohibited and businesses had to find other ways to get the word out about their goods and services. "If you can't afford billboard ads," Mentley told Harvey and Scott, "what you need are human billboards, a bunch of guys who'll stand on the streets holding up 'Milk for Supervisor' signs."[4]

What great theater that would be, Harvey thought; a lot better than static billboards that the eye gets used to and stops seeing. Scott hurried to organize volunteers, and a couple dozen promised to show up in the mornings and late afternoons when the thoroughfares were jammed with rush hour traffic. Scott met with them on Market Street and arranged them in a long row at the curb: smiling, waving gay men holding high their big signs that read Harvey Milk Supervisor. The "Super" part was underlined on every placard, to create a subliminal message. These human billboards also gave the impression that there were droves of volunteers who wanted to get Harvey Milk elected. That was the story the newspapers started reporting.

Mike Wong was a slight, bespectacled straight man in his early twenties, a staunch progressive who had run unsuccessfully for the Community College Board but still had dreams of someday becoming the first Chinese American on the Board of Supervisors. In 1973 he had been the San Francisco Young Democrats' representative to the meetings of the Alice B. Toklas Memorial Democratic Club, and that was where he was told by Jim Foster that Harvey Milk, the gay guy who was running for supervisor, was a nut. Despite what Foster said, when Wong attended that year's Candidates' Night meeting of San Francisco Tomorrow, he thought Harvey stole the show, talking passionately about issues dear to environmentalists' hearts, such as shutting down plans to expand the airport. Then Harvey's absurd joke—about how he would get the sympathy vote of liberals and also raise campaign money from them because a gay-hater would surely come after him with a gun—made Wong figure that Foster was right. The freaky-looking guy with long, scraggly hair might be eloquent on stage, but he was definitely a nut. Wong led the charge in 1973 to torpedo San Francisco Tomorrow's endorsement of Harvey.

Then, in 1975, he heard Harvey speak in support of the short-lived presidential bid of the ultraliberal U.S. senator Fred Harris, whom Wong was supporting too. Harvey awed Wong all over again with the progressive things he said about the working class, minorities, the environment—all causes Wong himself advocated; and Harvey did not look at all freaky anymore.

That is why Mike Wong came to Castro Camera, to join the droves of volunteers he read about in the newspaper. Only there weren't droves. Aside from the couple dozen or so gays who showed up to be human billboards, the campaign was mostly Harvey and Scott. As Harvey confessed to Wong, the media loved flash, so of course he let reporters think he had a huge team of volunteers. Young Mike Wong was once again impressed: he was looking for a model of how eventually to launch his own supervisor campaign, and this Harvey Milk seemed to have an instinct for making the media work for him.[5] Wong declared himself a volunteer, and Harvey was ecstatic: not only was Wong energetic and devoted to liberal politics but also, as a Chinese American, he would be bringing racial diversity to Harvey's campaign. Harvey appointed him as his political advisor.[6]

Jim Foster informed Mike Wong that he was "very disappointed" in him.[7] But Wong was unfazed. He was committed to helping Harvey Milk become San Francisco's first gay supervisor. Harvey, who never stopped being tasteless in his jokes with close friends, called Wong his "little yellow lotus blossom." Wong, always quick on the uptake, bantered back that Harvey was "a credit to your proclivity."

Harvey decided that to fill out his team he needed a political strategist and a speechwriter. Though he did not have the money to hire seasoned professionals, he had infectious enthusiasm that felt like compensation enough for key people to say yes.

Jim Rivaldo had been a political junkie since he was a kid in Rochester, New York, when he would wake up early so he could grab the newspaper and read it before anyone else in the family could monopolize it. At Harvard he majored in government. He had some notion of going into politics, but after graduation he took a job with *Ramparts*, a New Left political magazine headquartered in Menlo Park, California. By then he suspected he was gay and concluded that a political career was out. Once he knew for sure that he was gay he left for San Francisco, where he drifted for a couple of years.[8] When he was twenty-eight years old he wandered into Castro Camera, like so many young men of the neighborhood did, and he and Harvey hit it off. Rivaldo signed up to be one of Harvey's human billboards. When Harvey discovered that Rivaldo was a fierce politico with a degree in government from Harvard he knew he had found his political strategist. Rivaldo, already a believer in Harvey Milk, said yes.

Jim Rivaldo was a natural as a strategist. He studied every precinct; went through the voter lists; color-coded Jewish, gay, senior, working-class, and minority households; calculated how many votes could be expected from each precinct and where Harvey needed to focus his energy and where it was a lost cause.[9]

He went around the city with Harvey and saw for himself how people from all walks of life reacted to a gay man with good ideas and an extraordinary gift for communicating them.[10] It was therapeutic for Rivaldo to watch how positively straight people would respond to a gay political candidate if he had what it took. Rivaldo reciprocated in kind: if Harvey was down even for a minute, he pumped him up with what he observed about how Harvey's audiences loved him. He designed and polished the language in Harvey's brochures too. Harvey would write a rough draft, and Rivaldo, who was privately astonished that such an articulate speaker wrote so unintelligibly, would clean up his sentences.[11]

Harvey could not afford to pay a professional speechwriter—anymore than he could afford to pay a political advisor or a political strategist. But he thought he really needed someone to take his great ideas and put them into good prose. A year earlier he had met Frank Robinson, a man in his late forties who lived up the hill from the Castro. Robinson, sporting a Greek sailor's cap rain or shine, walked passed the store every morning on his way to breakfast at a nearby diner. One day Harvey was out front playing with The Kid, and Robinson stopped to pet the dog. He and Harvey started talking, and it was not long before Robinson told him his whole life story. He was a Chicago transplant. Like Harvey, he had been a navy man and served in Korea. He also served in World War II. He was gay but mostly closeted because until just a few years ago he wrote sex columns for men's magazines—*Playboy, Rogue, Cavalier.* He and Harvey shared a hearty laugh over the idea that this middle-aged gay man had been advising young and horny straight guys about how to get it on with women.[12] What particularly interested Harvey was that Frank Robinson was a real writer, who had a degree in journalism from Northwestern and had sold several books of science fiction to major publishers. One of his books,

The Glass Inferno, a techno-thriller, had just been adapted for the blockbuster film *The Towering Inferno.*

"Hey, why don't you be my speechwriter?" Harvey asked him. "It'll be a hoot. We'll stir some shit."

Robinson did not think a homosexual could win an election. "Back in Chicago we couldn't have elected an openly gay dog catcher," he said. But Harvey's talk had swept him up. Robinson saw in him the same kind of populist that he himself was: in favor of neighborhoods and against developers; champion of the elderly, the unions, the patchwork quilt of ethnic groups that made up the city's population. How could he say no?

They made a fine team. Harvey would tell Robinson what he wanted to communicate; then Robinson would write it up and give it back to Harvey, who would go through it with an actor's eye—adding repetition for effect, breaking up long lines with shorter phrases. Robinson was genuinely moved when he heard Harvey give the speeches—Harvey made them entirely his own. Every word seemed to come directly from his heart.[13]

Harvey would have been the first to say that in the 1973 campaign he did not really know what he was doing. Now, two years later, he believed he did. He had a political advisor, a political strategist, and a speechwriter. His professional team was in place. And he would be more cautious in his personal life too. He and Scott had agreed to an "open marriage," as gay male couples often did, and Harvey had frequented the gay bathhouses south of Market, such as the Club Baths, where lithe young men were abundant; and the Cauldron, where opera blared in the background. He also used to take a toke or two or three of pot. Those were peccadillos that could lead to a bust or at least a scandal, which a serious politician could not afford, he decided.

But despite his cleaned-up look and more cautious behavior Harvey still had his detractors. The Alice B. Toklas Memorial

Democratic Club continued to think of him as dangerous and to hope that if they just ignored him he would vanish. "They're a bunch of anti-Semites," Harvey told Scott, thinking of Jim Foster, Jo Daly, Rick Stokes—in fact, most of San Francisco's major gay leaders. Scott believed Harvey was too quick to find anti-Semitism everywhere. But whatever the reason, the gay establishment continued to be critical. While the San Francisco chapter of the National Women's Political Caucus endorsed Harvey, the major lesbian leaders did not. Del Martin and Phyllis Lyon, San Francisco lesbian icons and cofounders of Daughters of Bilitis, the first lesbian organization in the country, called him a flake and could not forget that they once heard him say that "men in drag were better than women were."[14]

His enemies in the gay community also criticized him for downplaying gay issues to curry favor with straight voters.[15] That was at least partly true. If his homosexuality came up when he addressed nongay voters, he would declare, "I'm not a gay candidate, but a candidate who happens to be gay." He butched it up too. His years as a high school and college athlete and a navy diver had taught him how to present himself as hypermasculine; and why wouldn't he do that when he spoke to firemen in their fire stations and construction workers on their sites?

But it was not easy to walk such a fine line. He had spent the previous years getting gay people registered to vote, telling them that only through the ballot box would they win their rights. Yet the fact was, they alone could not get him into office because elections were not by district. He needed straight votes too. But he also needed to mollify gays about his seeking the straight vote. "The gay vote *is* powerful. The gay vote *can* make a difference," he wrote in a campaign letter to gay constituents. "But to expect to carry an election on the gay vote alone is wishful thinking. I've gone into the straight community. At many functions I've been the 'token' Gay. I've tried to build bridges between 'us' and 'them' because I believe that contact with the straight community is . . . the only way we can gain all we want: equality and acceptance."[16] He explained too that he was "trying to break down stereotypes," which was crucial if gays hoped to win first-class American citizenship.[17]

He did break down stereotypes. George Evankovich, the cigar-chomping boss of the thirty-five-hundred-member Laborers Union Local 261, had to admit that a lot of union members used to think that "gays were little leprechauns, tiptoeing to florist shops." But they saw that Harvey was a fighter, "a man who had guts," as virile as any of them. "He could sit on a steel beam and talk to some iron worker who was a mean, ornery sonuvabitch who probably beat his wife when he had too many beers, and here he was talking to Harvey"—and promising to vote for him.[18]

Harvey had tried to appeal to heterosexual voters even in his 1973 run; but in 1975 he tried even harder. He attended every Candidates' Night to which he was invited. He raised issues of inequitable taxes and poor city services. His eloquence and good sense (and neat appearance) won him a remarkable list of endorsements, including the Democratic League, the Harry S. Truman Democratic Club, the Associated Democratic Club, the Frank R. Havenner Democratic Club, and the People's Democratic Club.[19] The Alice B. Toklas Memorial Democratic Club, however, still saw him as an embarrassment to the community and much preferred straight liberal candidates. Harvey dubbed Alice Club members gay groupies who salivated over the piddling attention they got from gay-friendly politicians. He wrote them off.[20]

The Teamsters endorsement was already his because of his role in the Coors boycott, but he also went after the endorsement of other workers' groups, such as the Laborers Union. He went after the black endorsement through the San Francisco Black Political Caucus; he went after the environmentalist endorsement through San Francisco Tomorrow. And he got them all. In 1973 the *San Francisco Chronicle* columnist Herb Caen had mocked Harvey for running for the Board of Supervisors on the "homo ticket." But in 1975 even Caen was mightily impressed when Harvey got the endorsement of the seventeen-thousand-strong Building and Construction Trades Council, which refused to endorse the six "do-nothing incumbents" who were on the ballot. Caen called this "a superslap at the incumbents." Never again would he refer to Harvey Milk as a homo.[21]

The most astonishing endorsement he got was from the San Francisco Firefighters Union. In other big cities, like New York, Los Angeles, and Chicago, firemen, along with policemen, were at the forefront of campaigns against gay rights. But Harvey had done his homework so thoroughly before he showed up to speak to the firemen of San Francisco that they came around. Better than any other candidate, he knew what their grievances were and told them his plans for fixing what bothered them once he got on the Board of Supervisors. As for the six incumbents who were running, Harvey argued, they had not addressed the firemen's grievances before, so why would they do it if they received another term? He brought a big jar of jelly beans to the firemen's meeting, and he passed it back and forth in clubhouse camaraderie. As he talked about what he would do as a supervisor, he mentioned in passing that he was gay; and then, as Leon Broshura, the young head of the firemen's union, observed with admiration, "the conversation moved on." Harvey seemed absolutely sincere, determined, the firemen agreed, not a guy who would ever shirk his duties on the Board of Supervisors, and they voted to endorse him.[22]

For Harvey, the conquest of unlikely supporters was exhilarating. But all of the campaigning took a toll on his personal life. Scott was getting worn out. He wanted their old life back. Why couldn't they just quit the campaign, he asked, when setbacks or frustrations occurred. But Harvey was addicted to the heady rush of it all. And he ardently believed it was time for an openly gay man to win political office—not only to fight for gay rights but also to show the world it could be done. Why shouldn't he be that man? His victory—his and Scott's victory, he said—would be a victory for all gay lovers. After one of their arguments, which were happening with increasing frequency, Harvey wrote Scott a not very convincing explanation of why he could not stop running: *"For you alone*—I could never 'quit' the race—because I would be quitting you. We fight, have problems and more, [but] when all is said, as long as you are there I could never quit."[23]

Scott stuck by Harvey until the bitter end of the 1975 campaign. But he later told their friend and neighbor Lee Mentley that a life in politics—for which Harvey had to wear a suit and tie and act bourgeois and stop smoking pot—was not what he had signed on for and was never what he wanted for them. In the end, it destroyed their relationship.[24]

* * *

On November 4, 1975, San Francisco voters went to the polls. That evening, surrounded by a throng of his supporters, Harvey watched as the election returns came in on a television at The Island, a gay Castro Street restaurant owned by a neighborhood buddy, Dennis Peron (who had started the restaurant with money he made as the friendly neighborhood drug dealer). Fifty-three thousand San Franciscans voted to elect Harvey Milk to the Board of Supervisors—over thirty-five thousand more votes than he had won two years earlier. But the field was crowded, and, with six seats open, Harvey came in seventh.

When it became clear that all the incumbents had been re-elected, Harvey put the best face on things that he could. He declared to his supporters that his campaign had made invaluable inroads and that he would keep them when he ran for the Board of Supervisors again in two years. Then he pointed to Scott, who looked somber and exhausted. "When people thank me for what I'm doing, they really are thanking Scott, the man

I love," Harvey announced. "He's the one who puts up with me. The world may one day be a little bit better because Scott was there."[25] Despite Harvey's brave and tender words, the disappointment they both felt at this moment was tremendous.

But not long after Harvey's defeat Jim Rivaldo took him to the backroom of Castro Camera and again pulled out his color-coded map. He showed Harvey how incredibly well he had done. He won by a landslide in the Castro district, despite the gay establishment being against him. His numbers were overwhelming in the hippie Haight-Ashbury district also. They were even significant in affluent Pacific Heights, with its big liberal Jewish population. And he did okay in a lot of the working-class and poor neighborhoods too. In the conservative districts he bombed completely, of course. That was what cost him the election.

However, if there had been district elections instead of city-wide elections for the Board of Supervisors, Jim Rivaldo pointed out—if Harvey Milk could have run just in his own district—he would have been a shoo-in.

8

Milk vs. the Machine

THE DAY AFTER Harvey lost the election he dismantled the Harvey Milk for Supervisor Headquarters that he and Scott had set up in Castro Camera, but he did not go back to being just a shopkeeper. He opened a George Moscone for Mayor campaign office in the same space. Harvey was excited about Moscone's candidacy because he really liked what he stood for, and he deeply disliked Moscone's Republican challenger, John Barbagelata. But also, Harvey thought that if he played his cards right there was a chance that having George Moscone as mayor might be his own best route to political office. Clearly, Harvey was not close to giving up his political aspirations.

Moscone was the majority leader of the California State Senate. A bon vivant with a perpetual tan, he was often spotted racing up and down the hills of San Francisco in his Alfa Romeo with the top down. During his tenure as majority leader he had pushed through a school lunch program for poor kids, championed bilingual education, and strengthened California's Department of Consumer Affairs. California liberals loved him.

Harvey was especially partial to Moscone because the senator had gone to great lengths to get California's sodomy law repealed. Only a handful of states had repealed their laws against sodomy when a bill came to the California State Senate floor on May 1, 1975. That day Moscone stood at the podium and directed the senators' attention to a Latin motto carved on the chamber wall above him: "Senators must guard the liberty of the republic." Then he argued eloquently that the sodomy law threatened such liberty because it encouraged blackmailers and police abuse. When the senators split 20–20 on the vote to repeal the law, Moscone asked the president pro tem of the Senate for permission to have the Senate chamber doors locked to keep the quorum in place. California's lieutenant governor had the authority to break a tie; but a proxy vote was not acceptable under law, and Lieutenant Governor Mervyn Dymally, a Democrat, was in Denver, scheduled to speak at a political dinner. Moscone's aide got on the phone with Dymally's aide and, posthaste, Dymally was hopping a plane to San Francisco, where he was flown by helicopter to Sacramento, then rushed to the Senate chamber in the State Capitol Building. The lieutenant governor broke the tie in favor of repeal, as Moscone knew he would.

There was no question that Moscone's liberalism was genuine, but he had also been gearing up for the San Francisco mayoral race that November, and he knew that a big gay vote would be indispensable to winning. In the primaries Moscone had had to steal the gay vote from Supervisor Dianne Feinstein, who had long worked diligently to earn her bona fides as a champion of gays. In 1969—at a time when almost all politicians still regarded homosexuals as criminals and crazies—she went after and received an endorsement from the biggest gay organization in San Francisco, the Society for Individual Rights, for her first supervisorial race. In 1972 she introduced legislation to prohibit contractors who wished to do business with the city from discriminating on the basis of sexual orientation—and she got it passed. She also helped Jo Daly, the lesbian vice president of the Alice B. Toklas Memorial Democratic Club, win appointment to a paid position as a staff member of the San Francisco Human Rights Commission, which made Daly one of the first out homosexuals on a government payroll. In the garden of the Feinsteins' Pacific Heights mansion, Supervisor Feinstein would even officiate at a much-publicized commitment ceremony for Jo Daly and Nancy Achilles. San Francisco's gay establishment had reason to adore Dianne Feinstein.

But Harvey still believed she was in the pocket of real estate developers; he also smarted a little because she had been reelected to the Board of Supervisors in the 1973 race, which he had lost. So in the midst of working on his 1975 campaign Harvey took time out to promote Feinstein's mayoral rival, George Moscone. California's sodomy law would not have been repealed if it had not been for Moscone, Harvey reminded the gay community.

Moscone easily defeated Feinstein, who came in third. The San Francisco supervisor John Barbagelata came in second and hence would be in a mandated runoff against Moscone in December. Barbagelata was ultraconservative—a staunch Catholic who was motivated to become a politician in the 1960s because he was horrified by the nude go-go dancers working in the North Beach night clubs.[1] He was a truly repugnant figure to Harvey.

However, Harvey was also looking to the future. He not only ran a Moscone for Mayor campaign office out of Castro Camera; he also stumped for Moscone. He would not let gay audiences forget that Barbagelata had opposed the Gay Freedom Day Parades. "I think he wants to be a priest and not a mayor," he said of Barbagelata.[2] He even hosted a fund-raiser for Moscone at the gay restaurant The Island. By now, even though Harvey had lost two elections, he knew more than a bit about how the game of politics was played. It was at that fundraiser at The Island that he did what he had been planning since he opened a George Moscone campaign office at Castro Camera. He took Moscone aside and told him he would continue to support him in the runoff—provided that Moscone promised that if he won he would make Harvey a commissioner on one of the city boards.

"Come by my office tomorrow," the mayoral candidate told him.[3]

On December 11, 1975, George Moscone beat John Barbagelata by only forty-four hundred votes. At the victory celebration in the ballroom of the San Francisco Hotel the mayor-elect announced to his supporters that because of Harvey Milk gays had come out in droves to give Moscone their vote; and that that had put him over the top.

On January 8, 1976, George Moscone was sworn in as San Francisco's mayor. On January 30, in Mayor Moscone's office, Harvey Milk was sworn in as commissioner to the Board of Permit Appeals. Commissioner Milk he was now called.

The Board of Permit Appeals had jurisdiction over all official permits issued in San Francisco. Harvey was jubilant about his new role, which would even allow him to promote progressive principles. The first meeting of the board was held three days after he was sworn in. The San Francisco Police Department had rejected the application of a Korean woman for a license to operate as a masseuse. The SFPD had argued that since the woman spoke only Korean, officials could not explain the regulations to her or interview her about her background. Two vice squad officers represented the SFPD at the appeals meeting. Harvey, never shy about jumping into the fray, led the charge to overrule the police, though his tenure on the Board of Permit Appeals had barely begun. He reprimanded the vice squad officers as though they were errant schoolboys. "Unless you have legitimate complaints, I don't want to hear this kind of complaint again!" he roared.[4] For Harvey it must have been a fantasy come true—to put the vice squad in its place in such an imperious fashion.

However, his tenure as a commissioner was very short. It had been his plan to stay on the Board of Permit Appeals for a year and a half, until it was time to run again for supervisor. But he got sidetracked. The year before he had become friends with an unmarried heterosexual woman, Carol Ruth Silver, a lawyer who served as legal counsel to San Francisco's liberal sheriff Richard Hongisto. Silver had been a red-diaper baby and a life-long freethinker. In 1973 she adopted a little boy from Taiwan, and three years later, still single, she gave birth to another child. She wore a short, straight hairdo and thick, squarish glasses and had a no-nonsense look about her; but, like Harvey, she was quick-witted and funny, and they laughed a lot together. She ran for district attorney in 1975, though political experts had warned her that there was no way a woman would be elected DA; and, like Harvey, she lost her bid narrowly. The two commiserated and grew even closer when they learned they were both secular Jews and Litvaks. They began having weekly breakfasts at her house, and sometimes Harvey's speechwriter, Frank Robinson, would join them.

At a breakfast not long after Harvey's glorious revenge on the vice squad, Silver mentioned to Harvey that she heard that Assemblyman John Foran would be running for George Moscone's old Senate seat. That meant that the seat in the 16th Assembly District, the district in which Harvey lived, would open up. Silver had been very impressed that Harvey had gotten fifty-three thousand votes in the previous election. "You ought to run for Foran's seat," she told him. "Yeah, that's what you ought to do," Robinson agreed. "You can count me in for help."[5]

Harvey was still exhausted from his 1975 run, when he would

wake up at six in the morning to hand out leaflets at bus stops and go to bed at one after attending two or three political events in a single evening. His old shoulder injury from his college football days had been acting up because he shook hands with every prospective voter he met.[6] He was looking forward to the year-and-a-half respite before he had to rev up again. Yet what Carol Ruth Silver and Frank Robinson said was irresistible. Why wait so long to run for the Board of Supervisors again when he could run for a more important office right now? He decided to go for it.

With that decision Harvey unwittingly walked into a lion's den. Although he had been getting more and more politically savvy, he was unaware of the existence of two rival Democratic cliques in Sacramento, which dated back to the 1960s and a bitter Senate race involving Moscone and Leo McCarthy, who was now the speaker of the California State Assembly. Nor did he know that the two cliques, which were made up of some of California's major political heavyweights, had now come together to strike a complicated backroom deal.

The previous year Assembly Speaker McCarthy had made some promises to his old foes: he would back George Moscone in the mayoral race; he would refrain from thwarting the re-election bids of two progressive U.S. congressmen from San Francisco, John and Phillip Burton, brothers whom he resented because they had supported Moscone in the 1960s race; and he would see to it that Moscone's best buddy, the black assembly-man Willie Brown, would get his pick of Assembly committee assignments. But the promises came with a price tag: first, McCarthy said, Moscone, the Burtons, and Willie Brown must support John Foran in his run for Moscone's old Senate seat. McCarthy and Foran went way back: they had been friends in high school, and in 1953, as students at the University of San Francisco, the two young men had survived a kidnapping at gunpoint by a man who had just killed a policeman. Foran went on to serve a brief stint as deputy attorney general and in 1962 was elected to the Assembly. Six years later he had helped McCarthy get elected. McCarthy owed him one.

McCarthy also pressured his old foes to support Art Agnos, his much-trusted chief of staff, who would be running for John Foran's old Assembly seat.[7] Agnos had impeccable liberal credentials, having started his career in San Francisco as a social worker with the Housing Authority, where he helped senior citizens. In December 1973, he was shot twice in the back in Potrero Hill, a poor neighborhood where he had gone to a meeting to discuss the building of a government-funded health clinic. His assailants were the so-called Zebra murderers, four extremist Nation of Islam members who gave themselves points for killing white people. Fifteen of the Zebra victims had died, and Agnos almost did. For that ordeal not only did he have name recognition all over San Francisco, he had public sympathy too.

But Harvey knew nothing of the story of the backroom deal. He had been on the Board of Permit Appeals barely a month when he announced to the newspapers that he might be running for John Foran's seat. Because Moscone had already endorsed Art Agnos, the *San Francisco Chronicle* sought the mayor's response to Harvey's announcement. Moscone declared that it was his "absolute duty to appoint commissioners who will use their time to serve the city," and if Harvey Milk ran for office he would be distracted from his commissioner duties. Therefore, Moscone threatened, "He will set the record for the shortest commissioner in history. And I'm not talking about his size."[8]

Harvey was shaken by Moscone's anger. He had worked hard to get the mayor to make him a commissioner, and now he was throwing away his accomplishment. He hastened to walk back his earlier announcement a bit, telling a reporter from the *San Francisco Examiner* that while it was true he had picked up blank petition forms from the Registrar of Voters, he had not yet filed a formal declaration.[9]

But he had already started a firestorm. Supervisor Quentin Kopp, who had been a fierce critic of Moscone's ultraliberalism, relished any opportunity to put the mayor in his place. Kopp became Harvey's very unlikely ally, declaring that the mayor had no right to "violate a fundamental principle of American democracy" by forbidding Harvey his wish to run for office. Kopp asserted that Moscone was a member of an "unholy alliance" together with the Burtons, Willie Brown, and Leo McCarthy and that they were plotting "machine politics" to seize complete control of San Francisco.[10] The newspapers dwelled on the controversy day after day. If Harvey Milk was not a household name before, he was now.

Harvey reveled in the language of the battle in which he suddenly found himself embroiled. He especially liked the way one gay paper characterized his struggle: "Harvey Milk vs. The Machine."[11] He was the small but valiant David taking on Goliath. It was an image he loved. The attention he was getting through Kopp's fulminations was too precious to give up.

Harvey tamped down his fear of upsetting Moscone and sat down to write his campaign statement, emphasizing all the chairs he had put up in recent years and all the community boards on which he had served—including the Board of Permit Appeals. He focused on the poor of the 16th Assembly District, which included Hunters Point, a neighborhood that was home to many black people. They had once been employed in the area's shipyards and slaughterhouses, which closed down in the early 1970s. He would bring jobs back to the unemployed. He appealed to other constituencies too, talking about "the beaten faces on Third Street, on the streets of Chinatown, and among the Senior Citizens of the Tenderloin." With populist fervor he billed himself as a candidate "who understands money, who understands the value of a dollar, who realizes that bread costs over 50 cents a loaf and milk 40 cents a quart, and if you don't have that 40 or 50 cents your kids don't eat."

In his campaign statement he adopted the language he had been gifted by Quentin Kopp and the media. The people must help him "fight the political machine, which doesn't serve the people," he declared, pleading for the people to understand that the "unholy alliance" had "immense financial support," and he, who had not been bought by the Machine, had only them. He pounded the point that the Machine had deviously hand-picked their candidate (Art Agnos), but he, Harvey Milk, was appealing directly to the people because "I think representatives should be elected by the people—not appointed."[12]

On March 9, 1976, Harvey appeared at a meeting of the San Francisco Press Club, where he distributed his campaign statement and officially announced that he was a candidate for the 16th Assembly District seat. Four hours later Mayor Moscone fired him from his position as a commissioner on the Board of Permit Appeals.

To fill Harvey's place George Moscone appointed Rick Stokes, the well-spoken, gentlemanly gay attorney who in 1972 had run for a modest seat on the Community College Board and lost. Stokes promised Moscone that he had no further political ambitions, so he would never do what Harvey Milk had done. His promise proved ironic the next year.

* * *

Harvey threw himself into the Assembly race, just as he had in his two earlier runs, campaigning seven days a week, seventeen or eighteen hours a day. This time Scott refused to be Harvey's campaign manager, which was upsetting to Harvey—though it had no effect on his determination to run. He was famous now, and it was not hard for him to get volunteers. John Ryckman, who had started out in politics twenty years earlier working on Adlai Stevenson's presidential bid and had been on Governor Pat Brown's reelection team, took over Scott's duties as campaign manager. Tom Randol, the artist friend from New York who had helped make posters for the first two campaigns, bought boxes of T-shirts wholesale, silk-screened them with a HARVEY MILK FOR ASSEMBLY logo, and got Harvey enthusiasts to carry the message on their chests all over San Francisco. Volunteers devised other ingenious ways to get the word out. They procured a stock of twenty-by-thirty-foot pieces of Masonite board and painted them with a blue background and bold HARVEY MILK FOR ASSEMBLY lettering; they also silk-screened large sheets with the HARVEY MILK FOR ASSEMBLY logo—and they distributed their various makeshift billboards to supporters all over the district, where they were affixed to friendly houses and business buildings.[13]

Since Harvey did not have money to rent a space for political headquarters, Castro Camera was converted once again: windows were covered with posters and bumper stickers, tables and counters were covered with leaflets, boxes overflowed with campaign materials. To Harvey it was all deadly serious—and delicious fun too. But his personal life was in dire trouble.

A student reporter from San Francisco State University came to Castro Camera to interview him one day. To get to the makeshift office at the back of the store the student had to navigate an obstacle course of paraphernalia and squeeze through ratty old brocaded draperies and a big sign hand-printed by Danny Nicoletta that said, "Fortunes told: 10 cents. With Lipstick: 50 cents." As the young man tripped over still more boxes to get closer to the desk where Harvey would sit for the interview, Harvey explained about the disarray: "We've always been more interested in the political situation than in the business part."[14]

But the "we," if it included Scott, was a lie. Scott wanted absolutely nothing more to do with Harvey's interminable runs for office. He just wanted his hippie clown back, the long-haired, bead-wearing, pot-smoking loving fellow who had picked him up in a Greenwich Village subway station five years earlier. The glory of victory at the polls had been Harvey's big dream, never Scott's. Scott had gone along with it for the first two races because he loved Harvey. But he came to detest Harvey's incessant campaigning for the elusive thrill of a win.

Scott was insecure, needy—like all the young men with whom Harvey fell in love; but Harvey was too busy to tend to Scott's needs. Harvey could be a tyrant too, and in their fights he blamed Scott for anything and everything that went wrong— in politics as well as in their personal life. Scott threatened to leave and then did leave. Then he came back, and left and came back again.

* * *

On top of Harvey's serious domestic problems he had serious campaign problems. A dilemma that had caused him anxiety in the earlier races seemed even more troubling in the Assembly race. How should he speak to very diverse constituencies? The 16th Assembly District covered the eastern part of San Francisco, which included the largely Latino Mission District as well as the heavily black Bayview–Hunters Point area, communities that were much less supportive of gay rights than communities of color later became under the leadership of President Obama. He believed his chances of winning were better running for an Assembly District seat than they had been in the general election, when he had had to appeal to voters all over San Francisco. But, still, he feared that if he spoke too loudly to the Castro, he risked turning off the other communities. He worried they would think that because he was a homosexual, homosexual rights were his first and only priority.

His solution was a compromise. He would speak ardently about gay issues, but only when he had a gay audience. He told readers of the *Advocate*, for instance, that he entered politics for the sake of a fifteen-year-old San Francisco girl who told him she feared she would be denied her high school diploma because she was "an upfront gay," and a seventeen-year-old San Francisco boy who told him that he was looking to Harvey as a role model. Harvey declared that he wanted all gay kids—not only in San Francisco, but in Des Moines, Iowa, and small cities and towns everywhere—to be able "to walk down the street relaxed and free."[15] However, he would never make such statements when he spoke to voters in Hunters Point or the Mission District.

Art Agnos, always a reliable defender of gay rights, was heterosexual, so he did not have Harvey's baggage. That meant he could speak about gay issues anywhere and not fear that his listeners would assume gays were his priority. Agnos took advantage of his position and accused Harvey at every chance of opportunism and insincerity. A week before the election Agnos took out a full-page ad in the *Bay Area Reporter*, the gay paper for which Harvey wrote his Milk Forum column, that asked, "Who is really upfront for Gay rights no matter who the audience is? . . . If Harvey Milk won't speak out for Gay Rights at the Labor Council in S.F. [which had endorsed him] what will he do in Sacramento?"[16]

Agnos's efforts to undermine Harvey did not work among most gay voters. They knew about the far reach of gay hating and understood what Harvey was up against. And they agreed that if an openly gay man were elected he would be a crucial role model for young gays. They trusted him to do the right thing for the community. (In the end he got 62 percent of the gay vote.)

Still, the major politicos of the gay establishment continued to regard him as an interloper with a New York accent and a kind of pushiness that they also associated with New York. They despised his attack on the Machine, which, as they pointed out, had served gays just fine. Every year since 1969 it was the Machine member Willie Brown who had reintroduced the bill for the repeal of the sodomy law. It was the Machine member

George Moscone who was largely responsible for the passage of that bill. The Machine members Leo McCarthy, the Burton brothers, and Dianne Feinstein were among the most gay-friendly politicians in the country. If gay people were ever to get their rights, it would be by the good graces of the Machine. Jo Daly, who was the Alice Club's vice president, proclaimed in the *Advocate* that gays had an obligation to support straight politicians who had supported gay issues, and that Art Agnos was "a longtime supporter of gay rights and . . . a voice for us in the capital" and had earned the gay vote.[17]

Apparently oblivious to Harvey's popularity among the majority of gays, all parts of the gay establishment seemed fixed on assuring his defeat, even the *Sentinel*, the first gay paper for which Harvey wrote. The paper's news editor, Randy Alfred, who had taken over Harvey's "Waves from the Left" column in 1975, believed that Harvey Milk was not ready for Sacramento, and Sacramento was certainly not ready for Harvey Milk.[18] The *Sentinel* backed Art Agnos.

Jim Foster went even further to make sure there would be no Assemblyman Milk. Elaine Noble, the first openly gay person to be elected to a state legislature, in 1974, was running again in 1976 for a second term as representative of her Boston, Massachusetts, district. She was looking everywhere for campaign funds when Jo Daly called to say that San Francisco lesbians would like to have a fund-raiser for her and would she come to California. Daly mentioned that Jim Foster, whom Elaine had met years earlier when he was a young man working as a waiter in Provincetown, Massachusetts, was looking forward to seeing her again.

At the fund-raiser Foster made a date with Noble to pick her up at her hotel the next day and take her to lunch. "Do you mind if we swing by someone's office?" Foster asked on the way to the restaurant. "I want you to meet this guy." It was Art Agnos. Foster, an amateur photographer who always had a camera at the ready, snapped a picture of Elaine Noble and Art Agnos beaming at one another like buddies. "So, do you like him?" Foster asked afterward. "Yeah, he's a nice guy," she said. A week or two later the picture Jim Foster had taken appeared in a full-page ad in San Francisco's gay papers. The statement that accompanied it said that Massachusetts State Representative Elaine Noble, the first openly gay person to be elected to a statewide office anywhere, endorsed Art Agnos. When Noble called Foster to complain that she had never said anything about an endorsement, he told her, "Harvey Milk is not the right guy for the job. Agnos has supported us for years." Furious, Noble thought about taking out an ad saying she had not endorsed anyone for the San Francisco race. But she dropped the idea when her friend Kevin White, the mayor of Boston, warned her that such an ad would "only make the whole thing bigger."[19]

Harvey was not above playing his own tricks as a candidate. During the Assembly campaign Jimmy Carter came to San Francisco to raise money for his race for the presidency. Harvey scraped together a hundred dollars to go to a fund-raising dinner. Word had already gotten around among gays that the presidential candidate was averse to being photographed with open homosexuals and had even made absurdly awkward moves to avoid the optics of proximity to a known gay.[20] When Harvey stood in line with others for a photo op with Carter, he did not introduce himself as the gay candidate for the California Assembly—but the picture, which Harvey used in his campaign, shows him shaking hands and exchanging broad smiles with the man who would soon be president.

* * *

Though Harvey was rejected by the gay establishment, he was again endorsed by many straight organizations that had supported him in his supervisor runs. He also got his first endorsement from an elected official, Milton Marks, a Jewish Republican state senator who was a longtime adversary of John and Philip Burton, members of the Machine. Harvey was helped by some new groups too. One of his supporters would come back to haunt him. Reverend Jim Jones was the minister at the Peoples Temple, a church he had founded in Indiana in 1955. After several moves Jones relocated to an old converted synagogue in the Fillmore District, which had been the center of San Francisco's immigrant Jewish community in the early twentieth century; by the 1950s the neighborhood was mostly black. Jones's sleek, dark hair and prominent cheekbones made him look like an American Indian, which he claimed he was; but he orated in the style of a black Pentecostal minister, wore hipster shades, and attracted a predominantly black congregation. "Oh, yes, you're a nigger. I'm a nigger. I don't care if you're an Italian nigger, or you're Jewish, or an Indian," Jones would tell his followers. "The only people that're getting anything in this country are the people that got the money, baby."[21]

But Jones also preached and practiced good works. He gained huge attention throughout San Francisco by setting up a free medical clinic and giving away food and clothing to the indigent. He played an active role on the political scene, too. Most of San Francisco's progressive politicians knew Jim Jones as a reliable supporter. At his direction, his thousands of followers campaigned hard to get George Moscone elected mayor. Moscone would eventually reward the reverend by making him chair of the San Francisco Housing Authority, which oversaw San Francisco's public housing.

Reverend Jones supported gay issues also. In 1975, when a gay couple, Richard Adams and Anthony Sullivan, procured a marriage license from a clerk in Boulder County, Colorado, which authorities refused to recognize, Jones preached in their favor, and the temple made a large donation to their defense fund.[22] The temple's newspaper, *Peoples Forum*, often carried outraged stories about how the police bullied homosexuals by raiding gay bars, beating up gay people, and using undercover vice squad officers to entrap gay men. State Senator Milton Marks wrote an enthusiastic proclamation commending Jim Jones and the Peoples Temple not only for their human services work but also for their defense of "constitutional liberties." The proclamation was passed by the entire Senate.[23]

So when Jones called Harvey to say that he knew Harvey was worried about the vote in the black Hunters Point precincts and that he would send his congregants there to canvass for him, Harvey was elated. Peoples Temple volunteers distributed more than thirty thousand "Harvey Milk for Assembly" brochures to black voters. Harvey, always skeptical about religion but full of gratitude for Jim Jones, attended a service at the Peoples Temple and afterward wrote to the reverend, "The words are not good enough, but lacking the words themselves I can only say in the fullest, deepest, and warmest meaning of the often overused expression Thank You. . . . It may take me many a day to come down from the high that I reached today. . . . I found what you wanted me to find. I shall be back for I can never leave."[24]

*　*　*

The Assembly District election was held on June 8. Once again Harvey watched the returns with a crowd of his supporters at The Island restaurant. For the first forty-five minutes he had a clear lead. "Hey, Harvey, you're winning!" the restaurant's owner, Dennis Peron, shouted to him, and his supporters cheered.

"I know, but I'm just not used to it," a dazed Harvey shouted back.[25]

His lead fizzled quickly. Agnos racked up 17,031 votes; Harvey got 13,401. He quipped that he was "the gay Harold Stassen," the governor of Minnesota who ran for the presidency nine times between 1944 and 1992 but never once succeeded in winning the Republican nomination.

Harvey had given the campaign his all. He even lost Scott because of it. One night, after hours of manning the campaign headquarters, Mike Wong went upstairs to the apartment above the store where Scott and Harvey lived to fix himself some soup. Scott was sitting in the front room, looking despondent. Wong had heard Harvey having one of his explosive fits with Scott a few hours earlier. Those fits happened often, but, as Wong liked to say, Harvey got over them "as fast as the sun rose and set." In the past it never took long for Scott to accept Harvey's apology and forgive; but as the race grew more intense, the fits grew more frequent and harsh. Harvey just could not control himself. Now Wong watched Scott sitting there, miserable and brooding. "Do you think you and Harvey are going to last?" he finally asked. "No," Scott answered simply.[26]

That summer, not long after the election, Scott moved out of their home permanently. They exchanged acrimonious letters. Harvey heard that Scott was parading around the Castro and other gay spots with new lovers and that he was carrying on a wild sex life, which everyone seemed to know about. Hurt and angry, Harvey threatened to sever every tie he had with Scott. Scott feared that Harvey would close Castro Camera— or, even worse, that he would reopen the store with someone else, a new lover. The store was Scott's only livelihood. If he were kicked out of it, he wrote Harvey, "all the three years of the sweat of my balls would be for naught." He had invested his all in it, and he would fight Harvey to keep it, Scott threatened.

"Well, I invested over five years in Scott!" Harvey wrote back, referring to Scott in the third person and excoriating him not only for once having been closeted but also for having been a tame lover: "At first he would not walk down a beach with me with my arm on him. Now he will do that—with others but not with me," Harvey complained. "At first he would not have erotic sex with Harvey—now he likes it—with others."[27] Scott stayed away. As happened with Joe Campbell years earlier, once Scott left, Harvey desperately wanted him back. Suffering the pangs of contrition, he wrote Scott an apology, imploring him to resume their relationship: "I was wrong in much of my treatment of you . . . I miss you, I miss your eyes, I miss your mouth, I miss feeling your chest. . . . There is so much beauty in the world, so much to see together. I love you."[28]

But Scott never returned as Harvey's lover. They remained partners in Castro Camera for as long as the store stayed open; and despite the acrimonious breakup, Scott never stopped being the most important person in Harvey's life. Until Scott died, seventeen years after Harvey's death, Harvey remained the most important person in Scott's life too.

* * *

But now Harvey was alone, and nothing was working out for him. He was broke also. Danny Nicoletta had tried to keep Castro Camera together as best he could, but Harvey and Scott had been of no help because the Assembly campaign and their tumultuous relationship had soaked up all of their attention. After the election Harvey realized that he had to rescue the only livelihood he and Scott had. When a reporter from the *San Francisco Chronicle* asked if he would ever again run for office, he replied that his "first priority was trying to get this camera store back into shape."[29]

He also had plenty of reason to be scared of remaining in the public eye. He had discovered that running for office as an out homosexual made you a target for wackos. He got piles of hate mail, such as a disjointed ten-page rant, supposedly from officers of a Black Muslim temple on Geary Street. The letter graphically threatened that Black Muslims were going to bomb his store; and also, "You will be stabbed and have your genitals, cock, balls, prick cut off"; and for good measure, the letter declared, his executors were going to "dump your homosexual gay body out at the city dump."[30]

* * *

On December 14, 1976, six months after Harvey lost the Assembly race, he also lost his father. As a politician, Harvey became passionate about urging gay people to come out to their families, yet Bill died without ever being told that Harvey was gay. Maybe Harvey urged other gays to do what he himself had never done because he understood the cost of hiding who he was from Bill. Their relationship had become so shallow that when Bill died, Harvey told his friend Frank Robinson, he "didn't shed a tear."[31]

Of course, he had never been close to his father. As a child, he could not please Bill, who was a tattooed cowboy at heart, while Harvey was enamored of supposedly effete pastimes such as listening to opera. Bill had a short fuse with Harvey, just as Bill's own father, Morris, had had a short fuse with Bill. Both whacked and hollered at their kids, who were so different from them. When Harvey was a young man he tried hard to be the right sort of son, the manly athlete who would make his father proud. But he could not change his deep desires, and he was certain they would have disgusted Bill had he known.

With Scott Smith, Galen McKinley, Joe Campbell—with all his young lovers—Harvey tried to re-create the father-son relationship and make it come out better. He would be the good, gentle, nurturing, accepting father. But he could not help exploding and belittling, just as his father had. He could not help his ambitions either—his desire for the spotlight, for the stage—which got in the way of his intentions to be totally available to his young lover, as his father had never been available to him. And now Harvey desperately needed the comfort of a lover, but Scott had walked out, and Harvey was alone.

Harvey's grandfather Mausche Milch, the Milk family patriarch in America (Courtesy of Sam Mendales)

Minnie Milk, Harvey's offbeat mother (Courtesy of Harvey Milk–Scott Smith Collection, San Francisco Public Library)

Bill Milk, Harvey's gruff, taciturn father (Courtesy of Harvey Milk–Scott Smith Collection, San Francisco Public Library)

Harvey (*right*), age three, with brother, Robert, 1933 (Courtesy of Harvey Milk–Scott Smith Collection, San Francisco Public Library)

In college Harvey played football, soccer, volleyball, and basketball; and he competed in wrestling and track (Courtesy of Harvey Milk–Scott Smith Collection, San Francisco Public Library)

Teacher Harvey, 1957 (Hewlett-Woodmere High School)

Harvey (*left*), a cutup in the navy, too; c. 1951 (Courtesy of Harvey Milk–Scott Smith Collection, San Francisco Public Library)

Harvey (*center*), a numbers cruncher on Wall Street, c. 1964 (Courtesy of Harvey Milk–Scott Smith Collection, San Francisco Public Library)

Harvey (*back*) with Scott Smith, c. 1971 (Courtesy of Harvey Milk–Scott Smith Collection, San Francisco Public Library)

Campaigning for the longshoremen's vote, 1976 (Daniel Nicoletta)

Campaign volunteers as "human billboards" because Harvey could not afford paid ads (Courtesy of Harvey Milk–Scott Smith Collection, San Francisco Public Library)

Harvey (*right*) and State Senator Milton Marks with Nicole Murray Ramirez (Empress de San Diego of the Imperial Court) in drag, 1976 (Courtesy of Nicole Murray Ramirez)

Harvey in a photo-op with soon-to-be-president Jimmy Carter, who did not know Harvey was gay (though Carter's disapproving staff did), 1976 (Courtesy of Harvey Milk–Scott Smith Collection, San Francisco Public Library)

Harvey the Clown, 1978 (George Olson)

Harvey before a meeting of the Board of Supervisors, 1978 (Courtesy of
Harvey Milk–Scott Smith Collection, San Francisco Public Library)

Part 3

A Serious Political Animal

9

Victory!

HARVEY WAS NOT being coy when he told the *San Francisco Chronicle* right after he lost the Assembly race that he had to tend to business at Castro Camera and was not considering another run for office. Not only was he broke; he was exhausted. But that exhaustion dissipated when he stood beside Jim Rivaldo in front of the color-coded precinct map that now hung on the wall at Castro Camera. Jim had again marked the vote tallies for each pertinent area on the map. He pointed to the Castro. In every one of those eleven precincts—despite the hatchet jobs Harvey got from the gay establishment—he won significantly. Proposition T would be on the ballot in November, Jim reminded him. If voters decided in favor of it, the old method of citywide elections for the Board of Supervisors would be no more. Instead, each district would elect its own supervisor. And, as the map revealed, if Harvey ran for the seat allotted to District 5, which comprised neighborhoods where he had always made a decent showing—the Castro, Haight-Ashbury, Duboce Triangle, Noe Valley, Eureka Valley—he could win next time.

That fall, Proposition T passed with 52 percent of the vote, and Harvey's resolve to tend to Castro Camera faded before all the ballots were counted. He was back in the fray, though it pained him that he would have no one at home to help him. Scott still ran Castro Camera, but he was living elsewhere now. He had made it clear he would never work in another one of Harvey's campaigns. Nevertheless, Harvey charged ahead. He could not stop now, when his chances seemed better than they had ever been.

He and Jim Rivaldo agreed that one of the first things they needed to do was start a gay Democratic club that could drown out whatever voice the leaders of the Alice B. Toklas Memorial Democratic Club had in San Francisco. Harvey loathed even the name of the Alice Club. It was a cowardly wink-wink—you knew it was a gay organization only if you knew that Alice B. Toklas had been a lesbian, and in 1971, when the club was founded, most people did not. With a half dozen other gay men, Harvey and Jim Rivaldo founded the San Francisco Gay Democratic Club, the first democratic club in the country that had the word "gay" in its name.

The San Francisco Gay Democratic Club's immediate purpose, all agreed, would be to get Harvey Milk elected in 1977 to the Board of Supervisors. Their manifesto would be a flat-out challenge to the Alice Club, which had wanted gay-friendly politicians to speak on their behalf. Gays did not need anyone speaking for them; they could speak very well for themselves. "No decisions which affect our lives should be made without the gay voice being heard," the manifesto of the San Francisco Gay Democratic Club said. "Openly gay people should be elected and appointed to city offices," it demanded.[1]

As soon as the gay establishment got word that Harvey was yet again running for office, they were yet again determined to stop him. Rick Stokes, who had been appointed the year before by Mayor Moscone to take over Harvey's barely warmed seat on the Board of Permit Appeals, now let himself be persuaded by Jim Foster and David Goodstein, the publisher of the influential gay magazine *the Advocate*, to throw his hat in the ring, to halt Harvey Milk.

Stokes was a polar opposite to Harvey. Though he grew up in a poor family in rural Oklahoma, he had the demeanor of a southern gentleman: pale, blue-eyed, soft-spoken, courtly. Where Harvey was passionate, Stokes was calm, reasoned, moderate. His leadership in the San Francisco gay community went back to the 1960s, when he was elected president of the Council on Religion and the Homosexual, the first organization ever to bring together prominent gays and liberal clergymen to fight for gay rights. He had been the Alice Club president too. And he was a lawyer who made his reputation defending gay men by arguing in municipal court that it was unconstitutional for undercover vice squad officers to entrap homosexuals in parks and public restrooms.[2] Stokes also had a second job: he and his long-term partner, another lawyer, ran the Ritch Street Health Club, an elegant, 24/7 gay bathhouse where men could make sexual contacts without having to resort to dangerous parks and public toilets—tea rooms, they were called. Though there were seventeen candidates running for the newly created District 5 seat, Harvey saw Stokes as his major competition.

Unlike Harvey, who had always much preferred running for office to selling film, Stokes took his paying jobs very seriously. His busy law practice and bath business already equaled two full-time jobs, Harvey argued, and Stokes had not resigned from anything before declaring his candidacy—not even his seat on the Board of Permit Appeals, from which Harvey had been fired by Mayor Moscone when he announced his 1976 run. Harvey pledged that if he won the election, "I won't continue to conduct my business or practice with occasional time out for playing Supervisor"—ignoring the fact that the job of supervisor was actually designed to be a part-time position.[3] (At a time when the median household income in the United States was $13,570, it paid a mere $9,600, so that citizens with day jobs, not career politicians, would run for the office.) Harvey would be a "*full-time* [*sic*] Supervisor," he reiterated in his campaign literature, implying that Stokes was too busy doing other things to serve the constituency well.

Stokes, as mild mannered as he seemed, tried to hit back hard, sometimes even blowing dog whistles to constituents who would be turned off by Harvey's "New York" qualities. Stokes went around saying that Harvey "gets too emotional" and (eerily) that he was "born to be a martyr."[4]

But Harvey's emotionalism, which he had learned how to calibrate to his audiences, could in fact be just what his key constituency wanted. At one Candidates' Night in the Castro, Stokes used a line that Harvey had often used—but only when he spoke to straight audiences: "I don't want to be referred to as the gay candidate for supervisor. I want to be known as the candidate who happens to be gay," Stokes coolly declared. The audience clapped politely. But when Harvey reportedly jumped to his feet and yelled, "Fuck that shit, motherfucker! I'm gay!" the audience went wild with approval.[5]

There were even members of the Alice Club who would approve. With the tidal waves of gays moving into the area throughout the 1970s, the club had grown, and the young new blood was altering Alice's identity. Older members too, roiled by recent events, were changing. That June, gays everywhere had been enraged by a high-profile campaign that started in Florida to repeal gay rights ordinances around the country. So not all Alice Club members were as content as the old guard was with moderation—nor were they turned off by Harvey's passion. When the Alice Club met to vote for whom they would endorse in the supervisorial race, the gay establishment assumed that Stokes, as past president of the club, would be a shoo-in. But his pallid style was a turnoff to many in the new order, and he fell one vote short of the two-thirds required for endorsement. In the most significant election of its history, the Alice Club endorsed no one. It was a stunning blow to Stokes's political credibility that his own group would not stand solidly behind him. Harvey, meanwhile, had the San Francisco Gay Democratic Club working for him night and day.

The Rick Stokes supporters in the Alice Club grew nasty in their determination to keep Harvey down. For instance, on weekends an army of Harvey's San Francisco Gay Democratic Club volunteers would go out to the residential streets of the Castro at one in the morning, an hour before the bars closed, and place "Harvey Milk for Supervisor" door hangers on every door. At one-thirty, Alice Club volunteers would follow their rivals' paths, pick up every one of the Harvey Milk door hangers, and throw them in the trash.[6]

* * *

Despite the absence of Scott from his campaign and his bed and despite his loneliness, Harvey soldiered on. The race was what mattered now, and he could not let himself be distracted. He once again got the endorsements of the local Teamsters, the Firefighters Union, the Building and Construction Trades Council, the environmentalist San Francisco Tomorrow, the major democratic clubs, senior citizens' groups, and neighborhood associations all over the city. But he hoped to expand his base with groups that had not been strongly in his corner in the past, such as feminists. He knew that might be tricky. Among the seventeen contenders for the District 5 seat was Rita George, the president of the San Francisco chapter of the National Women's Political Caucus. Her supporters were saying that Harvey was antiwoman. Desperate to open conversations but not sure how, when he passed women he recognized as lesbians on the streets of the Castro he turned around and said hello; he tried to schmooze them; he tried to interest them in his campaign. But why would they trust this aggressive stranger who was asking for their vote?[7]

The vocal community of radical lesbian feminists, who were well represented among San Francisco's gay population, had particular grievances with Harvey. After he once again wrote a column touting the importance of "gay economic power," calling it "almost as strong as the power of the ballot box," a bunch of them stormed Castro Camera, shouting, "Gay capitalism is no better than straight capitalism!" and apprising him that because of gay gentrification in the Castro small businesspeople like the straight Middle Eastern family who ran the corner grocery store were being pushed out. Harvey listened and admitted that they had a good point but stuck to his position. "It's important to have a gay neighborhood, owned and run by gays," he said.[8]

Yet he found a pragmatic way to respond to their distrust. He hired as his campaign manager Anne Kronenberg, his "little dykette," as he came to call her. Kronenberg was active in both the women's movement and the lesbian feminist movement. She had moved to San Francisco in 1975 from Bellevue, Washington, where, when she was fifteen years old, she opened the area's first environmental recycling center. Kronenberg became seriously interested in politics when she was a student at the University of Washington and worked on the 1972 McGovern presidential campaign. But in San Francisco the only jobs she could find were clerking at Earring House Imports or typing invoices, with two fingers because she had never learned to type, at a wholesale seafood company. She earned about four hundred dollars a month. But she was twenty-two years old and not very invested in her work anyway. It interfered with her real interests, working to get the Equal Rights Amendment passed, volunteering at the Women's Center, and spending nights in San Francisco's lesbian bars and discos.

Then a gay male friend of hers, Ken Lester, who had contributed one hundred dollars to Harvey's campaign, told him he knew a young woman who loved politics and would make a great staff person. "You ought to have some women involved in your campaign. You should call her," Lester said. Harvey desperately needed someone to take on all the campaign tasks that Scott used to do, and John Ryckman had gone on to other things. Harvey took Anne Kronenberg's telephone number from Ken Lester and called.

Anne immediately hopped on the used motorcycle she had recently purchased and rushed to Castro Camera, where she was scared upon entering by a disembodied voice somewhere in the background, screaming at the top of its lungs. It was Harvey, of course. ("I yell a lot," he would eventually tell her. "Everybody in my family yelled. You just need to yell back.")

"Ken spoke very highly of you. I'd like to hire you as my campaign coordinator," Harvey said when he finally appeared.

"But I don't know anything about coordinating campaigns," Anne answered.

"I do. I'll teach you," he told her. He could pay her only one hundred dollars a month, which would barely cover her rent, but he would also feed her while she was at work—ten to twelve hours a day, seven days a week, he informed her up front, and he would make sure she had money for motorcycle gas. "And you'll learn a lot and have a lot of fun."

"Okay," she told him, because she was already charmed by the funky barber chair, the maroon couch, The Kid—and especially the volatile, funny, charismatic guy whose vitality felt electric.

To supplement her income she would clean the apartment that Ken Lester shared with his partner, and she would do odd jobs, like painting the neighbor's stairs.[9] Harvey kept his word about feeding her. After his daily leaflet-distributing and hand-shaking at bus stops at six in the morning, he would come into the store by seven (Anne had already arrived on her motorcycle), carrying coffees and a box of sweet rolls and pastries. For lunch he would bring in sandwiches or pizza. Same for dinner.

In addition to doing her duties as campaign coordinator—organizing volunteers and arranging speaking engagements, fielding phone calls and soliciting potential endorsers and donors—Anne taught Harvey to talk about what women in general and lesbians in particular wanted and needed. He learned when it was important to say "gay and lesbian" rather than just "gay." He learned about the hottest feminist issue of the day, the struggle to pass the Equal Rights Amendment, which stated, "Equality of rights under the law shall not be abridged or denied by the United States or by any state on account of sex." Thirty-five states had ratified the ERA by 1977; it was three states shy of becoming the law of the land. Anne tutored Harvey, passing on to him her copies of the National Organization for Women newsletters that were primers on the ERA.[10] He learned to include in his talking points on the campaign trail why the ERA was important; how women were an oppressed group, just like gays, seniors, and black and brown people; and why all the oppressed, including straight women and lesbians, needed to stick together.

But what probably helped put female voters in his corner the most was the optics of Anne Kronenberg, a young lesbian-feminist activist who trusted Harvey Milk to do the right thing by women. In the end, Rita George, the candidate Harvey feared would take the women's vote from him, got less than 4 percent of the overall vote. The preponderance of the women's vote went to Harvey.

* * *

Though Scott worked faithfully in the store, he and Harvey fought constantly. "God, you didn't do *that!* You stupid idiot!" Harvey yelled at him several times a day. Scott yelled back. He was doing a lot more drugs at this point, not just pot.

"Medicine," he called his dope.[11] Anne Kronenberg, who came from a polite Swiss family where no one raised their voice, did not know what to make of their fights. The Bickersons, she called Harvey and Scott. But they would not be jollied out of their arguing. Scott had a seething anger, she sensed, and he could not let go of his bitterness over Harvey's relentless desire to hold political office.[12] It did not help matters when Harvey met a curly-haired, twenty-three-year-old Latino at a New Year's Eve party at the end of 1976.

Jack Lira was a high school dropout. He was born in West Texas and grew up in Fresno, California. As soon as he was able, he escaped to gay San Francisco, where, as he had heard, Latino youths who did not meet the culture's standard of machismo could find a welcoming home. Jack, who was high-strung and emotionally wobbly, was living with a wealthy older man in Pacific Heights when he met Harvey. Soon after, the man tired of Jack's instability and unceremoniously kicked him out.

Harvey tried to get Jack a job at the New York Deli on Market Street, which Mel Lefer—a straight New York Jew with whom Harvey liked to talk Yiddishkayt—had just opened. Jack worked for four or five weeks and then quit.[13] That should have been a warning signal to Harvey. But when it came to affairs of the heart, he was never good at reading warning signals. Jack perfectly fit the pattern of the waifs who had always attracted Harvey: troubled, needy, young, and pretty. Like Joe Campbell, Craig Rodwell, and Galen McKinley, Jack had made serious suicide attempts.[14] Yet Harvey could not relinquish the idea that he could save this young man, despite his history of failures. Hadn't Jack been physically abused by his father and thrown out of his family because he was gay, just like the youths Harvey talked about in his campaign? Once again Harvey undertook the role of loving father figure who would give his beloved everything he needed to make him happy and whole.

Though Harvey was busy running for office, he took the

time to immerse himself in his new love affair, so Jack would not feel neglected, as Scott had. He tried to make Jack know how deeply he was valued; he sent him tender, romantic letters. "Watching the ocean slam against the rocks—spraying its mist—the sun setting in the background," Harvey wrote Jack a few weeks into their relationship, "I could not help myself stop [*sic*] from looking into your wondrous face—& last night as I carried you to your bed I saw the day over & over & over—I needed no camera yesterday to capture glorious pictures—They are forever burnt into my heart."[15] He invited the younger man to move in with him.

But Jack was an embarrassment to Harvey in public. He would get obnoxiously drunk or high on pot, dress like a street person, and sulk by himself in a corner at fund-raisers. As the supervisor race heated up, Harvey reverted to his old patterns, and Jack felt neglected because Harvey was so often away campaigning. Jack would throw tantrums or call him on the phone incessantly, no matter how much scheduling pressure Harvey was under. Jack watched soap operas in the apartment when he was needed to address campaign envelopes or to register voters. Jim Rivaldo tried to tell Harvey that Jack was a detriment to his campaign and that he would be a disastrous partner if Harvey became a supervisor. "Harvey, he's not salvageable. You gotta get rid of him," Rivaldo warned after each antic Jack pulled. But nothing would make Harvey kick out the young man who had already been kicked around so much by others.[16]

* * *

Although Harvey had not yet won an election, San Francisco's straight world already seemed to acknowledge him as the city's major gay leader. In the midst of his 1977 campaigning, the San Francisco Police Department turned to him to prevent a gay riot. The police feared the community was on the verge of erupting when in Florida's Miami-Dade County, on June 7, 1977, a gay rights ordinance was repealed after a vicious battle.

The agitation for repeal was led by Anita Bryant, a fundamentalist Christian pop singer. Bryant was a household name because she touted Florida orange juice on television for the Florida Citrus Commission. She had founded a group she called Save Our Children, whose hysterical message was that homosexuals were child molesters and giving them civil rights would encourage their criminality and immorality.

Save Our Children flooded the media with ads that featured bits of articles from around the country about homosexual pornographers who sold dirty pictures of little boys and homosexual Boy Scout masters who raped the adolescents in their charge. This was a "holy war," Anita Bryant proclaimed, "a battle of the agnostics, the atheists, and the ungodly on one side, and God's people on the other."[17] And she won the war—or at least its opening salvos: Miami-Dade voters went to the polls, and, of the 446 precincts in the county, 385 of them voted in favor of repealing the gay rights ordinance.[18]

Gay people called the debacle Orange Tuesday and staged protests in big cities everywhere. In the Castro thousands congregated, fists raised and angrily shouting, "2, 4, 6, 8, separate the church and state!" and "Civil rights or civil war!" With so many livid gays demonstrating in one place, the SFPD feared that a Stonewall-style riot was imminent. Thus, the police came to Harvey and implored him to help.

He had mixed feelings. The Stonewall riots in Greenwich Village in 1969 had triggered a national gay movement that was much more effective than anything resulting from the polite homophile organizations of the 1950s.[19] Harvey had paid little attention to the riots at the Stonewall in the moment; but he acknowledged now that they had helped make possible the boldness of the Castro. However, people got hurt or killed in riots, and neighborhoods got destroyed. To guard the Castro and its inhabitants was his priority. The police were right to rely on him: he proved himself a trustworthy peacekeeper.

As Harvey stood facing the mob on Castro Street, Randy Alfred, the journalist who had taken over the "Waves from the Left" column on the *Sentinel*, handed him a bullhorn he had intended to use himself. Harvey was astute in knowing what would sway the crowd. He told them that Anita Bryant had done the gay community a service: her hatred had united them and made them tough. He called on the assembled to show their unified resolve not just in the Castro but where straight people lived too. For the next three hours he led them in a five-mile march up and down the hills of San Francisco—to Market, to Polk, to City Hall, to Nob Hill, to California Street, where they halted the cable cars, to Union Square, where they stopped to hold a midnight rally.[20] Harvey's march was a brilliant way to honor gay anger and keep the community safe: he encouraged the mob to let the whole city know their feelings while averting the injuries and destruction to property that would have been inevitable if rioting had occurred in the Castro.

The following spring there were copycat repeals of gay rights ordinances in St. Paul, Minnesota; Wichita, Kansas; and Eugene, Oregon. In San Francisco there were long marches again—gays working off their frustration by walking and shouting instead of tearing up their neighborhood. To keep the throng together, Harvey now brought with him the bullhorn that Allan Baird had given him after the success of the Coors boycott. Most of the time he handed the bullhorn to a slight, spirited, twenty-four-year-old college student, Cleve Jones, one of the young men of the Castro whom Harvey had taken under his wing and who was campaigning for him on college campuses. Jones shouted out directions to the marchers: to Market, to Polk, to California, to Nob Hill, to Powell, to Union Square, until everyone was ready to drop from exhaustion. The "disaster march route," he and Harvey called it.[21]

Anita Bryant's odious campaign bestowed another gift on gays: it ended forever the idea that homosexuality was "the love that dared not speak its name." During the flood of repeals of gay rights ordinances every major newspaper in the country had the word "homosexual" on its front page. *Newsweek* ran a cover story that dispelled the worst myths about homosexuals. National TV anchors were talking nightly about the subject of gay rights. Bryant had unwittingly prepared the whole country for taking the next steps toward gay freedom and equality; and Harvey was ready to lead the charge.

* * *

In a tight election, Harvey knew, every demographic was important. He pursued the drag queen vote through the Imperial Court, an organization of "female impersonators" that had been founded in San Francisco in 1965 by José Sarria, who crowned himself Empress José I. The campy group, which soon spread to several cities, had a charitable purpose too: to raise money for good causes with grand balls in which queens vied to outdo one another in elegance and gorgeousness. Harvey had always loved seeing the flamboyance and fun of drag. Sylvester, Queen of Disco, had been his friend since Harvey first came to San Francisco; he was also a great admirer of the gifted Empress José I, who performed brilliant parodies of women's operatic roles, such as Carmen and Madame Butterfly. But not only did Harvey genuinely appreciate drag queens—he also knew that within San Francisco's gay community the Imperial Court had real clout in raising money and awareness. One evening he ordered Danny Nicoletta, the young photographer who had helped run Castro Camera, to accompany him to a meeting at the Society for Individual Rights' community center. He would be voting in a competition to name the next Empress of the Imperial Court.

"It may seem silly, but it's really important that I be there," Harvey told Danny. "These are my potential voters, and they'll pay attention to whether I make the effort to come and vote for Empress." In fact, they did pay attention. When Harvey later appeared at an Imperial Court event, the rafters shook with applause for him.[22] Of the drag queen vote he could be certain.

He could also be certain of the youth vote. In a speech he gave several times during his 1977 campaign he made young gays a chief reason for his candidacy. At a time when Anita Bryant and her ilk were agitating for the repeal of gay rights, Harvey proclaimed that young gay people had to be given hope: "Hope for a better world. Hope for a better tomorrow. Hope for a place to go if the pressure at home is too great. Hope that it all will be all right." He concluded his "Hope" speech with the declaration that his election as an out and proud gay man would be much more than a mere personal triumph: "It will mean that a green light is lit. A green light that says to all who feel lost and disenfranchised that now you can go forward. It means hope, and we—you and you and you, and yes, you, have got to give them hope!"

In public discourse older gays had previously kept their distance from youths, lest they be accused of predatory interests. The subject of gay youth had been taboo because, according to the stereotype, a homosexual was someone who lurked in the shadows waiting to pounce on a young person. Harvey was the first politician to publicly declare his determination to help young gays.

* * *

To audiences outside the Castro, however, Harvey did not always make his concerns for gay youth so prominent. Asked in Noe Valley, a predominantly straight neighborhood of District 5, what his number one priority would be as supervisor, he answered simply, "Jobs—it affects taxes, welfare, crime, attitudes and the spirit of the city." To his Noe Valley constituency he even rejected the description of his views as progressive, saying, "I don't think in terms of labels. I only think in terms of issues."[23] So Harvey was furious when, two days before the election, a sensationalistic article, "A Walk on San Francisco's Gay Side," appeared in the *New York Times*'s "Sunday Punch" section, presenting him to the world in precisely the way he did not want to be presented outside the Castro.

Harvey had been thrilled when the writer of the article, Herbert Gold, made an appointment to come to Castro Camera to interview him. It would be the first time the newspaper of record paid any attention to him as a politician. On the day of the interview Gold sat with Harvey on the famous maroon couch ("a tattered couch," as Gold described it in the *Times*) and watched a procession of gay volunteers clad in tight jeans, Pendleton shirts, and leather jackets come in and out of the store while the candidate talked volubly to Gold about his campaign. In the article Harvey proclaims himself "a left-winger, a street person," and he is quoted as distancing himself from most gay leaders, whom he portrays as closeted and Republican. He sums up his campaign with the declaration, "Gay for gay. That's my issue. That's it. That's the big one."[24]

Harvey worried. He had let his guard down with Herbert Gold, who was best known as a novelist who wrote about the Jewish immigrant-family experience; perhaps they even exchanged a few Yiddish phrases, as Harvey loved to do with fellow Jews who had grown up, as he had, hearing the language of their grandparents. Perhaps Harvey had not realized that everything he said to Gold would appear in print. In any case, he felt betrayed. He sent off an angry letter to the "Sunday Punch" editor at the *Times*, claiming that Gold quoted him out of context. He had never characterized himself as a "left-winger" or "street person," not to Gold or to anyone else, Harvey wrote. He had never said that "Gay for gay" was his issue. The paramount issue to him, he emphasized, was that San Francisco was a city of "people of all creeds, ethnic origins, and sexual persuasions [who] are going to have to learn to live together," and that was what he wanted to help them do if he got elected. But the election was just two days away, he complained, and there was no way he could repair the damage Gold had done.[25]

The *New York Times* article did not appear to hurt Harvey in the least. Of the seventeen candidates running for the Board of Supervisors from District 5, Rick Stokes came in third. A straight liberal lawyer, Terence Hallinan, came in second. And Harvey finished first, with over 30 percent of the vote. District elections also brought to the new Board of Supervisors the first Chinese American, the first black woman, an unwed mother (Harvey's friend Carol Ruth Silver), and a Latino. The working-class District 8 elected a young fireman and former policeman with no political experience by the name of Dan White.

* * *

As Harvey told the media, his win made him feel like Jackie Robinson, the first black man to be permitted to play major league baseball. He drew the parallels, reminding himself at the same time about how he needed to behave from that point on: Jackie Robinson had had to be as good as possible and could not allow himself "to blow up out of anger." Just as Robinson had been a symbol to "every single black youth" in the country, Harvey was "a symbol of hope to gays and all minorities." That was the upbeat message he wanted to convey to America—and that his election, "against all odds, shows that the system can work."[26]

But just in case any of his straight constituents had read the *New York Times* article and gotten the wrong impression of their new supervisor, Harvey took the opportunity to stress to the media that he had never conducted a gay campaign—rather, it was "an issue-oriented campaign." He even downplayed the enthusiasm for him in the Castro District by insisting that "the gay vote was pretty well diffused" among his competitors.[27] He was vindicated when groups that were not gay, such as the Building and Construction Trades Council, rejoiced in his win, proclaiming that "labor had a great victory in Supervisorial District 5 in electing Harvey Milk."[28]

Yet it was with gays that Harvey celebrated his triumph on election night. They began coming to Milk Headquarters at Castro Camera just as soon as the polls closed. There were hundreds of them, spilling out onto Castro Street, expectant and excited.[29] But Harvey was not there. He had been driven to City Hall to watch election officials count the votes. Anne Kronenberg's lover, Joyce Garay, had taken him there on the back of her motorcycle. When he learned before the clock struck eleven that he was the victor, he jumped on Joyce's motorcycle, and, holding on to her leather-clad torso, he was sped to headquarters. Beaming, he made his way to a little clearing in the room as the sea of admirers parted for him. Somebody handed him a bottle of champagne. The crowd chanted in ecstasy as Harvey, a teetotaler, anointed himself by pouring the bubbly over his head.[30]

Harry Britt, one of the founders of the San Francisco Gay Democratic Club, was in the crowd. "He'll be a Moses for gay people," Britt thought. "He'll now be able to lead us to his promised land."[31] And he would lead all, not just gay men, Harvey seemed to vow when he announced that he would take with him to City Hall two of his aides: Dick Pabich, who had helped him organize his campaign, and his campaign coordinator, Anne Kronenberg. The lesbians present went wild.

The first morning after his victory Harvey was a kid delighted by a new gizmo. The victory party had left a lot of debris in and around Castro Camera. Harvey picked up the phone and called Sunset Scavenger: "Tell 'em Supervisor-elect Harvey Milk needs a dumpster immediately." He was thrilled when it arrived within the hour.[32]

He was also thrilled when those who had opposed him now tried to make nice with him. Even his archenemy Jim Foster, who had scoffed at his ambitions from the beginning, sent him a breezy note of congratulations saying, "We'll take the corner office at City Hall!"[33]

Neither did Mayor Moscone waste time in coming around. Right after his victory, Harvey claimed, Moscone called him to his office for a meeting and offered to pay off some of Harvey's campaign debts. Harvey—still bitter about being summarily fired from the Board of Permit Appeals after he announced he was running against Art Agnos—maintained that he replied, "Look, George, I'm the number one queen now, and if you continue to go against me I'm going to make sure you don't get reelected."[34] Whether or not Harvey really said that to George Moscone, there is no doubt that that was how he felt.

* * *

On January 9, 1978, the day of his swearing-in ceremony, Harvey walked the two miles from the Castro to City Hall with a retinue of 150 supporters behind him. He kept his arm around Jack Lira's shoulder all the way to convey to the media and the world that this is what a happy gay couple looks like. In the overflowing council chamber, after the other new supervisors had made a few comments, Harvey took his turn at the microphone, where he criticized state laws that banned homosexual marriage. The other supervisors had introduced their wives, husbands, or other relatives. Harvey announced, "And now I'd like to introduce my lover, my partner in life." But Jack had left the chamber just as Harvey had gotten up to speak.[35]

The evening after Harvey's swearing in, the owner of the *Advocate*, David Goodstein, sponsored parties in his honor at three gay venues. Goodstein, one of the few Jewish members of the old gay establishment, had thought in 1973—along with the rest of the establishment—that Harvey the hippie was an embarrassment to the gay cause. Even a suit and tie could not change Goodstein's mind: Harvey muddied the gay rights issue by talking about rights for all the oppressed. In the 1977 election Goodstein even tried to pressure Imperial Court members to swing their votes to Rick Stokes.[36] But once Harvey won, Goodstein acknowledged through the parties he threw for Harvey that the new supervisor was the preeminent gay leader of San Francisco. Harvey graciously showed up at all three, even though he surely knew that Goodstein, like the entire Jim Foster camp, had been his sworn enemy.

At one of the parties someone gave Harvey a congratulatory gift of a pure white long-stemmed lily, which he carried around with him à la Oscar Wilde for the rest of the evening. When Goodstein, who was weirdly decked out in a Stetson cowboy hat and buff suede jacket that January night, announced at I-Beam, a dance bar on Haight Street, that he was calling it a night, Harvey walked him out and offered to shake his hand. Goodstein took Harvey's hand and kissed it instead.

Some of those present claimed they heard Goodstein say, "Goodnight, Sweet Prince." Even if Harvey had not remembered his Shakespeare, he would have known from Ambroise Thomas's operatic adaptation of Shakespeare's play that the line is uttered by Horatio to the dying Hamlet.[37] If the incident truly happened that January night, it would surely have been disturbing to Harvey, who often imagined his early death by an assassin who hated homosexuals. Now, as the first openly gay man to be elected to office, he was the most prominent homosexual in America.

On November 18, 1977, ten days after the election, he went to the office of a lawyer friend, Walter Caplan, where, speaking from notes, he recorded three tapes of his "political will," which he distributed to Caplan, Frank Robinson, and his personal attorney, John Wahl. In all three versions he asked that the tape be listened to "only in the event of my death by assassination." He declared in the tape he gave to Caplan, "I fully realize that a person who stands for what I stand for—a gay activist—becomes the target or potential target for a person who is insecure, terrified, afraid, or very disturbed themselves."

He was worried about who would be appointed to take his place if he were killed. He had been part of the movement, he said, and he did not want his replacement to be someone like Rick Stokes, Jim Foster, or Jo Daly, who simply *used* the movement for their own gains. He named several replacements he favored, including Harry Britt and Anne Kronenberg.

In the tape he gave to Caplan he also spoke of a phone call he got right after his election, from a young gay person isolated in Altoona, Pennsylvania, who had been cheered by his victory. And that is what his election meant, Harvey declared: "It's not about personal gain, not about ego, not about power— it's about giving those young people out there in Altoona, Pennsylvania, hope."

In the tape he sent to Frank Robinson he declared, "If a bullet should enter my brain, let that bullet destroy every closet door."[38]

10

Supervisor Milk

HARVEY ALWAYS FELT wounded by his older brother's long-standing opinion of him as a lightweight who never grew out of being a showoff. It was not just an older brother's difficulty admitting that his kid brother was no longer a kid. Robert harbored a practically endless list of grievances against Harvey: Harvey was the hippie who could not make a decent living; Harvey was the failed man who did not do his manly duty to society and to the Milk family by getting married and having children; Harvey did not even have the wherewithal to put up a nice plaque in the synagogue in honor of their dead parents or to make a big donation in their name to a new hospital in Israel—as, Robert liked to remind Harvey, he himself had done.

But the day Harvey was sworn in as supervisor he received an enormously gratifying letter from his brother. Robert addressed him as "Dear Mr. Supervisor," wished him "continued success," and joked, "You may even replace that guy Nixon in the history books."[1] It was too bad that Harvey's father, who had also always doubted him, did not live to see his big victory; but at least his brother was now forced to acknowledge what an extraordinary success Harvey had become. And the best part was that he had done it by the sheer force of his determination— and on his own terms, as an open homosexual.

It was also important to Harvey that Tom O'Horgan know of his success. Tom had been a good friend; he had given Harvey work in the theater and had come to his aid financially more than once. But it had been Tom who was the celebrity, the star; and it had been Harvey who was nothing, the hanger-on, the gofer. Finally, however, Harvey was where he always felt he should be. There would be a victory dinner for him on January 10, the day after he was sworn in, and the lieutenant governor of California, Mervyn Dymally, who had cast the deciding vote to repeal California's sodomy law, would be there and would toast him. Harvey sent a printed invitation to Tom and Galen McKinley (who for years had witnessed Harvey in the lesser role). On the invitation addressed to them both he scribbled a droll note: "Who would have ever thought that the Lt. Gov. of the largest state would be the guest speaker for a fag? Well, you all come now, you hear!"[2]

* * *

As soon as Harvey took office he promised the radical press that had supported him that he was not going to become an insider—he was going to change what the inside looked like. He would do things his way, he told the *Berkeley Barb*. "I'm not concerned about the Emily Post attitude of life. Emily Post kept the blacks suppressed for hundreds of years. Emily Post kept Jews out of the boardrooms of the major corporations for hundreds of years. Emily Post kept the gay people where they are."[3] Deflating City Hall with a moniker he would often repeat, he boasted, "You can throw bricks at Silly Hall, or you can take it over. Well, here we are."[4]

At the very first board meeting Harvey jumped in with both feet by taking on the San Francisco "airport lobby," whose proposal for airport expansion the Board of Supervisors was set to rubber stamp. An expansion of the San Francisco airport was antithetical to Harvey's aim to keep the city livable; he had even promised the environmentalist group San Francisco Tomorrow, which had supported him in his victorious election, that he would fight expansion. A bigger airport meant more traffic, more pollution, and more noise.[5] But he had not figured out yet the game of being sure of his aye votes before he plunged ahead. Of the eleven supervisors, only three sided with him. Harvey's loss on this issue was embarrassing. If he wanted to win, he learned, he had to understand the practical politics of how to swing the majority of a board of eleven people to his side; he had to be able to count to six.

He had challenges with his constituency too. When he was campaigning for office he emphasized whatever it was he knew the group sitting in front of him wanted to hear; but to be the legislator for such diverse communities was more complicated. He had to please them all at once. His straight constituents sent him messages like, "I trust that Gay orientation will not cause you to ignore or avoid the broader problem of the district and the city. For example, District 5 includes a large percentage of non-Gays, Senior citizens, multi-ethnic groups and Single straights. All these constituents deserve the attention of you and the Board of Supervisors. . . . I hope you will attend to the duties of the office with the dignity it deserves."[6]

But when he tried to reassure straight constituents by promising that he would be no more a gay supervisor than John Kennedy was a Catholic president, he received outraged letters from gay constituents, such as the one reminding him that "you were elected AS A GAY PERSON [sic]. . . . We wanted a person on the board who was gay and would speak up as gay. We won't forget this, and I hope you won't either. Without your gayness, you would be just another white liberal man running for office."[7] Yet when he went to battle for gay issues, he received admonishments from other gays: "Straight voters aren't going to buy this 'second holocaust' argument ('if-you-aren't-for-gay-rights-you-want-to-put-us-in-the-ovens')," one self-identified "gay businessman" wrote. "There will be a second holocaust only if we are so masochistic as to insist on continually fueling the fire over and over again until people get fed up enough to throw us in it."[8]

Harvey also discovered that it was not a good idea to dispense with all formalities. He had hoped to cut through the usual pomposity associated with holding office by democratizing things at City Hall. He made it a point to know the names of all the clerks and their partners and kids and told everyone to call him by his first name. "No, not 'Supervisor Milk.' I'm Harvey," he had to remind them when they reverted to habit and addressed him formally. In the beginning he had an open-door policy for all his constituents, some of whom he truly enjoyed, such as Henrietta Abrams, an elderly Jewish lady who would often take a bus from Cole Street to City Hall, carrying a box of cookies she had made for Harvey's sweet tooth. They would sit together in his office, door closed, their chitchat interspersed with bits of Yiddish, and munch cookies. She called him her "little Jewish prince."[9] But as his office became a community center where anyone could drop by and ask for advice or just shoot the breeze, he realized that a wide-open door made it harder to get supervisorial work done. After a few weeks, he had to ask his aides to filter out most of the casual visitors.

* * *

Harvey threw himself into his duties, typically devoting fifteen hours a day to the job, including appearances at three or four official events in the evening. Jack frequently complained about being left alone at night; but for Harvey, once again, there was love and there was work, and they were in two different compartments. He explained to Jack as patiently as he could that he owed long hours of hard work to the voters who had had enough faith in him to put him in office. But the explanation did little to placate Jack.

One night Cleve Jones, who lived up the block from Harvey, was coming home around two, after the bars closed. There on the street was Supervisor Milk in his bathrobe. He was sweeping shards of glass from the sidewalk in front of Castro Camera. He told Cleve that Jack had just hurled a vase out the window of their apartment above the store.[10] Yet no matter Jack's fits, nothing altered Harvey's single-minded devotion to his work. It had taken him five years to get elected, and he had no intention of doing the job halfway.

* * *

Harvey did his homework better than almost any other board member, studying everything he could about each issue that came up for discussion—and he was not shy about letting this be known. At board meetings he spoke often and at great length, presenting copious proposals, asking many questions, raising points of procedure. Not all his fellow board members appreciated the verbosity and zeal of the smart-alecky newcomer.

He presented to the Board of Supervisors a blizzard of progressive ideas: there should be free public transit, a Department of Aging responsible for all of San Francisco's senior services, strong laws against animal cruelty, a permanent ordinance against housing discrimination for families with children, curbside collection of recyclables, a prohibition against construction of high-rise buildings in the downtown area, relaxation of laws against marijuana use, a Commission on Youth composed only of youth members, a demand from the Board of Supervisors that the U.S. State Department close the South African consulate in San Francisco in protest against apartheid in South Africa.[11]

His most critical proposal, which he presented at his first meeting of the board, was a gay rights ordinance that would expand and put real teeth into Dianne Feinstein's 1972 bill against antigay discrimination by city contractors. Under Harvey's bill, not only would gay people be protected in housing, employment, and public accommodations, but if their rights were violated they would have recourse in the courts.

To Harvey's exasperation, Feinstein, now the president of the Board of Supervisors, did not let the bill come to a vote: it would first need to be vetted by the Police, Fire, and Public Safety Committee, she announced. She had named as chair of that committee one of the new supervisors she hoped to mentor: the clean-cut, thirty-one-year-old Dan White, who had been both a fireman and a policeman. Perhaps she really did not consider how obstructive White would be with regard to Harvey's gay rights bill. Yet White had been elected by the voters of District 8, a conservative, largely Catholic, blue-collar area in the southeastern swath of the city, and he made promises to the voters of his district: if elected, he told them, he would fight against San Francisco's "radicals, social deviates, and incorrigibles." Harvey's signature piece of legislation would now have to pass through perilous hoops.

* * *

While Harvey awaited the verdict of Dan White's committee, he proposed a bill that he knew would make the press pay attention. He had gotten the idea soon after his election, when he received a letter from a constituent along with an Associated Press article about a new law that had just been passed in New York: it fined dog owners up to one hundred dollars if they did not clean up after their animals in public.[12] The letter writer implored the newly elected supervisor to do the same in San Francisco.

A dog-poop law! What a brilliant way to remind San Franciscans that Harvey Milk was on the Board of Supervisors and was working for them all. "Whoever can solve the dog shit problem can be elected mayor of San Francisco, even president of the United States," he had joked.[13] Two weeks after his gay rights ordinance was sent to Dan White's committee, where it was stalled, Harvey asked the board to have the city attorney draft a dog-littering ordinance, which would establish penalties for anyone who "permits a dog to defecate on public or private property or who walks a dog without carrying a container suitable for the removal and disposal of dog excrement."

Ever the showman, Harvey invited reporters to join him on an amble through Duboce Park, a popular site for dog walkers. A couple of minutes into the walk he stepped onto the green and right into a heap of dog turds, which he had had planted there. To everyone's amusement, including his own, he held up his dog-doo-covered shoe for all to see, especially the cameramen. The story made the six o'clock news, and hilarious little articles appeared in newspapers everywhere, including photos of Harvey and his soiled shoe. Harvey Milk became the man of the hour: the bold and funny champion of a cause everyone—gay, straight, liberal, conservative—could understand. It was good for the gays, as he said: "All over the country they're reading about me, and the story doesn't center on me being gay. It's just about a gay person who is doing his job."[14]

It was certainly "good for the gays" that America saw an out homosexual doing a civic-minded, nonsexual thing; but it was also a stunt. He devised other stunts that would get him media attention. A few months into his term the Ringling Bros. and Barnum & Bailey Circus came to San Francisco, and its PR people asked a few public officials to allow themselves to be decked out in clown regalia furnished by the San Francisco Clown School. Harvey jumped at the chance. In startling Pagliacci makeup and clown suit, he boarded cable cars or stood at the main cable car stop on Powell and Market and informed astonished onlookers that he, a clown, helped run the city. "If you're not having fun in politics, you're missing the boat. Why bother?" he told Danny Nicoletta, the young helper at Castro Camera, who trailed him all that day to take photographs of Harvey the Clown.[15]

He adored camping too, both for its theatricality and its shock to people's expectations about how an elected official and a masculine-seeming man ought to behave. Among the young people who surrounded Harvey at City Hall was Debra Jones, a black San Francisco State College student who was working for him as an intern. The supervisors' offices were on the second floor, and Jones had gotten into the habit of taking the elevator rather than walking down the majestic marble staircase. One day Harvey stopped her just as she was about to get into the elevator. "No, no, my dear!" he cried. "You should never pass up the opportunity to make a grand exit!" Taking her hand, he led her to the staircase. "Now I will show you how it's done," he said. They glided together down the stairs like a royal couple. "See?" Harvey whispered conspiratorially, "a Nubian queen and a Jewish queen."[16]

* * *

Harvey's gay rights ordinance, his signature piece of legislation, had much less smooth sailing than his pooper-scooper law. The bill had been languishing for two months in the Police, Fire, and Public Safety Committee chaired by Dan White. But suddenly, it seemed to Harvey, an opportunity emerged for a breakthrough. On March 6, White came to his fellow supervisors with what for him was a burning issue. Since 1932 the Sisters of the Good Shepherd had run a school in his district for wayward girls who had "fallen from virtue." However, changing times meant that unchaste females were not as penitent as they had once been. Since the school was almost empty, the Sisters agreed to sell the property to the San Francisco Department of Social Services, which planned to use it as a Youth Campus for disturbed boys: "juvenile delinquents," as White's constituents called them. They feared that the boys would be looting and raping on their streets. White promised the voters of his district that he would use his power as a supervisor to halt the establishment of a Youth Campus.

Harvey was no longer the novice he had been in January when he had not understood that supervisors got their bills passed largely by playing ball, or seeming to, with other supervisors. He went to White and vowed he would help him on the Youth Campus vote if White would help Harvey by getting his gay rights ordinance out of committee. Harvey's proposal to Dan White would prove to be the first act of a tragedy.

Dan White had won his seat on the board because of his boyish sincerity, his "old-fashioned values," and his all-American-boy good looks. He had gone door to door throughout his working-class district, visiting seven thousand houses and five thousand businesses, looking like an impeccable schoolboy with his pomaded hair and starched white shirt. He had shaken the hand of everyone in sight and promised to fight the "cesspool of perversion" that was shaming San Francisco in the eyes of the nation.[17] Danny Boy, the people of his district called him. But thus far on the Board of Supervisors he had had a hard time.

He had only a high school education and had never before held office. He was the youngest person ever to serve on the board. When he first became a supervisor, he tried to hide his nervousness behind a facade of charm; he even presented each board member with a gift (which he could ill afford): Chivas Regal for the men, flowers for the women.[18] But that could not make up for his weekly failure to do his homework by carefully reading the huge packets of material that board members were given in the days before each meeting. He was not like Harvey, who spent grueling hours maneuvering behind the scenes before the board meetings. For Harvey, the board had quickly become a stage, one on which he could show off his nimble-mindedness and audacity. Even when he lost on an issue, Harvey thoroughly enjoyed himself. Sitting in the supervisors' chambers at City Hall, he would laugh as loud and as long at his own jokes as he did at those of the other supervisors. But when things did not go Dan White's way, the six-foot-tall former cop had a temper tantrum, just like a little kid. His already high voice got eerily higher with every enraged sentence.[19]

But now White happily agreed to Harvey's proposal. Though White had campaigned on the promise to fight the "deviates," nothing was as imperative to him at this time as serving his constituency by scuttling the Youth Campus. If Harvey voted with him, White would have a good chance of succeeding.

Dan White kept his part of the bargain. On Thursday, March 9, Harvey attended the meeting of the Police, Fire, and Public Safety Committee, where his gay rights ordinance was scheduled for a vote. White spoke at length in favor of the ordinance. Harvey must have been astonished when he heard White say that as a paratrooper in Vietnam he had learned that gays and blacks and other minorities performed as admirably as anyone else in combat. "The sooner we get down to eliminating discrimination against any people, the better we'll all be," White concluded.[20] His words blatantly contradicted his campaign rhetoric; but White was figuring out—or so he thought—how to play the political game: you got your important bills passed by supporting other guys' bills. Even if you had to hold your nose to do it. To Harvey's elation, his gay rights bill sailed through White's committee with a unanimous vote.

Did Harvey know from the beginning that he could not keep his part of the bargain? To vote against a Youth Campus would have violated his conviction that society had an obligation to help the young and the disenfranchised. Even as far back as 1973, the first time Harvey ran for office, he filled out a candidate's questionnaire that asked, among other things, whether halfway houses and board and care homes should be placed in residential neighborhoods. He had responded in no uncertain terms: "If people who call themselves Christians are Christians then the only answer is 'of course.'" At his second meeting of the Board of Supervisors, in January 1978, he had a chance to show the depth of that conviction, and he did. He spoke out in favor of a proposal to locate a federally funded drug rehab center in a residential part of the Mission District. At the start of that meeting, only the four reliable progressives on the board had been in favor of it. But, led by Harvey, their enthusiasm overcame the reluctance of the more conservative majority, and Harvey's side won. A drug rehab center would be built in a residential area of the Mission District.[21] Wasn't White's issue almost identical to that one—people wanting to deny much-needed help to those in desperate straits just because they did not want pariahs in their neighborhood?

The following Monday, March 13, Dan White arrived at the board meeting with a gaggle of admiring constituents. He felt sure of a victory. With Harvey's support, White could get to the required six votes. That meant the Youth Campus project would be scuttled, just as the residents of District 8 wished. He was eager for them to witness how well he was safeguarding their interests.

But Dan White was humiliated in front of his constituents when Harvey—despite what White thought was an inviolate promise—voted with the five supervisors who favored the Youth Campus. It was a betrayal White would never forgive.

The following Monday, at the next supervisors' meeting, Harvey's gay rights ordinance, cosponsored now by Carol Ruth Silver and the only Latino supervisor, Robert Gonzales, was finally presented to the full board for consideration. In retaliation against Harvey, Dan White moved that the bill be returned to his Police, Fire, and Public Safety Committee for further study. But his motion was too transparent to be seconded. As

White sat visibly fuming in his seat between Harvey and Carol Ruth Silver, the board voted 10 to 1 to advance the gay rights bill to the next step in the approval process.

The bill had its second reading on March 27. Again, the board voted 10 to 1 to move it forward. White must have felt the sting when Harvey also got the supervisors to approve a "certificate of honor" for Matthew Coles, a gay attorney who had written up the gay rights ordinance in the appropriate legal language. On April 3 the board gave Harvey's ordinance its final vote. It passed, 10 to 1. All that was left now was for Mayor George Moscone to approve.

Eight days later press cameras at a public ceremony in City Hall caught a beatific Harvey Milk handing Mayor Moscone a lavender-blue pen, with which the mayor signed the gay rights bill into law. When a reporter asked Dan White his opinion of it, he answered, "This bill lets a man in a dress be a teacher. People are getting angry!"[22]

In the following months Dan White's grudge against Harvey became fanatical. He tried to block whatever Harvey proposed to the board, especially if it had to do with gay rights. But he was no match for Harvey, either in smarts or wiliness, and his maneuvers always failed. In May, Harvey proposed that the Board of Supervisors pass a resolution in support of a State Senate bill that would ban employment discrimination against gays all over California. The lone nay vote against Harvey's resolution was White's. In June Harvey asked the board to order a temporary street closure along the route of the Gay Freedom Day Parade. All the supervisors voted in favor of the closure except Dan White. From their seats on either side of White, Harvey and Carol Ruth Silver began passing notes behind his back, laughing at his inane predictability. In July Harvey's friend Dennis Peron, the owner of The Island restaurant in which Harvey had held fund-raisers, was arrested for selling pot. Harvey was questioned about his acquaintance with Peron by a reporter from the *San Francisco Chronicle*. When Harvey told the reporter that Peron was a good man and an upstanding member of the community, Dan White requested that the Board of Supervisors ask the city attorney "for an opinion as to whether members of the Board may personally support a convicted drug dealer."[23]

Despite the annoyances perpetrated by Dan White and the problems of Harvey's home life, Harvey was joyous in his role as a San Francisco supervisor. Finally, he was who he was always meant to be. Marc Cohen, the young man who had lived with Tom O'Horgan and had been the stage manager on *Lenny* in New York, showed up one day at Harvey's City Hall office, and Harvey was delighted to take him all over the impressive Beaux Arts building. He pointed with pride of ownership to the gorgeous rotunda with the copper dome. "Higher than the one in the U.S. Capitol," he said. He pointed out the great ring of Corinthian columns, the pediment decorated with intricate Grecian friezes, the gorgeous marble staircase. "So what do you think of my theater?" Harvey asked Tom O'Horgan's assistant at the end of his City Hall tour.[24]

* * *

Mayor Moscone, whose term would end in 1979, knew he would run again, so he went out of his way to curry favor with Harvey, the man he had fired two years earlier. Moscone needed the gay vote, and he believed that Harvey alone could guarantee it. Harvey, for his part, was flattered that the mayor acknowledged his power and put himself in his hands. Moscone even went with him to an empress coronation for José Sarria's Imperial Court of drag queens because Harvey assured the mayor that Sarria and his court had an influential voice in San Francisco's gay community.

Moscone also gave Harvey an occasion to imagine himself on a higher stage. Each year before the mayor went on vacation he appointed acting mayors from the Board of Supervisors. In

April 1978, Moscone was going off to Europe and chose Harvey to temporarily assume a role he adored. Harvey called a press conference to announce to reporters that he was America's first openly gay mayor. The *San Francisco Examiner* featured a front-page picture of Harvey looking very mayoral as he sat behind the mayor's desk. At lunchtime he piled his staff into the mayoral limousine, and they were chauffeured in style to a Castro Street restaurant because he supposedly had "district business" to do there. "Wait a minute and I'll think of what it was," Harvey kidded.[25] As acting mayor, he also cut the ribbon at the opening of a friend's business, and he invited the press to watch. "I'm probably the only mayor of a major American city who cuts the ribbon and puts it in his hair," he joked to reporters.[26]

He had Danny Nicoletta take pictures of him in his new role while Mike Wong, the friend who had been Harvey's political advisor a few years earlier, looked on. "Hey, you seem to be enjoying this so much people will speculate you want to be mayor," said Wong. "Who said it's speculation?" Harvey asked. "Let them think I'm interested."[27]

It was not an impossible dream. The speed at which he was winning over those who had doubted him was remarkable. Even Art Agnos, the rival who beat him two years earlier in the Assembly race, now regarded him as a promising leader. It was not just flattery that made Agnos tell Harvey that he saw in him "the kind of potential" that would make him "mayor of San Francisco inside of ten years."[28] Agnos had sponsored a bill to amend the state labor code to outlaw employment discrimination against gays and lesbians. When it got stuck in the Ways and Means Committee, Agnos wrote to Harvey exhorting him to come to Sacramento and testify because, he believed, Harvey's eloquence, his stature as a prominent gay, and his demonstrated leadership could help Agnos get the bill out of committee.[29] One of the most powerful figures in Sacramento, Willie

Brown, who had opposed Harvey's run for the Assembly in 1976, now saw his gifts too, as did Phillip and John Burton—and all the members of the Machine who had once worked against him. They were all getting in line to promise they would endorse Harvey when he ran again. Willie Brown volunteered to be the honorary chair of his next campaign committee.[30] Harvey Milk had reason to dream big.

11

Leading

Harvey took his responsibility to serve all of District 5 and all of San Francisco very seriously. He put immense energy into even the most nitty-gritty issues—getting the Public Works Department to sweep Castro Street daily rather than once a week, as it had been doing, getting the Municipal Transportation Agency to put up fifty new stop signs in his district. But he also kept a sharp eye out for a larger political stage. The Board of Supervisors has often been a stepping-stone for San Francisco supervisors: George Moscone, for instance, had been a supervisor before serving in the California Senate and then becoming mayor; Supervisor Dianne Feinstein would become mayor, make a failed run for the governorship of California, and eventually become a multiterm U.S. senator. But what was unique about Harvey's aspirations was that at a time when openly gay politicians were rare, in 1978, he believed his success would be more likely if he made himself *more* prominent as a gay-activist leader. The constituent who had admonished him that "without your gayness, you'd be just another white liberal man running for office" was not off the mark.[1]

Assisted by his old speechwriter friend, Frank Robinson, Harvey delivered stirring speeches. Martin Luther King's rhetoric was a conscious influence on him. In his "I Have a Dream" speech in 1963, King had declared on behalf of black people that the Declaration of Independence and the Constitution were "promissory notes" to which every American was a rightful heir. Every American was guaranteed the riches of freedom and the inalienable rights to life, liberty, and the pursuit of happiness. America could be a great nation only when it recognized that its minorities, too, are heir to its founding documents.

At San Francisco's Gay Freedom Day rally on June 25, 1978, Harvey was decked out not like Martin Luther King, in a formal dark suit and tie, but in 1970s gay style: tight jeans and a white T-shirt. He wore a lei draped around his neck. But he addressed the crowd of more than a quarter million people with a speech that had clear echoes of King. Gays, too, held a promissory note for the inalienable rights to life, liberty, and the pursuit of happiness. "No matter how hard you try, you cannot erase those words from the Declaration of Independence," Harvey declaimed to his cheering audience. Nor can the words "yearning to be free" be chipped from the base of the Statue of Liberty; nor can "The Star-Spangled Banner" be sung without the words "land of the free." "That's what America is," he shouted, as the crowd went wild. He proposed that on July 4, 1979, gay people from all over the country gather in Washington, D.C., "on that very same spot where, over a decade ago, Martin Luther King spoke to a nation of his dreams." There, Harvey said, gays would tell the president of the United States "about America and what it really stands for."[2] But at home, life could be shaky. Jack felt neglected. He was resentful and depressed. When he wasn't holed up in their apartment drinking or calling Harvey at City Hall demanding that he come home, he was wandering the streets, or he would stumble into a gay bar demanding free drinks because he was the boyfriend of the most influential gay in San Francisco. If Harvey let himself think about what was going on at home, he was distressed. Most of the time he focused on carrying out his duties.

* * *

In envisioning a larger stage for himself, Harvey began to envision a larger world for gay people, where they would not need to live in ghettos to feel at home. He once composed a sort of love letter to Castro Street in which he wrote that after he had his first gay experience, at the age of fourteen, he felt that he never again would have a home in his parents' house because he had to hide who he was. Even as an adult, wherever he went, he had had to suppress himself, so he always felt that he had neither home nor hometown—until he came to Castro Street, where "for the first time in my life, there was a place to live, to shop, to play, to be, that I felt was home."[3] Harvey never stopped loving the Castro, but his thinking was beginning to change: not only did gays have a right to feel at home anywhere they chose to live but also straight people everywhere needed to know that gay people were there too.

Harvey's new mission was to shatter the myth that gay people live only in San Francisco or Los Angeles or New York. He wanted heterosexuals to recognize that gays are everywhere, in all parts of society, even in their own families. He proposed that gays show up at gay pride parades—where people often held signs such as "Gay Rights Now"—with only one sign, displaying the name of the town and state where they were from: their hometown, a place to which they would now lay claim.[4] In the San Francisco parade that year he rode atop his Volvo, legs dangling from the sunroof, holding aloft his own sign: "I'm from Woodmere, N.Y.," it read.

* * *

Harvey made a giant leap onto a larger stage through his role in defeating California's Briggs Initiative, Proposition 6. If passed, Proposition 6 would have prohibited homosexuals as well as all other public school employees who said anything positive about homosexuals from working in any capacity in California's schools. The proposition, which was on the November 1978 ballot, was inspired by the barrage of right-wing successes in rolling back the modicum of civil rights that gays had been slowly achieving.

California state senator John Briggs, a far-right Republican from Orange County, hoped to run for governor. When polls showed him far behind in the gubernatorial race, he sought surefire issues to boost his campaign. He had gone to Miami with his Spanish-speaking wife, Carmen, during the Anita Bryant campaign so that Carmen could help Bryant get her message across to Miami's large Cuban community. Bryant's huge victory was eye-opening to Briggs.[5] But he hoped to go even further than she had. He would put an initiative on California's statewide ballot that would speak not only to the disgust Americans obviously still felt toward homosexuals but also to parents' anxieties when they put their schoolchildren in the hands of strangers every day. His initiative would remove any public school employee not only for engaging in relations with members of the same sex but also for "advocating, soliciting, imposing, encouraging or promoting [such relations] in private or in public." Briggs needed 312,000 voter signatures on his petition in order for the initiative to qualify for the November ballot. "Politicians do nothing. Decent citizens must act," he proclaimed in a dramatic appeal, censuring all the other California lawmakers for turning a blind eye to homosexual immorality.

Briggs got 500,000 signatures in his petition drive, almost 200,000 more than were required by California law. "It's the hottest social issue since Reconstruction," he boasted to the press. As Briggs's campaign progressed, his rhetoric became increasingly outrageous. "The teaching profession," he told one reporter, "is terribly attractive to the homosexual, and if the initiative is defeated, all of them are going to come out of the closet [as] legitimized role models for our children to emulate." "One-third of San Francisco teachers are homosexual," he told another. "I assume most of them are seducing young boys in toilets."[6]

Gay people knew they had reason to panic. If Prop 6 won in the liberal state of California, the firing of gay teachers and their allies would only be the start. Reactionaries would be emboldened even further and it would lead to homosexual witch hunts all over America, like the ones of the 1950s and 1960s, when to be known as homosexual nearly guaranteed unemployment. Yet the juggernaut of antigay legislation beginning with Anita Bryant's victory seemed unstoppable, even to many gay activists. The Briggs campaign kept sending out panic-inducing propaganda, such as a widely distributed flyer with a picture of innocent little boys and girls going off to school that said, in boldface type, "Preserve Parents' Rights to Protect Their Children from Teachers Who Are Immoral and Who Promote a Perverted Lifestyle. Vote 'Yes' on 6!"[7] Money raised in fundamentalist churches and huge, Bryant-style "God and Decency" rallies poured into the "Yes on 6" coffers. Reverend Jerry Falwell, a celebrity minister who spoke at Briggs's rallies, predicted that Proposition 6 would lift good people out of their apathy and get them to the polls, and "a landslide will begin across the country."[8]

Gay people despaired that Falwell was right and that a landslide was inevitable. Harry Britt, a human billboard in Harvey's 1975 campaign and an openly gay activist ever since, lamented in the newsletter of the San Francisco Gay Democratic Club, "I know of no informed person who holds any real hope for defeating the Briggs Initiative."[9]

David Goodstein, the influential *Advocate* publisher, was as pessimistic as most about defeating Prop 6, but he believed it was crucial to keep fighting to prevent Briggs from winning by the predicted landslide. If gays lost in California as dramatically as they had in Wichita or even in St. Paul, that surely would be the death knell for all gay progress. Goodstein teamed up with Harvey's old nemesis, Jim Foster, to try to do damage control.

Goodstein and Foster had made steps toward reconciling with Harvey when he won the supervisorial race in November 1977 because they admired winners. But the reconciliation was tenuous. Though Harvey had gone through a gigantic metamorphosis in his appearance since 1973, on a more substantive level his style—brash, bold, and confrontational—continued to be abhorrent to them. For instance, fervently believing that the only way to stop antigay prejudice was for all gays and lesbians to be out, he did not scruple to out gays who were in the public spotlight, such as the ex-marine Oliver Sipple, who briefly became a national hero when he averted the assassination of President Gerald Ford by grabbing the arm of his would-be killer and deflecting the bullet. Sipple had been closeted with his family, but Harvey made sure that major newspapers reported that President Ford's rescuer was a homosexual.[10] The gay movement needed heroes, Harvey said, and the public needed to see that gays could be heroes. Harvey also kept insisting that it was important for gay people who were not public figures to come out to everyone—parents, friends, coworkers, neighbors—because it was impossible to fight the lies, myths, and distortions about gays if they remained in the closet. To defeat Briggs, Harvey argued, all gay people must tell those who already know them as human beings and not malevolent stereotypes that *they* are who gay people are.[11]

Goodstein's and Foster's approach was the opposite. As Goodstein wrote in his column for the *Advocate*, he believed that the only way to run a campaign that would defeat Briggs was to pretend Prop 6 was not really about gay people. Gays could register gay voters and stuff envelopes in headquarters, but they must "keep out of sight of non-gay voters." He was jabbing at Harvey when he added, "Gay media freaks must get off the television." Only straight allies should do the talking against Proposition 6—and their talk should cover only "non-gay issues," like how Proposition 6 would invite the government into people's lives and homes and violate privacy; how Proposition 6 would add another layer of unnecessary bureaucracy to the government; and how taxpayers would have to pay to enforce it.[12]

To fight back against Briggs, Goodstein and Foster started an organization they called by the ultraneutral name Concerned Voters of California. They decided they needed to hire a high-powered PR person, one who would know how to get endorsements from people who counted, that is, influential heterosexuals; and they found a heterosexual to do the job: Don Bradley, who had helped John Kennedy and Lyndon Johnson win their presidential bids in California. At the first organizational meeting of Concerned Voters of California, U.S. congressman Phil Burton, an "influential heterosexual," was there to declare his support for the fight against the Briggs Initiative and to read aloud from the group's brochure. The brochure addressed the necessity of defeating Proposition 6 because it threatened human rights and violated the sacred protections of the Constitution. In the entire brochure there was not one word about how homosexuals would be the primary victims of Proposition 6.

Harvey was at the meeting, and he sat quietly while Congressman Burton read aloud. Burton was one of the politicians he was counting on to endorse his next political run; but Harvey was repelled by the way the Concerned Voters of California was dressing up the issue in the generalized guise of human rights instead of confronting head-on the fact that gay citizens deserved the same protections granted to other minorities. The approach of Concerned Voters of California had been the approach in Miami-Dade, too. Harvey was certain that gays had been overwhelmingly defeated there because most straight voters had no idea that they had ever met a gay person—let alone that they had a beloved child or kindly aunt or uncle who was gay. In the fight against the Briggs Initiative, Harvey would urge gay people to say bluntly to everyone in their lives, "I'm asking you to help protect *me.*"

When Congressman Burton finished reading, Supervisor Milk jumped to his feet. "This is masturbation!" he shouted.[13]

But if Goodstein's and Foster's Concerned Voters of California was too buttoned-down for Harvey, another San Francisco group, the Bay Area Committee Against the Briggs Initiative (BACABI) was too unbuttoned. BACABI was a grassroots organization started by members of the Socialist Workers Party, including Howard Wallace, the gay truck driver and union activist who, years earlier, had worked with Harvey on the Coors Beer boycott. There were things Harvey really liked about BACABI. It had a Third World Outreach Committee that focused on sending out lesbians and gays of color to speak to straight groups of color in order to show the straights who they are and to deliver the message that if rights could be taken away from gays, they could be taken away from other minorities too. BACABI also had a labor committee, and it sent out working-class gays to speak to groups like the Teamsters union, to deliver the message that Briggs was not only against gays but also against collective bargaining and other issues dear to labor's heart. Harvey also liked BACABI's take-to-the-streets, door-to-door politicking.

But there was much that bothered him about BACABI. As a duly elected politician he scorned decentralized chaos. He did not like it that anyone who showed up at a BACABI meeting could vote on any issue—and did not have to do any homework to educate himself or herself—just like in the old, radical Gay Liberation Front meetings. He wanted an organization that did the things BACABI did but was also well-organized and spoke not just to the radicals but to middle-class, mainstream people too.[14]

Because neither Concerned Voters of California nor BACABI suited him, he formed a third group, San Franciscans Against Prop 6, through which he could represent the campaign as he thought it should be represented. He set up the headquarters for his new organization in an old building south of Market that had once housed The Shed, a popular dance club that used to attract hordes of young gays. He put together a steering committee, and, to manage the running of San Franciscans Against Prop 6, he hired Bill Kraus, a young man who was working on his doctorate at UC Berkeley and who had been the coordinator of Get Out the Vote for Harvey Milk in 1977. Kraus became a canny strategist, mapping out the crucial areas into which San Franciscans Against Prop 6 had to put its greatest energy. Under his direction, eight hundred volunteers of every stripe went door to door, traversing the city according to his map, registering those who had never registered to vote, telling their own gay stories if they were gay, saying why Proposition 6 was hurtful to them personally and would be hurtful to everyone because it threatened privacy and would be the start of witch hunts.

Harvey also hired Kraus's friend Gwenn Craig, a twenty-four-year-old black lesbian activist from Atlanta, to coordinate the operation and do outreach. Harvey's detractors called her "the black woman in the window," meaning he had hired her as window dressing. But it was proof of his sound political sense that he understood how Craig would be crucial to the success of their battle. She met with groups such as the Black Leadership Forum and the Black Ministers Alliance as well as San Francisco's black congregations, which were often fundamentalist.

Her task was to shift a knee-jerk focus on sin to a focus on the harm inherent in Proposition 6. Yes on 6 proponents assumed they would have a sympathetic audience in the black churches, but Craig was a counterbalance, telling the congregants how Briggs's ideas were dangerous not only to her as a black lesbian but also to all of them as black people.[15]

Harvey's job was to be the face of the battle against Briggs—the spokesman for San Franciscans Against Prop 6 and very soon a key personality in the entire campaign. He was the one whose face was seen most often on TV and whose words were quoted most often in the newspapers. But radical gays did not like that. In September 1978, less than two months before voters would go to the polls, Harvey was invited to speak about the Briggs Initiative on *News Talk*, a local TV show hosted by a young Latina, Juana Samayoa. Spiffed up for the interview in a suit and tie and a very white, pressed shirt, looking and sounding very much like a mayor (at the minimum), and ready to talk sense about why Proposition 6 was pernicious, Harvey must have been taken aback when Samayoa announced on air that a BACABI spokesperson had told her, "You shouldn't have Harvey Milk on. He's just doing it to further his political career." As BACABI members saw it, Harvey was destroying their group through his opportunism. He was getting headlines in the *San Francisco Examiner;* he was getting support from the Democratic Party leadership; he was sabotaging BACABI's fund-raising efforts by badmouthing the dominance of the Socialist Workers Party in the leadership of BACABI.[16]

Harvey had suffered for years from horizontal hostility in the gay movement but had worked around it, and he had been triumphant. Now all gays were facing a lethal enemy. Polls of likely voters were frightening. A Field Survey showed that a whopping 61 percent of the California electorate had made up its mind that it would vote in favor of Proposition 6. Only 31 percent were saying they opposed it.[17] And still, incredibly, some gays took time off from attacking the foe to attack each other, in front of the straight public. It could not have been easy for Harvey to keep his temper. But with the KBHK-TV audience watching, he took the high road, seamlessly explaining that the fight against Briggs had "three major campaigns" in San Francisco, and each—BACABI, Concerned Voters of California, San Franciscans Against Prop 6—worked on "three distinct levels," all in the service of defeating a dangerous proposition.

Samayoa persisted: "So how close are you, then, to the gay community?" she asked. Harvey's politic answer surely won him more of the mainstream admirers he now sought: "Nobody can be close to the entire gay community, because we go from the extreme left to the extreme right. And I am a good, old-fashioned Harry Truman–Adlai Stevenson Democrat. I sit in the middle. Those on the extreme left think I'm too conservative. Those on the extreme right think I'm too liberal."[18] Harvey Milk was ready for prime time.

*　*　*

John Briggs was an enigma even to his colleagues in the State Senate. He was apparently a right-wing populist, but he did not really give a damn about following the party line; he was a loner. The other senators on the right resented that he was less interested in their agenda than in grabbing headlines for the sake of his own advancement. Briggs would stoop to anything for that and did not care when he enraged even his own party. As Senator H. L. Richardson from the conservative bastion of Glendora told the *San Francisco Chronicle*, "Anybody can get attention by dropping his pants. That's how Briggs operates."[19]

Briggs dreamed up Proposition 6—as well as Proposition 7, which would expand the list of crimes that warranted the death penalty—because he thought those were the big issues that would get voters on the right off their couches and into the voting booths. His gubernatorial fund-raising campaign fizzled early, but when polls showed that a huge majority of Californians favored both of his initiatives, he decided he might take advantage of the headlines he was getting as their author to run for the U.S. Senate seat occupied by Alan Cranston, a liberal Democrat.

As Harvey would learn, Briggs was not really emotionally invested in destroying gay people; he was emotionally invested in advancing his career.[20] But whether or not Briggs truly believed that homosexual teachers raped children and should not be allowed in the classroom, he said it, and his initiative was designed to make voters believe it. Harvey, as the leading voice against Briggs, had to make voters understand Briggs's dangerous malevolence.

The grimmest instance Harvey knew of dangerous malevolence had been forever impressed on his psyche when he was a child listening with his parents to radio reports of the destruction of European Jewry. The Holocaust became the metaphor he kept returning to in his speeches against Proposition 6. When he spoke to Jewish groups, the metaphor poured out of him in a torrent of emotion: "I cannot remain silent anymore," he told the congregation at Oakland's Temple Sinai. "There was silence in Germany because no one got up early enough to say what Hitler really was. If only someone did, maybe the Holocaust would never have happened."[21] A coalition of lesbian and gay Jews, Hashevet Ha'avud, the Lost Tribe, encouraged his Holocaust comparisons with materials they sent him: "Just as Proposition 6 would prevent gay people from teaching in the public schools"—Harvey bracketed the statement to incorporate in his talks—"so, forty-five years ago, did the German law prohibit Jews from teaching or holding any other civil service positions."[22]

Even with non-Jewish groups the metaphor seemed apt to him. To ignore the deadly threat Proposition 6 would lead to, he warned readers of a national gay newspaper, was "to be like Jews in Nazi Germany as they were being loaded into the boxcars and hoping they will be treated nicely and not put into the ovens."[23] "Senator Briggs is using the gay community as scapegoats, much as Hitler used the Jews as scapegoats," he said on a panel with United Farmworkers and NAACP members.[24]

In October, before the election, BACABI's leaders challenged John Briggs to a debate, saying they would get KQED, a PBS station, to televise it. To their astonishment, Briggs said yes. Now they had to find someone who could hold his own in a debate with Briggs. Millions of Californians would be watching, so the stakes were high. Howard Wallace, the Socialist Workers Party truck driver and cofounder of BACABI, was the first choice of some. Wallace was articulate, good-looking, and had all the right political sentiments. But as others in BACABI pointed out, he was barely known outside of leftist circles. Harvey Milk might have been persona non grata in BACABI, but he was prominent, an elected official, and if he was there, the media would be there to cover it. "Let's not be stupid," they argued. "Milk may be a pawn for the Democrats, but that doesn't mean we can't use a pawn to a good end."[25] A BACABI delegation showed up at Harvey's City Hall office to say, "We have Briggs and we have Howard Wallace, but we'll take you over Howard."[26]

This was an offer Harvey could not refuse. It was a chance not only to let Briggs have it in front of a large television audience but also to unite disparate elements of the anti–Prop 6 campaign, so that together they could crush the opposition. He had been trying to unify the factions. When asked in public which of the anti–Prop 6 groups someone should support, he had inevitably answered, "All of them." He had even helped to form a statewide No on 6 campaign to bring together, in a very rare collaboration, gay groups from Northern California and Southern California, which were often hostile to one another. "I'd be delighted to debate John Briggs on PBS," Harvey told the BACABI delegation.

Harvey also knew that he had to unify the perpetually war-ring factions of lesbians and gay men. That animosity had sur-faced yet again in the battle against Prop 6. Many of the anti-Briggs organizations, including BACABI, did try to defuse this infighting by ensuring that there would always be a man and a woman as cochairs. But lesbians in Gay Teachers and School Workers, a group led by two gay men, split off and formed their own group, Lesbian Schoolworkers. Harvey was opposed. He thought that separating at this time was a drain on energy that needed to be spent on the Briggs battle; and he redoubled his efforts to build coalitions with the lesbian community.[27] To that end he worked closely with lesbians to help start A United Fund to Defeat the Briggs Initiative. He told a reporter at the *San Francisco Examiner*, "If you'll look at the letterhead of our group, it says in bold headlines, 'A UNITED FUND.'" After the proposi-tion was defeated, Harvey said, the United Fund was going to unite to fight for the Equal Rights Amendment, which would have mandated the federal government to prohibit discrimina-tion against women.[28]

So when Anne Kronenberg—among whose jobs it was to tug at Harvey's coat if he was about to screw up on issues relat-ing to women—told him, "You need to have a lesbian debating Briggs alongside you," he listened.[29] Cleve Jones, the young man who lived up the street from Castro Camera and was a poli sci major at San Francisco State University, had the perfect person, a professor: "Her name is Dr. Sally Gearhart, a lesbian feminist, teaches Speech and Women's Studies—and she *exudes* dignity," Cleve promised.[30] She did. And when Harvey asked, she agreed to be his debate partner. Poised, stately, handsome, a fine match for Harvey's new "well-turned-out" appearance, they joked that together they looked like "Mom and Pop of Middle America." They became a duo not only in the PBS debate but also at many anti–Prop 6 rallies, where onstage Harvey would raise Sally Gearhart's arm and call her "San Francisco's next Supervisor!"

a tacit promise that he would help bring lesbian feminists into mainstream politics.[31]

John Briggs chose as his debating partner Ray Batema, the crusading minister of the Central Baptist Church in the small Southern California town of Pomona. Batema was cochair with Briggs of Citizens for Decency and Morality. Looking anxious and lost in the debate, he let Briggs do most of the talking. Briggs came unhinged when a member of the live audience, former governor Ronald Reagan's campaign chair, Mike Curb, rose to say that Reagan, who remained beloved by Republicans, told him he was opposed to Proposition 6. "I don't care what Governor Reagan says," Briggs sputtered, before impugning Reagan's judgment and morality because "he comes from the same Hollywood crowd" that was financing the No on 6 campaign. "And ninety percent of the films that come out of Hollywood that are pornographic films are homosexual films!" he added.[32]

Cool and composed, Sally Gearhart came armed with real figures and facts instead of Briggs's nonsensical math. In response to his usual assertion that homosexuals were child molesters she calmly cited the FBI, the National Council on Family Relations, and the Santa Clara County Child Sexual Abuse Treatment Center—whose statistics all showed that most child abusers were heterosexual men.

Harvey dominated the debate from the start. "How many teaching careers are you willing to see destroyed?" he asked the senator directly. "How many lives will you destroy in your lust for power?" In the service of showing up Briggs's absurdity, Harvey was funny too. In response to Briggs's claim that homosexual teachers can actually teach their students to be homosexual, he quipped, "How do you teach homosexuality? Like you'd teach French?"

Not even the most committed Yes on 6 supporter could imagine that Briggs and Batema had won that debate.

*   *   *

John Briggs was not only an opportunist; he was also deeply cynical. While he was promoting Proposition 6, Briggs, a nominal Catholic, and his young aide, Don Sizemore, often attended fundamentalist prayer meetings, where Briggs declared himself "born again" and knelt in the aisles while people all around him spoke in tongues. At one point Briggs whispered to Sizemore out of the side of his mouth, "Gibberish!"[33]

Surprisingly, in the course of the campaign the personal dynamic between Briggs and Harvey changed. Contemptuous as the two men were of each other in their public debates, they actually developed a sort of camaraderie behind the scenes. On Briggs's part the feeling verged on admiration. As he told Sizemore, he thought he recognized a lot of himself in Harvey, who was "a natural politician, very gifted." They were "the same species," Briggs said—both superaggressive, hyper; they were guys who used angry language even when they were not truly angry and who respected the campaign process. Their debates were "nothing personal," Briggs thought.[34]

Like Harvey, Briggs knew a lot about theatrical performance —never mind that what he was performing could destroy people's lives. After one knock-down, drag-out debate Briggs remarked to Sizemore, "Well, that was lively. That oughta wake people up." In their spirited duels, Briggs saw Harvey as a worthy opponent. "You've got to hand it to Harvey, the anti-side isn't well funded like we are, but he's really making something out of nothing," Briggs would often say to his aide.[35]

For his part, Harvey came to understand that Briggs really did not care what homosexuals did, he just wanted to be governor, or U.S. senator. On Halloween, just a week before the November 7, 1978, election, Briggs informed the San Francisco Police Department that he and his aide, Sizemore, would be going to Polk Street to see the grand Halloween bacchanalia in which gays participated every year, thousands frolicking in orgiastic nudity, fabulous drag, glitter and greasepaint every-where. The senator stood side by side with Harvey, whom ev-eryone recognized. Hardly anyone recognized Briggs, perhaps because it was so unbelievable that he would be there, standing next to his most famous opponent. The press knew he would be there, though, and had sent reporters and cameras. "I'm here because this is a children's night and I'm interested in chil-dren," Briggs told the press. The next day the *San Francisco Ex-aminer* ran a story headlined "Polk Street's Odd Couple," with a picture of Harvey next to the far-right senator. Briggs looked as though he was having the time of his life. As he admitted to his aide, he was not particularly shocked by or disapproving of what he saw there.[36] Standing in the midst of the revelry, Har-vey put his arm around Briggs's shoulder and said, "John, if you hadn't come along we would have had to invent you."[37]

* * *

By early October it was clear that the tide of support for Proposition 6 was waning: the yes and no sides were in a dead heat. Harvey was not solely responsible for that, of course. Concerted efforts by all manner of activists in both the north and the south of California; anti-Briggs editorials in the major newspapers and on radio and TV; statements by major politi-cal figures, especially Ronald Reagan, who told the press that Proposition 6 "has the potential for real mischief"—all of those things contributed to its rapid loss of favor. Harvey, however, remained the face of the battle to the end and its most eloquent spokesman. It was he whom the leading pollster, Mervin Field, quoted when he reported on the dramatic shift in voter senti-ment: the proposition was "un-American," Harvey said, "based on the same abuse of civil liberties that gave us witch hunts and McCarthyism."[38] On November 7, when voters went to the polls, Proposition 6 lost by a landslide: 58.4 percent to 41.6 per-cent, with a margin of over a million votes.

Harvey orchestrated the victory celebration in a big hall

near Castro Street. The central decoration was a large card-board Statue of Liberty wearing a No on 6 sign, a jockstrap peeking out beneath it. Harvey had assigned to Dick Pabich, his aide, the job of blowing up hundreds of red, white, and blue helium balloons. When it was clear that Prop 6 had gone down, Pabich released the balloons over the heads of the cheering celebrants. It was like a national presidential convention when the nominee is announced.[39]

12

Dark Clouds Gathering

The gay establishment had once ridiculed Harvey the Hippie's uniform of jeans and denim work shirts. Now, when Supervisor Milk appeared before the straight media, he mirrored the nattiness of the dashing Mayor Moscone and the dapper State Assemblyman Willie Brown. Though Harvey's clothes were secondhand, it amused him to look as good as the man who was mayor and the man who was a star of the State Assembly. In fact, he was becoming increasingly confident that those were roles that were not beyond his reach. He found he really liked his new look, too. He even applied for a charge account at Brooks Brothers. On the application he gave his address as "City Hall," maybe hoping that would compensate for the unimpressive figure he had to list as his income.[1]

In truth, Harvey could not afford a Brooks Brothers charge account or much else. Although his political star was in its ascendency, his finances had tanked. On Schedule C of his income tax return for 1977 he told the IRS that Castro Camera had lost $43,977.45 that year.[2] His supervisor's annual salary of $9,600 ("less than a field hand picking artichokes earned," he once said) and the little that he took in from Castro Camera did not cover his expenses.[3] In the spring of 1978, shortly after he filed his 1977 tax return, which reminded him how poor he was, the owner of the building at 575 Castro Street raised the rent on the store from $350 a month to $1,200. The irony was not lost on Harvey that his Herculean efforts to make the Castro a better place to live had also made it much more expensive. He had to look for cheaper digs and relocate Castro Camera. Although he devoted little time to the store now, it was Scott Smith's only source of income.

Together with Jack Lira, Harvey moved to a small apartment at 18 Henry Street, a few blocks away. Harvey's friends had tried to persuade him not to take Jack with him when he made the move, but Harvey refused to give up the illusion that he might still be able to save the young man. The flat was owned by a friend, Carl Carlson, an airline pilot who had worked on Harvey's campaigns and now volunteered as the transportation expert on his staff at City Hall. Carlson made the rent cheap for him. Harvey also rented a little kiosk in a corner of a building that had once been a movie theater, on Market Street off of Castro; and there he and Scott relocated Castro Camera. Harvey made light of his poor finances. If he and Jack did not have the money to eat the best, he liked to say, they could always eat eggs scrambled in matzo brei.[4]

In October Harvey gave up the Volvo he had been leasing since 1975. To the press he announced he did not need a car because he intended to ride the Muni, San Francisco's public transit, everywhere. That's what all government workers should do, he said. It would support the city and it would cut down on traffic. But Harvey gave up the car mostly because he could no longer afford it. The State Board of Equalization had threatened to seize his earnings because of unpaid taxes on the camera store, and he was overwhelmed by the debts that had accrued during his four political campaigns.

Also in October, six months after they had opened the camera store in its new location, he and Scott were forced to close it. Harvey had seldom found time to set foot in it because he was so busy being Supervisor Milk, and without the draw of his personality the store attracted few customers. In November Carl Carlson offered to loan Harvey three thousand dollars so he could breathe more easily for a while. Harvey did not hesitate to take it.[5]

But Harvey's money woes were actually the least of his problems. He was now barraged with venomous threats from those who hated gays in general and hated him, San Francisco's most famous gay, in particular. At City Hall his aides worked alongside the other supervisors' aides in a single room divided by cubicles, and to amuse themselves they set up a bulletin board on which they all posted the most bizarre correspondence sent that week to the supervisor for whom they worked. Harvey's aides always got the Letter of the Week Award. Correspondents addressed him as "Ms. Harvey" or "Milk the Faggot" or "Dirty lowdown good for nothing cocksucking son of a bitch." They threatened to firebomb his store or take potshots at him. Some letters were frighteningly graphic—threatening to decapitate him or chop him into pieces after making him suffer prolonged torture. "We can't let it bother us. We've just got to keep doing what we're doing," Harvey would tell his assistant, Anne Kronenberg. But though he put a brave face on it to shield his aides from panic, Anne sensed his nervousness.[6]

To the press and even to friends he shrugged off the threats with humor or philosophizing. "If I turned around every time somebody called me a faggot," he would say, "I'd be walking backwards, and I don't want to walk backwards"; or, "If they're going to blow my head off, there's nothing I can do, so why think about it?"[7] But he did think about it. In the Gay Freedom Day Parade in June 1978, Anne Kronenberg drove his Volvo so Harvey could sit atop the car holding his "I'm from Woodmere" sign in one hand and waving at the crowd with the other. Not long after the procession started he bent down through the sunroof to ask her solemnly, "Do you know the closest route to the hospital? You've got to be aware, Anne."[8]

* * *

He had plenty of enemies and critics in the gay community too. Those who did not love his intense and colorful style often found it objectionable. For instance, at the same Gay Freedom Day rally in 1978 where he gave his eloquent "That's What America Is" speech echoing Martin Luther King's "I Have a Dream" speech, the lesbians in charge of the stage thought he was going on too long. After twenty minutes one of them sat down at the piano onstage and banged loudly to shut him up.[9]

Around that time Harvey also attended a California Democratic Council convention in San Diego. Governor Jerry Brown, who was up for reelection, was there to seek support; and Harvey, taking for granted his role as the preeminent spokesman for the community, led a gay caucus in submitting to the governor several questions about gay rights. When Brown did not respond to the caucus's satisfaction, Harvey announced, "The governor almost answered our questions and we almost endorsed him."[10] Not everyone in the gay caucus was pleased with his bluntness. Indeed, the membership of the gay San Diego Democratic Club was unanimous in its resentment of Harvey Milk. They found him loud, "New-York-in-your-face," presumptuous, abrasive—a know-it-all who had the audacity to pretend to speak for all gays.[11]

The most virulent internecine attack on Harvey came from the San Francisco Gay Community Center, which ran social programs, a gallery and performance space for gay artists, rehab programs for alcoholics, free legal clinics for the poor—all things that Harvey fervently championed. In September 1978, while Harvey was busy fighting the antigay Briggs Initiative, the Pride Foundation, which ran the Gay Community Center, was busy filing a complaint with the federal government that triggered an FBI investigation of him.

Since 1976 the Gay Community Center had been located in an old warehouse at 330 Grove Street owned by the city. In April 1977 the Pride Foundation was notified that the San Francisco Redevelopment Agency had decided to go through with plans that had long been in the works: the building, which was directly behind the Opera House, would be torn down, and a Performing Arts Center Garage would be built in its place. Mayor Moscone, still sympathetic to gay causes and still needing the gay vote, promised Paul Hardman, the director of the Pride Foundation, that he would help him get money from the San Francisco Office of Community Development and the federal Department of Housing and Urban Development. Together they would raise a million dollars to build a new community center. Members of the Pride Foundation wrote the requisite proposal and turned it in to the mayor. Moscone handed it over to Harvey for review, as he considered him the gay community's chief spokesman.

According to the Pride Foundation's federal complaint, Harvey then rewrote portions of the proposal and applied for funding in his own name, cutting out the foundation. Harvey claimed that his version emphasized things that were important to the community that the original proposal had ignored: a VD clinic, a mental health facility, a big meeting hall. The complaint further alleged that when Hardman protested that Harvey stole the Pride Foundation's proposal, Harvey told him, "Without my approval you will get nothing."

Even more egregious, Hardman and the Pride Foundation lawyer complained to the FBI; Harvey then filed legal papers to establish a San Francisco Gay Community Corporation. He had found a vacant old funeral home behind a Safeway super-market in the Castro district and declared that it would be the site of a new gay community center. But Harvey's supposed corporation was nothing but "a shell designed to compete with Pride." The Office of Community Development had fallen for Harvey's ruse, the complaint stated, and Harvey had been awarded $375,000 of the money that should have gone to the Pride Foundation to build a new San Francisco Gay Community Center. In the words of Hardman and the Pride Foundation lawyer, Harvey had perpetrated "a fraud against the government." The mayor, too, was named in the federal complaint, which said that Moscone had been in cahoots with Harvey. He had knowingly appointed to the Citizens Review Board a buddy of Harvey Milk's who would push through his proposal and cheat the Pride Foundation.[12]

An artist who sided with the Pride Foundation published in the gay press a cartoon of a big milk carton, with the words "Harvey Milk Homogenized Community Center" printed on its front. The caption read, "WHO SAYS WE NEVER OUTGROW OUR NEED FOR MILK?" Maybe before he got elected Harvey Milk was all about empowering people, his detractors said, but he had changed. Now he wanted to strip all power from grassroots people and control all public money intended for gay causes. It was a power grab. His success had gone to his head.[13]

While Harvey continued to busy himself fighting against the Briggs Initiative, the U.S. attorney general authorized the FBI to look into the Pride Foundation's allegation that Harvey Milk had, with Mayor George Moscone's assistance, tried to divert federal funds from the Gay Community Center for his own nefarious purposes.[14]

* * *

But Harvey's financial and legal problems paled by comparison with the disaster of his personal life. Things at the Henry Street apartment were imploding. Jack Lira often staggered around in public, scruffy, disheveled, beer can in hand. His depression had worsened since he watched, at Harvey's prodding, a four-part TV miniseries called *Holocaust*. It was about the destruction of a German Jewish family and the simultaneous rise of a young Nazi who became responsible for coordinating the mass murder of Jews. Harvey had hoped to educate Jack about a period of Jewish history that had haunted Harvey his entire life. But Jack saw the TV series only through his own lens, and Harvey's emotional response to the film and to the history of the Holocaust was of little interest to him. *Holocaust* triggered in Jack traumatic memories of the abuse he had suffered at the hands of his father.

Harvey was disappointed in his failed attempt to educate Jack, but he chalked it up to the young man's wounded nature, and he kept looking for ways to mend him. He had encouraged so many young gays to go to college, make something of themselves. Jack was smart enough. Maybe he could do that, too. "Why don't you go to school? I'll pay for it," he told Jack earnestly, though Harvey could barely pay the rent and buy food at that point. Jack was not interested anyway. Harvey did all he could to cheer him up, to pull him up with tenderness, to shake him up with threats. Nothing helped. Jack was at the mercy of his demons. Harvey felt responsible for Jack, but he was beginning to feel trapped too.[15]

On Monday, August 28, Harvey spent the morning preparing for his Board of Supervisors meeting, which started at 2 p.m. He also squeezed in some study for a debate with John Briggs that was scheduled for the next day. At the board meeting that afternoon he did yeoman's work, shepherding his pooper-scooper law through its third and final reading and then trying to get the support of the other supervisors to pressure the Recreation and Parks Department to extend the summer hours for the city's public pools.[16] In the midst of it all Jack kept calling

Anne Kronenberg and demanding that she go into the chambers of the Board of Supervisors, get Harvey out, and bring him to the phone. Jack was, as usual, drunk. Anne kept telling him that she could not interrupt the meeting but that she would let Harvey know he called as soon as possible. She left City Hall about four o'clock that afternoon because she was not feeling well.[17]

About 6 p.m., when the phone rang in the Henry Street apartment, Jack must have assumed it was finally Harvey returning his call. But it was a troubled eighteen-year-old in Minnesota who had telephoned Harvey a half dozen times over the past year asking for reassuring words that it was okay to be gay. "Why are you trying to take Harvey away from me?" Jack screamed into the phone before he hung up on the young man.[18]

The board meeting adjourned at 6:55. From there Harvey rushed to an evening committee meeting that did not adjourn until 9 p.m. Then, he walked the mile and a half to Henry Street, as he often did after work.[19]

On the rare occasions when Jack had lent a hand to Harvey's supervisorial campaign, it had been to register voters. Now, when Harvey opened the door to his apartment he saw a paper trail of voter registration forms and No on 6 flyers taped to the floor. The trail led from the front door to the hallway, through the dining room, to the kitchen, to the little bedroom that Harvey used as a home office. Jack was nowhere in sight, but on the desk was a legal pad on which he had written in big letters, "Harvey, you are a lousy lover." There were empty beer cans strewn about also—all of them Coors, the company against which Harvey had once led a boycott.

He followed the beer can trail to the bedroom he shared with Jack. A black curtain was draped over one of the ceiling beams. A note pinned to it said, "You've always loved the circus, Harvey. What do you think of my last act?" Harvey pulled the curtain back and saw Jack Lira's dead body hanging from the second beam. It was stiff and cold. He must have been dead for a couple of hours.

Panicked and sickened, Harvey ran to the kitchen for a butcher knife, cut the rope from Jack's neck, and lowered him to the floor. Shaking, he called Anne Kronenberg. "Are you sitting down? Jack killed himself," he blurted.

"Oh, Harvey!" Anne said. "I'm coming right over."

"No. Don't," Harvey told her. He wanted to spare the young woman the terrible sight. But she sped to Henry Street on her motorcycle. When Harvey opened the door to let her in, they fell into each other's arms.

Harvey had also called Scott Smith, who rushed over too. While they waited for the police and the coroner, Harvey blamed society for being so hard on gay people that a lot of them imagined suicide as an escape. But mostly he blamed himself. He had been away too much, had neglected Jack, had been absorbed too much with campaigning and then with the board and then with fighting Briggs. And all those lovers he had had in the past who had tried to do exactly what Jack Lira had just succeeded in doing—Craig Rodwell, Joe Campbell, Galen McKinley. He could not understand how his good intentions to love them and help them could end in such disaster.

After the coroner left with Jack's body, Scott offered to stay the night, and Anne offered to take Harvey back to her place. He thanked them both and said he needed to be alone. They left him about 11 p.m.[20] But staying alone in the apartment where Jack's body had just been hanging from a beam was harder than he had thought. He had loved Jack so much at the start, had had such hopes for their relationship, had announced to the world just seven months earlier that they were "lovers and partners."

Harvey left the empty apartment and walked over to Toad

Hall, the bar that had been in the Castro since before he and Scott moved there six years earlier. He needed to be where there were people. Usually in a gay bar Supervisor Milk would have been swamped by men wanting to talk or even flirt, but Harvey's grim expression that night made it clear to the other patrons that he did not want company. He sat alone and silent, nursing a soda, until closing time around 2 a.m.[21]

He had to call Jack's sister and let her know the awful thing that had happened. She was the only family member with whom Jack had been close, and Harvey had met her several times. "Didi, there's nobody to blame," he told her, though he was not sure he believed it himself.

Later, she wrote to him, alluding to the traumas Jack had suffered while growing up and hinting that their parents were implicated in his confusion and unhappiness. She said that though Harvey had told her there's nobody to blame, "I am sure that in the back of your mind there is a voice that says 'maybe or if'"; but, she assured Harvey, her brother's death wasn't Harvey's fault.[22] That was a thought Harvey had to hold on to because he had to keep functioning. His debate with John Briggs, which had long been scheduled for August 29, the day after Jack killed himself, was postponed—but only until the following week.

* * *

Perhaps Harvey felt guilty relief with Jack out of his life. But he was also in shock, and there was no way he could or would turn to his extended family in New York for consolation. He ignored an invitation to the wedding of his cousin Sherrie Feinberg, though he might have enjoyed being with his seventeen-year-old nephew Stuart Milk, who he suspected was gay. When Stuart was twelve years old he told Harvey that he felt he was different, and Harvey was pleased to give him avuncular assurance that being different was a tremendous gift. It was the same encouraging message Harvey would give all young gay people when he became prominent. But not even for Stuart did he want to show up at Sherrie's wedding now and have to explain that he was in mourning for a lover who had killed himself. His brother, Robert, did not want to explain either. "Harvey is very busy with his work as a San Francisco Supervisor," Robert told the wedding guests if they asked why his younger brother was not there.[23]

The shock of Jack's suicide made Harvey reexamine himself in surprising ways. As early as adolescence he had rejected organized religion, and he continued to reject it for most of his adult life. But he was not an atheist. He even emphasized in one of the tape recordings he had made on November 18, 1977, after his election that he had disgust for organized religion "because of what most churches are about *and not because of a disbelief in God*" (italics added). Jack's terrible death, however, seemed to make him think, at least briefly, about his connection to the religion into which he had been born and about the synagogue as a communal place to share that religion.

A few weeks after Jack's death Harvey received an invitation from the consul general of the People's Republic of China to attend a reception at the Chinese consulate in San Francisco on October 10. Ordinarily, Harvey would have been delighted to hobnob at an official international affair. But he sent his regrets, saying he could not attend because of the Jewish New Year. (October 10 was actually the start of Yom Kippur.)[24] He did indeed go to High Holiday services that October, perhaps for the first time since his boyhood. On Rosh Hashanah, when, according to the Talmud, God reinscribes the names of the righteous into the Book of Life for the coming year, he attended Congregation Sha'ar Zahav, San Francisco's gay synagogue. He returned there on Yom Kippur. After the service he spoke to the young gay rabbinical student who had officiated—to tell him how good it was to "be home" with his Jewishness.[25]

* * *

The story of the suicide of Supervisor Harvey Milk's lover was front-page news. Condolences poured in from around the country and the world. The strangest ones, fifty of them, came from a little jungle outpost in South America. All of the letters said almost the same thing, as though someone had dictated to a letter-writing committee what each must contain—a mention of Harvey's loss, a reference to his struggles on behalf of the oppressed, an invitation to join the letter writers in the beautiful jungle.

"I know this is a not too bright period in your life. As a member of Peoples Temple living in Jonestown, Guyana, where the weather is always pleasant and people of all races work and play together and are not oppressed, I find you can be optimistic about the future, even in your most troubled times. . . . Would you please consider this offer and come visit with us?" one letter implored. Another declared, "All of us in Jonestown feel stronger ties with you because of the honesty and bravery you have shown for others through the years of struggle. We hope that *soon* [sic] you too can come to Jonestown." Some letters were dated as early as August 31, only three days after Jack Lira's death. Clearly, Reverend Jim Jones in distant Guyana had immediately been informed of Harvey's tragedy, and he ordered fifty of his followers to get to work writing invitations in the guise of condolences.

Rumor in Jonestown said that Harvey had already expressed interest in going to live there—so he just needed a little nudge. "I understand that you may be coming to live with us here," one resident obediently wrote on September 1, four days after Jack's suicide, "and I wish to encourage you and say how much we would like to have you here."[26] What a radical coup it would have been for Jim Jones to bring to the Peoples Temple in Jonestown, Guyana, the man who was arguably the most famous gay in America.

Reverend Jones had hurriedly moved several hundred of his flock to the South American jungle the year before, in July 1977, after he learned that *New West Magazine* would soon be publishing an exposé of the Peoples Temple based on interviews with disaffected members. Jones had telephoned the magazine's publisher and persuaded her to read the article to him. She read for several minutes before Jones put down the phone and announced to an aide who was at his side, "We're leaving." In the wee hours of July 31, six hours before the article was scheduled to hit the newsstands, Jones and scores of his followers hurriedly left San Francisco and flew out to Guyana, where a few years earlier he had investigated the possibility of starting a community three hundred miles into the jungle.[27]

The *New West Magazine* exposé included accusations that Jones faked his laying-on-of-hands "miracle" healings, that he commanded that followers who disagreed with him be savagely beaten, that he condoned and participated in sexual assaults, that he forced members to hand over their Social Security and welfare checks and to sign their property over to the Peoples Temple.[28] Shortly before Jones left for Guyana he had called those supporters he considered most influential and explained that the allegations in the forthcoming article were nothing but a right-wing pack of lies.

Harvey had been one of the recipients of Jones's phone calls. "Hearing your voice Sunday gave me a warm feeling," he wrote Jim Jones the next day in the emotional language he often used with the reverend; and he vowed, "My name is cut into stone in support of you and your people."[29]

Harvey was far from alone in his gullibility: every progressive politician in San Francisco considered Jones a paragon of goodness who fed the hungry, clothed the naked, and welcomed the stranger. Assemblyman Willie Brown even interceded with the prime minister of Guyana to smooth the way for Jones to establish Jonestown. The assemblyman wrote Prime Minister

Forbes Burnham that Reverend Jones was "a rare human being. He is a leader of the first order. He cares about people. His inspirational involvement in a solution to the everyday problems of the world is unmatched. . . . Having him as a resident in your country can only be a plus."[30]

So it is no wonder that even as rumors continued to mount about scary goings-on in Jonestown, Harvey never hesitated to come to the reverend's defense. At Jones's request, in December 1977, Harvey even wrote a heated letter to the U.S. secretary of health, education, and welfare, with a copy to President Jimmy Carter, protesting the refusal of HEW and the U.S. Postal Service to forward Social Security checks to Peoples Temple members who were living in Jonestown. It was outrageous, Harvey argued, that the Peoples Temple, which "has done so much for elderly, minority, and disadvantaged citizens is now being deprived of its elderly members' right to receive benefits which have been earned through entire lifetimes of hard work." Harvey vouched even that Jones's followers at the Guyana outpost of the Peoples Temple had developed new methods of agriculture that were especially suited to the jungle: these methods would "contribute to alleviating the world food crisis through implementing and spreading such technology," he wrote.[31]

By the fall of the following year, 1978, over nine hundred members of Peoples Temple had followed their leader to Jonestown, where Jones continued to preach about creating "a world of total equality, a society where people own all things in common, where there's no rich and poor, where there are no races." The jungle into which he had taken the faithful was lush and gorgeous, full of scarlet ibis, russet and gold hoatzin, and pink and white flamingoes. Bananas and mangos, cassava and sweet potatoes were abundant. An interracial choir sang rousing songs like "Never Heard a Man Speak Like This Man Before."

But throughout the day loudspeakers all over the compound boomed the tapes of Jim Jones preaching. "Give us our liberty or give us our death," he repeated in his rants about America as a prison. "It's blasphemy to talk about going home," he raged.

When word got back to America that Peoples Temple members were being held in Jonestown against their will, several of their relatives contacted U.S. congressman Leo Ryan and implored him to investigate. Together with several of his aides and a TV crew, Ryan flew to Guyana on November 17, 1978.

What they saw was impressive: Jim Jones and his people had carved out a vibrant community in the middle of the jungle. They even staged a very grand reception for their visitors. "There are people here I talked to who believe this is the best thing that ever happened to them in their whole lives," Congressman Ryan said to Jim Jones's cheering, whistling followers. Reverend Jones was assured that the representative's visit was going extremely well.

However, early the next day, November 18, several Jonestown residents surreptitiously passed to the congressman notes that said, "Please get us out of here." That same morning the TV crew had been wandering around the compound to find residents to interview for their story. To their astonishment, several people furtively told the crew, "We're being held prisoners. All we want is to go home." When the crew confronted Reverend Jones about what they had said, he was caught off guard. "People play games. They lie," he responded. But he was terrified that the congressman would believe them.

Ryan's party got as far as the airport's tarmac before they were ambushed by faithful Jonestown members. Ryan and four others were shot and killed. When the returning assassins reported to Jones that the congressman was dead, Jones knew it was all over. He announced over the loudspeaker, "They won't let us live in peace, we'll die in peace." Then he commanded everyone to "an act of revolutionary suicide protesting the conditions of the inhumane world." Before the sun set and plunged the jungle into darkness, 909 people, about 300 of them children, drank—willingly or by force—Kool-Aid laced with cyanide.[32]

* * *

"My name is cut into stone in support of you and your people," Harvey had told Jim Jones the day the reverend left for Guyana. Harvey must have felt overcome with guilt and shame when he remembered those words. He must have felt more than a little responsibility: he had written to the secretary of health, education, and welfare and to President Carter demanding that people's Social Security checks be sent to Jonestown.

And he must also have been deeply disturbed that such gruesome suicides and murders—Jack Lira, Jim Jones, over 900 of Jones's innocent followers, Leo Ryan, members of Ryan's investigative team—had so closely touched his own life.

Part 4

Martyr

13

"If a bullet should enter my brain . . ."

AFTER JACK'S SUICIDE Harvey found it hard to be alone at night. During the day it was okay because he was busy being Supervisor Milk and still fighting against Proposition 6. But when the sun went down he could not bear it. Not only was there the visual memory of Jack's grisly death, but he had spent most of his adult life in some sort of committed partnership. He was not used to coming home to no one.

In early September 1978, not long after he returned from Jack's funeral in Fresno, Harvey met Billy Wiegardt, a twenty-two-year-old from a small town on the Washington peninsula. Wiegardt worked as a bartender in a Castro gay bar. After a brief courtship, Harvey invited him to move into the Henry Street apartment. Wiegardt did, but if Harvey thought they would be a couple, he had to have been disappointed. Wiegardt, who had come to San Francisco because he craved the great variety of sexual pleasures the Castro had to offer, had no interest in domesticity. Still, Harvey asked him to stay on as his room-mate. Wiegardt helped pay the rent—and, perhaps even more important, was a living, breathing presence in the sad apartment where Harvey had so recently found Jack Lira's body.

If Harvey had had time enough he surely would have managed to find another needy young man whom he thought he could save, and he would have jumped again into a long-term relationship. That was his deepest emotional need. The pattern, which seemed to hold out the promise of righting his troubled relationship with Bill Milk, was as unbreakable as it was doomed to failure. But he did not have time enough. He filled the last months of his love life not only with several sexual partners but also with familiar joys of wooing. When he did not spend the night with a lover, Harvey called him early in the morning to wake him up with sweet, funny words. He brought flowers that he had picked himself from neighborhood front yards or flower boxes. He sent romantic, sexy notes.

He met Bob Tuttle, a boyish-looking twenty-eight-year-old, when Harvey spoke at a gay rally in Los Angeles in 1977. Whenever Harvey returned to the L.A. area to campaign against the Briggs Initiative, he arranged his schedule to include romantic interludes in Tuttle's Venice Beach apartment. Back in San Francisco, Harvey also took up with Doug Franks, another boyish twenty-something, who had just enrolled as a graduate student at San Francisco State University. Harvey had met Doug at a No on 6 fund-raising party.[1] Not long into their relationship Harvey took him as his date to an official dinner hosted by a delegation from Nationalist China. It was as bold a public statement as the one he had made at his inauguration when he introduced Jack Lira as his lover and partner, and it was in keeping with his conviction that straight people needed to deal with the fact that homosexuals had relationships, sexual and romantic, just as heterosexuals did.[2]

At the Castro's annual Beaux Arts Ball, Harvey met another

twenty-something-year-old, Steve Beery, with whom he was also enamored. Steve not only had the boyish look Harvey loved, but at the ball he was costumed as Batman's boy sidekick, Robin. Harvey's corny pickup line—"Hop on my back, Boy Wonder, and I'll fly you to Gotham City"—worked, and they started a relationship. Though Steve was the youngster in their duo, Harvey relished putting him in the role of the sensible, serious one. It was Steve who had to rein in an irrepressible Harvey by pretending shock at his outrageous antics, such as when Harvey called Steve at his job at a Geary Street credit agency to tell him, "I'm reading the most god-awful boring garbage. . . . Why don't you take the afternoon off? Come down to City Hall and get under my desk."

Steve Beery was Harvey's last boyfriend. Steve had been invited to Thanksgiving dinner at the home of friends who would have loved for the famous Supervisor Milk to join them. Harvey wrote down the address Steve gave him, but he never showed up.[3]

*   *   *

The $9,600 a year that San Francisco supervisors were paid—about $37,000 in today's money—meant that a supervisor either had a regular job with flexible hours (Carol Ruth Silver, for instance, had a law practice) or was independently wealthy (Dianne Feinstein was married to a rich man) or went hungry (as Harvey did). Supervisor Dan White had quit his day job as a fireman, at which he made $19,000 a year, to devote himself full time to the half-time position; but he found it impossible to support his wife and baby on $800 a month. To supplement his income White bought a franchise from the Hot Potato, a modest fast-food chain, and he opened a little place at Pier 39, where it was wedged among seafood restaurants and shops that sold tourist trinkets. He had to take out a mortgage against his house to pay for the franchise. He also had to hire a babysitter to take care of his baby while his wife worked long shifts at the Hot Potato. He worked there, too, whenever he was not at City Hall. Around midnight, late diners leaving the seafood restaurants and passing the Hot Potato could glance through the open doors and see the San Francisco supervisor Dan White himself scrubbing pans.[4] And still he and his wife could not make it financially.

On top of that, his position as a supervisor was becoming painful. He played a dunce's role on the board; at least that was the way Harvey Milk and Carol Ruth Silver made him feel—as though everything he said or did was ridiculous. Then, the election on November 7 made him realize that conservatism had become hopelessly embattled in San Francisco. Out of more than nine hundred precincts, only four voted in favor of Briggs's Proposition 6—and all four were in Dan White's district.

He decided he had to find a better way to support his family and spare his dignity, too. Three days after the election that revealed to all of San Francisco how out of sync his district was with the rest of the city, he strode into the mayor's office and handed Moscone his resignation. That afternoon White celebrated with his wife and one of the few other conservative supervisors, Lee Dolson. They went to a ballgame at Candlestick Park, where White told Dolson he felt "terribly relieved" that he had resigned.[5]

But the relief did not last. White was besieged by people telling him that his resignation was a huge mistake and that he had to demand his seat back. San Francisco's Board of Realtors was the most adamant. The Board of Realtors had endorsed his candidacy and really depended on him to stay in office. He was the one who had argued emotionally to his fellow supervisors that rent control "went against the free enterprise system." He had also supported the Board of Realtors against the repeal of a San Francisco measure specifying that each year that you owned a place 10 percent of your profit would be forgiven; so after ten years you could sell your property without having to pay any tax, no matter how much it had appreciated. The Board of Realtors was grateful when Supervisor White championed their cause by declaring, "People wouldn't want to buy rental property if owning a building meant their taxes would be high as the sky but the rent would be capped."[6] Supervisor Milk had been the most vocal in fighting White's realtor-friendly ideas. Harvey had even sponsored an ordinance to control real estate speculation that had been drafted by a progressive group called the Housing Coalition, which fought for affordable housing and against the developers.[7] Harvey Milk was the supervisor the Board of Realtors would have loved to get rid of; Dan White was too valuable to lose.

The San Francisco Police Department also thought White was too valuable to lose. A civil rights suit by blacks and Latinos about hiring discrimination in the SFPD was pending, and the police were certain that if White vacated his seat the mayor would appoint a liberal, who would side with the minorities. White's aides, too, were unhappy about his resignation. If he quit the Board of Supervisors they would be jobless. Dan White was overwhelmed by the pressure to retract his resignation that was coming from so many directions. And he himself was ambivalent about having quit: he had always seen himself as a fighter, not a quitter.

On November 14 he showed up at Mayor Moscone's office to say he had decided not to resign. Moscone reminded him that the Board of Supervisors had convened the day before, at its regular Monday meeting, and that they had been read his resignation letter. They had voted, without any objections, to accept it. His resignation could not simply be withdrawn after the supervisors had accepted it.

Though Moscone and White were very different in their political views, the mayor had always seen something of his younger self in Dan White. Like White, he had been a San Francisco supervisor when he was in his early thirties. They were both very ambitious. They were both devout Catholics. When Moscone saw how upset the former supervisor was, he agreed that "a man has a right to change his mind"; and he promised he would figure out what needed to be done. White left the mayor's office feeling assured that Moscone would call him as soon as he knew what steps to take in order to give White his job back.[8]

When Harvey heard that Moscone was thinking about voiding White's resignation he was livid. Why would the mayor want to keep a reactionary fool on the Board of Supervisors when he did not have to, when he could bring in someone whose political ideas were like his own?

In the role Harvey had been assuming as top gay of San Francisco, he immediately called Moscone with a threat; he went to Moscone's office at least three times to repeat it, not holding back on the expressive language that had become his style with the mayor: "You reappoint Dan White and you're finished in the gay community. You won't even get elected dog catcher!" Harvey proposed replacements. There was Helen Fama, the only woman to run against White in District 8. She had come in third, but her credentials included chairing the Legislative Committee of the San Francisco Commission on the Status of Women. There was Don Horanzy, who had worked for the Department of Housing and Urban Development and was now leading a progressive group called the All People's Coalition. There was a black woman who, Harvey told his boyfriend Doug Franks, would be great—"another minority, another woman, someone who can relate to gays."[9]

Harvey was right that the gay community would be furious if Moscone blew the chance to get rid of the man who had run on the promise that he would fight against San Francisco's "social deviates," the very man who had said to the media about Harvey's gay rights bill, "This bill lets a man in a dress be a teacher."[10] The gay community despised Dan White, and—as

Moscone acknowledged when he won his mayoral election in 1976—it was the gay community that had put Moscone over the top.

To complicate matters, if there was one other group that had been a huge help to Moscone in his mayoral campaign it was the Peoples Temple. Jim Jones had directed temple members to distribute tens of thousands of slate cards in San Francisco's black and poor neighborhoods endorsing Moscone's candidacy.[11] But Jones and the members of the Peoples Temple had died in Jonestown. Moscone would not have campaign help from them anymore. If he could not count on the gay vote either, how would he win his bid for reelection the next year?

*   *   *

Wednesday afternoon before Thanksgiving: almost everyone at City Hall was already gone or about to leave for the holiday. But Debra Jones, the intern Harvey had called a Nubian queen months before, was stuck in the office. She had to finish a project that was due the following week. Harvey was there too, and they both worked into nightfall. "I'm leaving now," she finally called out to him. Harvey came out of his office to say good-bye and ask how she planned to spend the long weekend. "Going to Santa Cruz for the holiday. See you Monday," Jones said. They wished each other a happy Thanksgiving.[12]

Saturday, November 25, was the highlight of the Thanksgiving weekend for Harvey. He was given a VIP box seat at the San Francisco Opera House to hear one of his favorite sopranos, Magda Olivero, singing the title role of *Tosca*. Olivero was making her San Francisco debut at the age of sixty-eight. To make things even more exciting, Harvey was sharing the opera box with Bidu Sayao, the Brazilian soprano who had been a star at the Met when the fourteen-year-old Harvey had listened breathlessly in the standing-room section of the opera house.

Now, sitting in the most coveted box of the San Francisco Opera House, he found a piece of paper in one pocket and the stub of a red pencil in another, and he scribbled an ecstatic note to Tom O'Horgan, telling him that at that very minute he was sitting next to Bidu Sayao in an opera box and listening to Olivero "in her San Francisco debut at the age of 71 [*sic*] !!!!" He gushed that "the ~~audience~~ crowd [*sic*] went so wild that Mick Jagger would have been jealous." The last line in his note to O'Horgan was, "Oh—life can be so worth living."[13]

Sunday, November 26, at sunset in New York: Harvey's brother, Robert, lit a *yahrzeit* candle for Minerva, the mother of Harvey and Robert, who had died sixteen years earlier on November 27. Robert was surprised to find that, hours after it should have gone out, it was still burning.[14]

Ten thirty that evening in California: Dan White's phone rang. He had spent sleepless, angry nights waiting for Moscone's call. He suspected that Moscone was toying with him. Two days earlier White had asked a lawyer friend to get a temporary court order to prevent Moscone from appointing another supervisor—because White could prove that the people of District 8 wanted him reinstated. The judge refused to issue the order. But now, almost two weeks since he had gone to Moscone's office to say he changed his mind and wanted his job back, he was sure that at last the mayor was calling, ready to share his plan for reinstating White.

The caller was a woman, Barbara Taylor, a reporter for KCBS, a San Francisco radio station. She just heard that Mayor Moscone had decided on a replacement for Dan White: Don Horanzy. What did Dan White think about that? she wanted to know.

* * *

Monday, November 27, about eight thirty in the morning: Harvey stopped by George Moscone's office before going to his own. Don Horanzy was to be sworn in that day as supervisor for District 8. Harvey was very pleased. He and Moscone chatted briefly, and Harvey left soon after the mayor's secretary, Cyr Copertini, arrived, about a quarter to nine.[15]

Nine o'clock: Cleve Jones, who was getting class credit at San Francisco State University for serving as Harvey's intern, arrived at work. But he had left a file of research material at home. It contained a list of possible opponents that Harvey might face when he ran for supervisor again in 1979. Leonard Matlovich, the air force sergeant who had come out in 1975 and fought successfully against discharge, was at the top of the list. Matlovich made the cover of *Time* magazine for his pioneering battle with the military. He could be someone to worry about in a district election. Another worrisome challenger might be Chuck Morris, the publisher of the *Sentinel*, the gay paper for which Harvey once wrote. There were a lot of possible candidates from the Castro who would have loved to unseat Harvey. The election was almost a year away, but it was not too soon to begin preparing. He asked Cleve to go back home and fetch the file. He intended to study it that afternoon. "But take your time," he said. "Local 2 is picketing at the Patio Café. Stop by and say hi for me."[16]

About a quarter to eleven: Dan White, spiffily dressed in a three-piece, light beige suit, though it was late November, stood at the main entrance to City Hall on Polk Street. Under his vest, in a holster strapped to his belt, was a .38 Smith & Wesson revolver from his days on the police force. He had cleaned the gun that morning and loaded it with five cartridges; he had wrapped another ten cartridges in a handkerchief concealed in his pants pocket. The policeman who usually monitored the metal detector at the Polk Street entrance knew White well and always waved him on. But in his place this morning there was another man who did not know White and would surely detect what he was hiding under his vest.

White went around the corner to the McAllister Street

side of the building and jumped through an open window of a ground-floor soil-testing lab. A lab worker in an adjacent room heard the noise and came running. "It's okay. It's okay," White said quickly. "I'm Supervisor Dan White. I forgot my keys." The explanation made no sense—but the lab worker was not comfortable questioning a well-dressed, perfectly sane-looking man who identified himself as a San Francisco supervisor.[17] White took the back stairs up to the second floor, where the mayor's office was on one side and the supervisors' offices on the other.

He went to Moscone's office first. "May I speak with the mayor?" he politely asked Cyr Copertini. She was dismayed to see him. In a little over half an hour Don Horanzy was scheduled to meet with the press and be sworn in as White's replacement. But she went through the double doors into the mayor's office to tell him that Dan White was there and wanted to talk with him. Moscone was preparing his remarks for the press conference at which he would introduce Horanzy. He seemed upset to hear that White wanted to see him. "Give me a minute to think about it," he told his secretary. But a second later he said, "Oh, all right. Tell him I'll see him." She asked Moscone if he wanted anyone to be present at the meeting; she suggested his press secretary, Mel Wax. "No, I'll see him alone," Moscone said. "But he'll have to wait a couple of minutes." He needed to finish writing his remarks about Don Horanzy.

In the outer office Dan White looked nervous, but he made small talk with the secretary. He asked if she was having a nice day. They chatted about Caroline Kennedy, who was turning twenty-one that day. In ten minutes Moscone buzzed and told Copertini to bring White to the sitting room in back of his office, which he sometimes used to rest or have lunch or when he wanted to strike a level of intimacy with someone rather than speak formally across his mayoral desk. He understood that White was hurting. Perhaps Moscone thought he could sit down with him and make him see that his not being a supervisor was not the end of the world and that he should not take it so hard.[18]

Moscone offered White something to drink and began to ask about his plans. White said the constituents in his district wanted him back in office—they had signed petitions; they were demanding he get his job back. "That will be impossible," Moscone said. That was when White pulled out his gun and fired two bullets into the mayor's chest. When Moscone fell, face down, White straddled him and fired two more bullets into the back of his head. Cyr Copertini, sitting in the outer office, heard four loud bangs. She went to the window, wondering if a car was backfiring.

The supervisors' offices were down a very long marble corridor. White, his gun concealed again under his vest, walked quickly to his old office. He still had the key. There, he reloaded the Smith & Wesson and went to find Harvey, who was in his office talking to Carl Carlson, the friend who had recently lent him three thousand dollars. "Harvey, I need to speak to you," White said. "Come into my office."

Harvey hesitated only a beat before he followed his former colleague. From Dan White's office window you could see the Opera House, where Harvey had written Tom O'Horgan two nights earlier, "Oh—life can be so worth living." The Opera House may have been the last thing Harvey saw.

Later, Dan White testified that Harvey had smirked at him, and that was when he took out his gun and fired three shots into Harvey's body and two into his head, penetrating Harvey's brain.

* * *

Cleve Jones retrieved the file of Harvey's possible opponents from his apartment and stopped by the Patio Café to say hi from Harvey to the Local 2 picketers. Cleve had just hopped on a bus that would take him back to City Hall when a woman whom he knew from events at the Women's Building called out, "Cleve, have you heard that Mayor Moscone has been shot?" He jumped off the bus, hailed a taxi, and sped to City Hall, spooked that Harvey had said repeatedly that there were threats against his life, that one day he would probably be assassinated. As Cleve ran up the stairs to the supervisors' offices, Dianne Feinstein, her sleeves and hands streaked with blood from trying to find a pulse on Harvey, ran past him. The door to Dan White's office was open. The first thing Cleve saw was Harvey's wingtip shoes, their soles worn and patched, and then his lifeless, bloodied body.[19]

14

Aftermath

THE OTHER bullets Dan White had carried in his pocket were intended for Carol Ruth Silver. He had not been blind to the notes she and Harvey passed behind his back at Board of Supervisor meetings, or to how she joined Harvey in smirking whenever White opened his mouth to speak. Carol Ruth Silver, Dan White thought, "was the biggest snake of the bunch." If she had kept her usual schedule that day, White would have encountered her walking up the steps of City Hall about a quarter after eleven, just as he was leaving. But that morning she had gone to have coffee at the Daisy, a mile away, with "Mighty Mo" Bernstein, an avid liberal and big political donor. After their coffee Silver dropped by her law office to pick up some papers. She survived White's murderous intent only because she arrived at City Hall late that day.[1]

Not finding Silver, White ran off, looking for a pay phone from which he could call his wife. He found one in a fast-food restaurant and asked her to meet him at the Cathedral of St. Mary of the Assumption. In the empty church he told her what he had done. Together they went to the Northern Station of the San Francisco Police Department, a ten-minute walk from the cathedral. There, White turned himself in. He chose that particular station because several of the officers at Northern were close friends. He gave his weeping confession to Police Inspector Frank Falzon, under whom White had once served. Falzon had been a buddy too. He and White were raised in the same neighborhood, attended a Catholic grammar school together, had the same friends.[2]

In his confession Dan White said that he killed Mayor Moscone and Supervisor Milk because "I saw the city going kind of downhill."[3]

* * *

When Harvey won his election, he gave Cleve Jones the bullhorn that the union head Allen Baird once presented to him. Harvey had said to Jones, "We'll play bad cop/good cop. You go out in the streets and make the demands. Be the radical. I'm gonna stay inside and fix things."[4] The evening after Harvey was killed Jones took his bullhorn out on the street with him, but he did not need it. By seven o'clock a huge crowd, gays and straights alike, thousands, had gathered spontaneously on Castro and Seventeenth Streets. The San Francisco Gay Democratic Club had asked those they alerted to bring candles. But everyone seemed to know to bring them. Led by a drummer and three gay men carrying a big American flag, a California State flag, and a flag of the City and County of San Francisco, they began marching toward City Hall on the route Harvey had walked, his arm around Jack Lira, the day he was inaugurated. As they marched, thousands more joined in. In the dark the marchers seemed to be a flowing river of light.[5] Local news stations estimated they were thirty thousand strong. This was "the greatest single outpouring of grief since Martin Luther King was killed," one newscaster declared.[6]

Gwenn Craig, who had been hired by Harvey to coordinate the San Franciscans Against Prop 6 campaign and to do black outreach, had gone to Hawaii for Thanksgiving and to celebrate the election victory. Her friend Bill Kraus, whom Harvey had hired to be the campaign's strategist, called her the minute he heard the news that morning. Kraus was sobbing uncontrollably. "Harvey's been killed!" he blurted out.

Craig threw her things together and rushed to the airport. In San Francisco she grabbed a cab. "Market Street, near Valencia," she told the driver. She had expected to see a big demonstration but was shocked to find the streets empty. Then she looked up the hill and saw thousands of little flames.[7]

Except for the sounds of weeping, the procession marched in silence toward City Hall. Some, like Debra Jones, Harvey's Nubian queen, were in the throes of such grief that they had to be held up by friends as they walked.[8] A black man standing on a corner watched the quietly weeping marchers in disbelief. "Where is your anger?" he shouted. "Where is your anger?"[9]

Many placed their candles at the base of the statue of Abraham Lincoln that sits in front of City Hall. Dianne Feinstein, who, as president of the Board of Supervisors, had already assumed the position of acting mayor, promised the mourning crowd that "social change will continue in San Francisco. Harvey is gone, but he will not be forgotten." Joan Baez led the crowd in "Amazing Grace." The folksinger Holly Near was there too. A few hours earlier she composed a song for that evening, "Singing for Our Lives": the lyrics she belted out referred to gentle, angry gay and lesbian people.[10] That night the gay and lesbian people were only gentle. The anger would come later.

* * *

Harvey's most intimate friends gathered to make funeral arrangements. Jim Rivaldo, who had been Harvey's political strategist, volunteered to go to the mortuary and pick out a casket. Walter Caplan, at whose home Harvey had attended Passover seders at which he always wore a yarmulke, was certain, as he instructed Rivaldo, that Harvey would want an unpainted wooden casket, no nails or metal of any kind, in keeping with Jewish tradition.[11]

There was an outdoor memorial service in front of City Hall on November 29, with speeches by dignitaries such as Lieutenant Governor Mervyn Dymally, who had made Harvey so proud when he spoke at Harvey's victory dinner less than eleven months earlier. Out of respect for George Moscone, the benediction was given by Archbishop John Quinn. Out of respect for Harvey, Rabbi Alvin Fine, a civil rights champion and the retired head of Temple Emanu-El, San Francisco's main Reform temple, gave the eulogy. Harvey's unpainted wooden coffin rested near the shiny mahogany and gold casket of George Moscone, under the ornate City Hall rotunda that Harvey had so loved. Flowers were strewn on every step of the beautiful marble staircase. More than ten thousand mourners stood in line, waiting to file by the closed coffins.

George Moscone's services, both a public funeral and a private funeral Mass, were held at St. Mary's Cathedral, home of the archdiocese of San Francisco. There were several memorial services for Harvey. In the tape recording he had left with his lawyer friend Walter Caplan shortly after his election in 1977, Harvey said that if he was ever assassinated there should be no religious services for him. "I would turn over in my grave if there were any kind of religious ceremony," he had declared. But there were many kinds of religious ceremonies for him.

One was at the Gay Community Center (which had been the cause of the federal investigation against him that was mooted by his death); Rabbi Martin Weiner of the Reform Temple Sherith Israel officiated.[12] Another service was organized by the gay Congregation Sha'ar Zahav; the gay rabbinical student Allen Bennett officiated. Sha'ar Zahav members even raised money to fly Harvey's brother, Robert, from New York to San Francisco to attend the service. They rented an auditorium too, Dovre Hall, which seated four hundred; and they arranged with the city's Municipal Transportation Agency for a special bus to bring people directly to the door. The hall was overflowing, and the service had to be amplified so that the hundreds unable to get in could hear it outside. Sha'ar Zahav was a tiny congregation before stories about the service and Sha'ar Zahav's gay membership appeared in San Francisco's newspapers. Because of the publicity, it grew exponentially, and San Francisco's Jewish Community Center finally recognized the gay congregation and welcomed the members to hold Friday and Saturday services at the JCC until the money was raised for Sha'ar Zahav to build its own home. Harvey would have liked that, at least.[13]

But neither of those Jewish memorials was the official one. Acting Mayor Dianne Feinstein was a member of Temple Emanu-El, which was not only San Francisco's wealthiest Reform congregation but also its largest, seating two thousand people. It was decided that the official Jewish service be held there, right after Harvey's lying in state at City Hall. Temple Emanu-El's senior rabbi, Joseph Asher, had always been committed to civil rights; in 1958 he had even participated in sit-ins in the South. But he was not a proponent of homosexual equality, and he was not at all charmed by the proposal that Allen Bennett, the only openly gay rabbi in San Francisco, give the eulogy at Temple Emanu-El. Under pressure from City Hall, however, Rabbi Asher could hardly say no. Harvey would have liked that too—and he would have liked that at the podium of stuffy Temple Emanu-El an openly gay rabbi talked about Harvey Milk's pride in his Jewishness.[14]

The memorial service that would have pleased Harvey the most was held at the Opera House. Not only was the lieutenant governor of California at this service: Governor Jerry Brown and the chief justice of California, Rose Bird, were also there. Robert Milk, because he was Harvey's brother, sat with the dignitaries in the front row. Robert did not know yet that Harvey's will excluded him from inheriting anything of the meager estate because Harvey had never gotten over his anger that his brother was contemptuous of him for being gay.[15]

At the Opera House, Robert had to have recognized what a somebody his younger brother had become. Every one of the more than three thousand seats was taken, as was every space where people could stand. Another thousand mourners listened to the service over a loudspeaker outside.

Acting Mayor Feinstein told the dignitaries and Robert and the thousands of others there that "the fact of [Harvey's] homosexuality gave him an insight into the scars which all oppressed people wear. It was undoubtedly the genesis of his admirable commitment to the cause of human rights." The eulogy was given by Harvey's friend the Reverend William Barcus, a gay priest at St. Mary the Virgin Episcopal Church. Barcus turned his eulogy into an exhortation that all gay people exit the closet "as a tribute to Harvey Milk and as an affirmation of our own freedom and integrity and wholeness." He called upon "every gay person in this room, in this city, in this country" to come out en masse on the following Monday. He echoed the words of the slain supervisor: "Come out to your friends, your employers, your clergy, your bankers, your neighbors, your families. Come out!" He also reiterated the call Harvey had made at the last Gay Freedom Day rally for a gay march on Washington on July 4, 1979, to tell the president of the United States "about America and what it stands for."

* * *

Harvey was cremated on the Thursday after he was shot. On Friday, December 1, Scott Smith and Galen McKinley drove together to the mortuary to pick up his ashes. Tom Randol, who had helped Harvey and Scott silkscreen the first campaign posters and who had led Veterans for Harvey Milk during the 1976 and 1977 campaigns, drove with them. They argued about who would get to hold the urn in his lap.[16] Scott took the urn home, to keep until Saturday.

Saturday morning, December 2, the three men wrapped the urn in Harvey's favorite comic strip, "Doonesbury," from the *San Francisco Chronicle*. Over the comics they pasted rhinestones that spelled out "RIP" and "December 2, 1978." About thirty of Harvey's closest friends, including Tom O'Horgan and men who had been his lovers through the years, including Joe Campbell, had chartered a vintage sailing ship, *Lady Frei*. As the *Lady Frei* sailed past the Golden Gate Bridge they scattered Harvey's ashes, along with peach-colored roses that represented his beloved opera *Der Rosenkavalier*. They also scattered bubble bath and the contents of a packet of grape Kool-Aid in remembrance of the victims of Jonestown, who had died two weeks earlier after drinking the cyanide-laced Kool-Aid under Jim Jones's command. The bubble bath and Kool-Aid created a coral-colored wake. They fired a little cannon to salute their martyred friend and lover.[17]

* * *

John Briggs had gotten two propositions qualified for California's ballot in November 1978. Though Proposition 6 went down to defeat, Proposition 7, called the Death Penalty Act, won by a landslide: 71 percent to 29 percent. It affirmed a law passed by the state legislature the year before that reinstated the death penalty in California; it made capital punishment mandatory for first-degree murder under "special circumstances." Those circumstances included murder of multiple victims and assassination of a public official. Who could doubt that Dan White, who had assassinated two public officials, would be executed?

White spent six months in jail as he awaited trial. Rumor had it that those months behind bars were made easy by White's former colleagues in the San Francisco Police Department, who allowed him to order take-out meals from his favorite restaurants and feast on chocolate cakes baked by his admirers.

Another rumor held that police officers passed the hat and raised a hundred thousand dollars for White's defense fund.[18] There was, in fact, little doubt on whose side the police were in this city that was, in their perception, being co-opted by progressives while those on the right were left to stew. Despite Moscone's chief of police appointee, the reformist Charles Gain, who had declared on taking office that he would welcome gays into the force, most policemen were conservative, if not reactionary. In fact, the Police Officers Association had held a no-confidence vote on their new chief. The assassinations of the mayor who had foisted Gain on the department and of the man who was famous for flaunting his homosexuality were no great tragedy to the force.

* * *

San Francisco's district attorney, Joe Freitas, whose job it normally would have been to prosecute the case, recused himself because he had been personally acquainted with the mayor and both supervisors. The job fell to Thomas Norman, the assistant district attorney. Norman intended to ask for the death penalty. He queried all the potential jurors about their views on capital punishment to be sure they had no scruples against it. Norman thus inadvertently dismissed liberal prospective jurors, who would have been most reliably outraged about the murders of a gay man and a gay-friendly mayor. The defense lawyers, Douglas Schmidt and Steve Scherr, were many steps ahead of the assistant D.A. They dismissed any prospective juror who was not white, straight, and conservative. The jury on which the defense and the prosecution agreed was composed of seven women and five men, mostly from working-class backgrounds very similar to Dan White's own.[19]

Assistant D.A. Norman made another grave mistake by playing for the jury the tape of White's twenty-four-minute police station confession. In the hushed courtroom the jurors heard White weeping audibly as he told Inspector Falzon about the murders. White's confession was so affecting that the jurors wept too. He had not intended to kill Moscone and Milk, White had said to his former schoolmate, colleague, and friend. He had been upset because he was so worried about how he was going to support his wife and little baby. All he wanted to do was take care of them and take care of the city that he loved so much. He had worked so hard to get elected supervisor because he wanted to fight corruption and keep San Francisco from deteriorating. True, he had carried a loaded gun to City Hall, but a lot of supervisors carried loaded guns, for self-protection—even Dianne Feinstein carried one. The day Moscone and Milk were killed he had gone to City Hall just to talk to them; but "I got kind of fuzzy; my head didn't feel right," White told Falzon in a pathetic-sounding voice.[20]

Each of the eleven days of the trial, the jurors saw before them, sitting in the courtroom, a pale, clean-cut family man. His grief-stricken wife, Mary Ann, was there too. Dan and Mary Ann looked devastated—the sight of the attractive young couple was heartbreaking, just as White's lawyers knew it would be. Defense Attorney Schmidt pointed out to this jury of White's peers that he'd had a spotless and honorable record before the tragedy—Vietnam vet, policeman, fireman. "Good people, fine people with fine backgrounds, simply don't kill people in cold blood," Schmidt summed up.

So how had it happened that Dan White, by his own confession, had killed two people? An expert witness testified that the upstanding young man had been so shaken by the loss of his position that he could not eat. He had been subsisting on Coca-Cola and Twinkies, and that had made it impossible for him to think clearly. The jury paid no attention to the fact that White had been deliberate in planning the murder of two public officials: he had cleaned his gun, loaded it with five bullets, put ten more in his pants pocket, dressed in a three-piece suit with a vest that would conceal his weapon, evaded City Hall's metal detector by climbing through a ground-floor window. On May 21, 1979—the day before Harvey Milk would have been forty-nine years old—the jury found Dan White guilty of voluntary manslaughter. For assassinating two public officials he was sentenced to seven years and eight months in prison.

But how was that possible? a *San Francisco Chronicle* reporter asked the foreman of the jury. Dan White had admitted to killing a mayor and a supervisor. He had committed a double capital offense. "Well, no one could come up with any evidence that indicated premeditation," the foreman explained.[21]

* * *

"Where is your anger? Where is your anger?" the man watching the silent candlelight march had cried out six months earlier. The jury's outrageous verdict now detonated that anger. A crowd began to gather in the Castro as soon as the verdict was announced. Cleve Jones ran to get the bullhorn to shout, "Out of the bars and into the streets!" thinking he would lead another mournful march. Five hundred people had congregated already, and they started walking to City Hall. By the time they got to Civic Center Plaza the number had swelled to thousands. It was almost dark. A mob massed in front of City Hall's main entrance on Polk Street. One man struggled to pull down a piece of the ornate grillwork to make a battering ram. Others joined him, pulling down rods of the grillwork and using them to smash the glass doors. Some broke off chunks of the aggregate trash bins on the streets, others pulled up chunks of pavement, others uprooted parking meters and newspaper vending racks, and they hurled them at the windows of City Hall. People yelled, "He got away with murder!" "We want justice!" "Avenge Harvey Milk!"

Cooler heads, hoping to calm the mob, located Harvey's beloved debating partner, Sally Gearhart, in the crowd. They rushed her up to the City Hall steps and put Cleve Jones's bullhorn in her hands. "There's nobody in the city angrier than I am tonight," she shouted through the bullhorn. "But Harvey Milk would not be here tearing down the doors of this building. Harvey Milk would say, 'I don't want my death avenged by violence. There are better ways to deal with our rage!'"

Her plea fell on deaf ears. Rioters broke limbs off of trees and used them to smash every car window in sight. They hurled burning shrubs through the broken windows of parked police vehicles.

Dianne Feinstein watched, peeking from behind the curtains of the mayor's office. She ordered the SFPD to call in every off-duty policeman in an attempt to restore order. She summoned the police departments of Oakland, San Mateo, Santa Clara, and Marin, pleading for backup. The streets looked like they had in Greenwich Village ten years earlier at the Stonewall riots. Policemen wearing riot shields and helmets tried to drive the angry mob from City Hall and the Plaza. The rioters ran north to Larkin Street, setting fire to trash cans, breaking plate-glass windows, looting stores. "Political trashing," they gleefully dubbed their deeds. "Make sure to put it in the papers that I ate too many Twinkies," one of them screamed at a *Chronicle* reporter while torching another police car.

Five hours after the riot began, it was finally over. Seventy rioters and fifty-nine policemen had to be treated for injuries from billy clubs, rocks, and flying bottles. The damage was over one million dollars.[22]

* * *

Hoping to quiet the crowd, Sally Gearhart had told them that Harvey would not have wanted a riot, but that was not quite accurate. Harvey had seen the impact of the 1969 Stonewall riots. He understood that militant action could be necessary to the gay movement if nothing else would make straight people sit up and take notice. Once the straight world started listening, then more reasonable-looking and -sounding spokesmen—like Harvey Milk in a suit and tie—could deliver the message of gay rights.

The day after the riot the *San Francisco Examiner*, trying to make sense of what had happened, interviewed Harry Britt. He had been a founding member of the San Francisco Gay Democratic Club, which was formed to help Harvey in his 1976 Assembly run; after Harvey's assassination it was renamed the Harvey Milk Democratic Club. Britt was one of the four people Harvey had named in his political will as his possible successor on the Board of Supervisors; and he was the one Dianne Feinstein appointed.

Like Harvey, Harry Britt understood the uses of riots. He explained to the newspaper and the world, "Now the society is going to have to deal with us not as nice little fairies who have their hair-dressing salons, but as people capable of violence. This was gay anger you saw. There better be an understanding of where this violence was coming from."[23]

Harvey Milk's Legacy

MOVEMENTS YEARN for heroes who can be immortalized, and Harvey's murder has cast him in that position. He has become larger in death than he was in life. The title of a museum exhibition in 2003, "Saint Harvey: The Life and Afterlife of a Modern Gay Martyr," even bestowed sainthood on Harvey Milk, the lowly Jewish boy who worked in a modest camera store, was killed for his views, and catalyzed a movement.[1] In the light of Harvey's deeply human flaws and unsuppressed excesses, the appellation "Saint Harvey" is, of course, tongue in cheek. But the exhibit's title also conveys the gay community's need to endow Harvey's murder with a mythic meaning that inspires action.

At Harvey's Opera House memorial service Anne Kronenberg read an earnest little poem Harvey had written a month or two earlier, during his campaign against the Briggs Initiative:

I can be killed with ease.
I can be cut right down.
But I cannot fall back into my closet.
I have grown.
I am not myself.
I am too many.
I am all of us.

Then with fist raised to rally the mourning crowd, she cried, "Harvey knew that our time would come. And our time is now!" Dan White's immediate motive for murder—his fury that Moscone, egged on by Harvey, decided not to give him back his job—was subsumed in a compelling narrative about the gay (and then later the LGBTQ) struggle: namely, Harvey Milk was martyred because of society's irrational hatred of gays; and gays and their allies must assure, "Never again!" by fighting for their human rights and equality.

Like the deaths of other leaders who were cut down in their prime, such as President John F. Kennedy, Harvey's early death made a space for people to imagine what could have been had he not been killed by an assassin's bullet. He would have become mayor within a few years. He would have been the first openly gay governor. The first openly gay U.S. congressman. He would have had the wisdom and political skills to solve the gay community's most intractable problems.

Immediately after his death, he was dubbed by some, including his successor, Harry Britt, the Martin Luther King of the gay movement. "Harvey was a prophet, like Dr. King; he lived by a vision," Britt declared to the candlelight marchers who were mourning Harvey's murder.[2] Harvey's significance has not diminished with time. As one writer emotionally observed thirty years after his death, Harvey was "Our Kennedy, our King, our Malcolm X. Our bullet in the head."[3] The similarity between Martin Luther King's initials MLK and MILK has been given the weight of prophecy.

As extravagant as some of the claims for Harvey and his legacy may be, there is no doubt that he was a singular force in the gay community and that his charismatic leadership helped effect significant change. The shock of his death triggered some change almost immediately. Harvey's proposal at San Francisco's 1978 Gay Freedom Day rally—that there be a gay March on Washington modeled on Martin Luther King's March on Washington for Jobs and Freedom in 1963—did not originate with Harvey. Talk of a gay March on Washington had been kicking around for some time. The homophile leader Frank Kameny, who had attended the MLK march, had even considered organizing a homosexual march in the mid-1960s, but, fearing that not enough people would show up, he settled for a series of pickets at the White House and other public places. Harvey had also worried that not enough gays would show up to make a March on Washington effective, but he changed his mind. He realized that a march would be great theater. It would also unify gay people nationally; and it would let the world know that gays were now willing to show their faces, that there were millions of them, that they were demanding the rights of first-class citizenship. A week before his death Harvey had issued a press release, once again calling for a march in the summer of 1979, on the tenth anniversary of the Stonewall riots.[4]

Soon after he was murdered, his aides met with San Francisco gay groups to promote Harvey's call for a March on Washington. This had been Harvey's dream, they said: "We have to do it for Harvey's sake. The time is *now* to make his dream come true." In a rare show of gay unanimity, audiences rose to their feet and cheered the idea.[5]

In New York the Coalition for Lesbian and Gay Rights had been vaguely talking about a march for months. But on the afternoon of November 27, 1978, they were busy planning their renewed battle for the passage of a New York City gay ordinance. In the midst of the meeting a call came from San Francisco. Harvey Milk had just been killed. The coalition member Joyce Hunter said, "Now we *must* do a March on Washington. For Harvey." A march would give purpose to his death. Nothing could be more appropriate than a March on Washington to honor the dream of the martyred gay Martin Luther King, the members of the Coalition for Lesbian and Gay Rights unanimously agreed.[6]

The March on Washington for Lesbian and Gay Rights was held on October 14, 1979. One hundred thousand gay people showed up to tell President Carter "about America and what it stands for," as Harvey had said. Many carried posters with large photos of Harvey. "Harvey Milk lives," they chanted. That same message was spray-painted around Dupont Circle.

The sight of so many gays congregated in the capital, demanding civil rights, daring to show their faces to the media and to all of America, had the effect that Harvey had envisioned: it encouraged more gay people to come out. In the years that followed they marched in bigger and bigger gay pride parades in cities all over America. They also marched again on Washington. The second March on Washington, in 1987, drew six hundred thousand marchers. The third, in 1993, brought almost a million. In the tapes that Harvey asked to be played "in the event of my death by assassination," he had pleaded for all gays, not just the radicals but mainstream gays too, "every gay doctor, every gay lawyer, every gay architect" to come out, to "stand up and let the world know." The marches on Washington that his death triggered went a long way toward making that happen.

* * *

By 1977—the year Harvey finally won an election—two out lesbians, Elaine Noble and Kathy Kozachenko, had already been elected to political office, but no gay male politicians had come out prior to winning a race. Harvey saw his unique victory as important to gay progress, and he was determined that his hard-fought battle for gay political representation would not be in vain. Should he be killed, he said on the tapes he made ten days after his victory, there must be no going back. His replacement *must be* one of four openly gay people that he named. Mayor Dianne Feinstein honored his will when she appointed Harry Britt to serve out Harvey's term. It marked the start of a succession that remains unbroken. Thanks to Harvey, San Franciscans learned to accept the notion that gay people really did belong in public office. Ever since his pioneering win there has been at least one gay or lesbian San Francisco supervisor.

But also, at a time when most people deemed it impossible, Harvey had aspirations for openly gay men and women to hold even higher elective offices. It has happened. As of 2016 forty-three states have elected at least one out LGBT person to their state legislature. One state elected an out LGBT governor. Seven out LGBT people have been elected to the U.S. Congress. Five more members of Congress came out while in office and kept their seats in their subsequent races.

Had Harvey not succeeded in 1977, when running as an openly gay man, would there still have been a paradigm shift in voters' view of who can be an elected official? Possibly. But it was certainly through his dramatic story that America first learned that an openly gay man had been an admired and credible politician. That surely helped voters take seriously the candidacy of other openly gay people; and it encouraged more openly gay candidates to dare to run.

* * *

While Harvey lived he brought to politics a perspective that had its genesis in what he had learned of *tikkun olam*—the obligation to repair the world—from his mother, Minnie, and his grandfather Morris. From his earliest political campaigns Harvey had argued that gay people had to make coalitions with all dispossessed people. Not only did they have common enemies: the "them"s that kept the poor and minorities in positions of powerlessness; but also it was the morally right thing to do.

He claimed his election victory as a triumph for all minorities: "Because if a gay person makes it, the doors are open to everyone," he often said.

His vision went far beyond San Francisco. One of his first acts as supervisor was to propose a resolution urging the State Department to banish the South African consulate from San Francisco because of South Africa's policy of apartheid. What right did San Francisco have to meddle in the policies of South Africa? Dan White and other conservatives on the board had asked. "Nearly half of San Francisco's population is composed of minorities," Harvey responded. "If any of these persons were to visit South Africa they would be treated as second-class citizens." He shepherded the resolution until he got the six votes to pass it.[7] By June he had also convinced the Board of Supervisors that San Francisco must not invest in corporations or banks doing business in South Africa. That was the start of municipal divestment movements across the country. By 1990, 112 cities and counties had followed suit.

Harvey's most ardent political efforts, such as his battle for rent control, were almost always focused on the disenfranchised. The disenfranchised included young gay people, and Harvey was a visionary in championing their rights. His fight on behalf of young gays was especially brave because activists of his generation, from the beginning of the homophile movement in the 1950s, had carefully excluded gay youth from their purview. No one under the age of twenty-one had been allowed to join groups such as Mattachine or Daughters of Bilitis or even to subscribe to their magazines or newsletters. "Responsible" homosexuals were worried about accusations of "child abuse" if they reached out to help the young. But Harvey, remembering how alone he had felt as a gay adolescent, thought that one of his most important roles as a public figure was to give hope to "the young gay people in the Altoona, Pennsylvanias and the Richmond, Minnesotas."

It was a revolutionary idea. National campaigns to prohibit the practice of so-called conversion therapy on gay youngsters; antibullying projects such as It Gets Better; programs that are focused on gay youth in LGBTQ centers, in the Human Rights Campaign, in the National LGBTQ Task Force, all would have been inconceivable in Harvey's day. But his pioneering conviction—that gay adults have a responsibility for the well-being of gay youth and must work for their causes and serve as their role models—is no longer debatable.

* * *

Two and a half years after Harvey's assassination the first cases of AIDS were diagnosed in America. The epidemic raged for fifteen years before protease inhibitors were finally developed to halt the inevitable fatalities caused by the devastating disease. By then hundreds of thousands of gay men had died. It took so long to develop effective drugs because the federal government was shockingly slow to fund the medical research that would save gay lives. Patrick Buchanan, the paleoconservative White House director of communications under President Ronald Reagan, did not hide the blind hatred that explains why foot-dragging on AIDS was federal policy: AIDS, Buchanan wrote in the first years of the epidemic, was simply "nature exacting retribution" for the homosexual's insult to "the natural."[8]

In the midst of the AIDS tragedy Harvey's leadership was sorely missed. His admirers were convinced that had he been alive when the epidemic struck he would have had a crucial role in the battle against the likes of Patrick Buchanan and President Reagan, who refused to even mention the term "AIDS" during his entire first four years in office. At the initial sign of the epidemic, Harvey, with all his energy and conviction and powers of persuasion, would have led a national charge to demand that money be put immediately into AIDS research.

But it is possible too that, had he lived into the 1980s,

Harvey would have been an early victim, felled himself by the disease that ripped like a cyclone through the Castro and wiped out countless numbers of his friends and constituents. If he could have chosen his fate—meaningless suffering and death by AIDS or martyrdom and the glory that followed—we can easily surmise what Harvey Milk would have preferred.

ACKNOWLEDGMENTS

MY HEARTFELT THANKS for helping me bring this biography of Harvey Milk to fruition go to my agent of almost forty years, the incomparable Sandra Dijkstra, and to my editor at Yale University Press, Ileene Smith. My gratitude goes as well to Ms. Smith's excellent assistant Heather Gold and to the talented copyeditor Lawrence Kenney.

I am grateful to members of Harvey Milk's extended family who shared with me family lore and unpublished documents and gave me invaluable insights into Harvey's life at its various stages: Michael Salem, Sam Mendales, Leslie Berg Milk, and Sherrie Feinberg.

In the course of my work on this biography I have been fortunate to encounter many generous individuals who guided me to invaluable material that helped me reconstruct Harvey Milk's life, introduced me to people who knew him personally and were willing to share their stories about him, or read my manuscript in its various stages and offered valuable feedback. I thank Randy Alfred,

David Carter, Marc Cohen, Vince Emery, Oliva Espin, Rabbi Bruce Ginsburg, Tory Hartmann, Gerard Koskovich, Paula Lichtenberg, Patricia Loughery, Glenne McElhinney, Lee Mentley, Dan Nicoletta, Nicole Murray Ramirez, Janice Steinberg, Anne Marie Walsh, Mike Weiss, and Michael Wong.

Thank you to the dear friends who graciously hosted me on my extended research trips to San Francisco and Los Angeles: Rosalind Ravasio, Linda Garber, Barbara Blinick, Katherine Gabel, and Eunice Shatz.

I cannot say thank you enough to the archivists and librarians who made my life easier by their great helpfulness and deep knowledge of the collections they administer: Susan Goldstein, Christina Moretta, Karen Sundheim, and Tim Wilson of the San Francisco Public Library; Michael Oliveras of the One National Gay and Lesbian Archives at USC; Elizabeth Cornu of the GLBT History Museum, San Francisco; Walter Meyer of the Lambda Archives, San Diego; Brian Keogh of the M. E. Grenander Special Collections and Archives at SUNY, Albany; Millie Vollono of the Hewlett-Woodmere Library on Long Island; and Jane Parr and Alex Rankin of the Howard Gotlieb Archival Research Center at Boston University.

Elva Smith, mother of Scott Smith, gifted the Harvey Milk Archives–Scott Smith Collection to the San Francisco Public Library, where it is open to scholars. This book would not have been possible without her generosity.

Nor would this book have been possible without the many people who knew Harvey Milk personally or worked on extensive projects that touched on his life and were willing to be interviewed by me and share their knowledge. My gratitude to Randy Alfred, Tom Ammiano, Rabbi Allen Bennett, Walter Caplan, Daniel Chesir, Marc Cohen, Kathleen Connell, Gwenn Craig, Nikos Diaman, John Durham, Sherrie Feinberg, Rink Foto, Sally Gearhart, Tom Greany, Robert Greenbaum, Tory Hartmann, Joyce Hunter, Cleve Jones, Debra Jones, Anne Kronenberg, Ron Lezell, Paula Lichtenberg, Bob Lynn, Ruth Mahaney, Glenne McElhinney, Sam Mendales, Lee Mentley, Dan Nicoletta, Elaine Noble, Naphtali

Offen, Nicole Murray Ramirez, Michael Salem, Sharyn Saslafsky, Carol Ruth Silver, Don Sizemore, Rick Stokes, and Susan Stryker.

Finally, I would like to thank Phyllis Irwin, my partner and now my spouse, who has made everything possible for forty-five years.

Introduction

1. Cleve Jones, San Francisco, interview #1, with author, April 12, 2013; and Anne Kronenberg, email correspondence, April 12, 2017.

2. Harvey Milk, keynote speech, at Gay Conference 5, Dallas, Texas, June 10, 1978. Transcription of speech in *An Archive of Hope: Harvey Milk's Speeches and Writings*, ed. Jason Edward Black and Charles E. Morris III (Berkeley: University of California Press, 2013), 198–210.

3. Gallup poll taken May 2–7, 2013.

4. John Schogol, "Ships to Be Named after John Basilone and Harvey Milk," *Military Times*, August 11, 2016.

5. "Not theologically oriented": Rabbi Allen Bennett, San Francisco, interview with author, March 22, 2016. The evidence for his belief in God can be found on p. 196.

6. Randy Shilts, *The Mayor of Castro Street: The Life and Times of Harvey Milk* (New York: St. Martin's, 1982), 21.

7. See, for example, the poll conducted by the Pew Research Center on October 1, 2013, "A Portrait of Jewish Americans," which found that a majority of those polled said that for them, "being Jewish is more a matter of ancestry, culture, and values than of religious observance."

8. Harvey Milk letter to Susan Davis, July 11, 1960, Susan Davis Alch Collection (GLC 19), box 1, folder 21, San Francisco Public Library. Sharyn Saslafsky, San Francisco, interview with author, December 31, 2015; Anne Kronenberg, San Francisco, interview with author; April 29, 2016; and Mel Lefer, "Memories of Harvey Milk and the Castro," *Bay Area Reporter*, May 19, 2016.

9. Harvey Milk quoted by his nephew Stuart Milk, in Iris Mann, "'Milk' Captures Doomed Life of Gay, Jewish Politician," *Jewish Journal*, December 10, 2008.

Chapter 1. The Milchs

1. I am grateful to members of Harvey Milk's extended family for permitting me to interview them and sharing family lore with me: Michael Salem, New York, April 4, 2016; Sherrie Feinberg, email correspondence, May 21, 2016; Leslie Berg Milk, email correspondence, August 4, 2016; and Sam Mendales, email correspondence, November 1, 3, 8, 14, 28, 2016. Information was also gleaned from the U.S. Census of 1900, Kansas City, Kansas; the 1910 U.S. Census, Nassau County, New York; the 1915 New York State Census, Nassau County, New York; the 1940 U.S. Census, Hempstead, Nassau, New York; the July 17, 1897, manifest for the ship *Taormina*, frame 85, line 1; and the July 5, 1903, manifest for the ship *Moltke*, frame 339, lines 24–30. The manifest shows that a sixteen-year-old niece, Frumine Milch, accompanied Hinde and the five children on their voyage to America.

2. Family lore said that Milk's Department Store was established in 1898; an ad for the store in 1952 in the "Five Towns Yellow Book" affirmed that date (Hewlett-Woodmere Public Library Local History Collection). However, the 1900 U.S. Census for Kansas City, cited above, shows that Morris was still living with his stepbrother at that time.

3. Email correspondence with Sam Mendales, whose mother, Helen Milk Mendales, was Harvey's first cousin and the extended family's historian and archivist.

4. Ibid.

5. Morris Milk obituary, *Brooklyn Eagle*, May 3, 1947; and proclamation from Congregation Sons of Israel honoring Morris as a chief supporter of the Hebrew school and "a man of charity and good will": I am grateful to Sam Mendales for sharing a copy of this proclamation with me.

6. Harvey Milk quoted in Francis J. Moriarty, "Cityside: Good Night, Sweet Prince," *Bay Area Reporter*, December 7–20, 1978.

7. Minerva Eleanore Karns's Honorable Discharge Papers, Harvey Milk Archives–Scott Smith Collection (GLC 35), box 2, folder 46, San Francisco Public Library.

8. Carol Pugash, "Brother Learned Recently Milk Was Gay— and Afraid," *San Francisco Examiner*, November 30, 1978.

9. I am grateful to Michael Salem, Harvey Milk's cousin who was the subject of the *pidyon haben*, for sharing this video with me. It can be seen on YouTube: "Harvey Milk Home Movies."

10. Recollection of Robert Milk in Randy Shilts, "The Life and Death of Harvey Milk," *Christopher Street*, March 1979, 25–43.

11. David Behrens, "Ku Klux Klan Flares Up on Long Island," *Newsday* (1998): LIHistory.com.

12. "Klan Parade a Mile Long: Men and Women Take Part in Bay Shore Demonstration," *New York Times*, November 8, 1923.

13. Beherns, "Ku Klux Klan Flares Up."

14. Ryan Shaffer, "Long Island Nazis: A Local Synthesis of Transnational Politics," *Long Island History Journal* 21/2 (Spring 2010); and Nicholas Casey, "Nazi Past of Long Island Hamlet," *New York Times*, October 19, 2015.

15. Letter from Robert Milk to Harvey Milk, January 4, 1978, Harvey Milk Archives–Scott Smith Collection (GLC 35), box 5, folder 6, San Francisco Public Library.

16. Randy Shilts, *The Mayor of Castro Street: The Life and Times of Harvey Milk* (New York: St. Martin's, 1982), 10.

17. Proclamation from Congregation Sons of Israel.

18. Harvey Milk, interview with Davidlee Rinker, *Kalendar* (San Francisco), August 17, 1973, Harvey Milk Archives–Scott Smith Collection (GLC 35), series 2a, box 3, San Francisco Public Library.

19. Rabbi Elias Blackowitz, "A Letter to Parents," *Congregation Sons of Israel Newsletter*, November 1945. Elias Blackowitz was the rabbi at Congregation Sons of Israel from 1942 to 1946. I am grateful to Rabbi Bruce Ginsburg of Congregation Sons of Israel and the librarians of the Hewlett-Woodmere Public Library for sharing with me historical documents related to Congregation Sons of Israel.

20. Stuart Milk, interview with Randy Hope, "Remembering Harvey Milk," *Gay and Lesbian Times*, May 21, 2009.

21. Pat Vesey, interview with Douglas Marshall-Steele, April 2009, Towardequality.org.

Chapter 2. Deep, Dark Secrets

1. John Anderson, "Got Milk? Long Island Did with Harvey's Family," *Newsday*, November 28, 2008; and Randy Shilts, *The Mayor of Castro Street: The Life and Times of Harvey Milk* (New York: St. Martin's, 1982), 6.

2. Harvey Milk, Gay Freedom Day speech, printed in "Milk Forum," *Bay Area Reporter*, June 25, 1978.

3. Harvey Milk, draft for article, "Castro Street—Home," Harvey Milk Archives–Scott Smith Collection (GLC 35), box 9, folder 55, San Francisco Public Library.

4. Harvey Milk, interview with Davidlee Rinker, *Kalendar* (San Francisco), August 17, 1973.

5. Robert Milk, interview with Carol Pugash, "Brother Learned Recently Milk Was Gay—and Afraid," *San Francisco Examiner*, November 30, 1978.

6. Eileen Mulcahy (Harvey Milk's classmate), interview with Randy Shilts, November 7, 1980, in Randy Shilts Papers (GLC 43), box 29, San Francisco Public Library.

7. Dick Brown (Harvey Milk's classmate), interview with

Randy Shilts, November 10, 1980, in Randy Shilts Papers (GLC 43), box 29, San Francisco Public Library.

8. Artie Schiller, interview with Douglas Marshall-Steele, Towardequality.org.

9. Pugash, "Brother Learned Recently Milk Was Gay."

10. In 1962 the New York State College for Teachers became SUNY, Albany. The most complete history of the campus is Kendall Birr, *A Tradition of Excellence: A Sesquicentennial History of the University at Albany* (Virginia Beach, Va.: Donning, 1994).

11. Arnold Newman et al., "B'nai Chaim, Brothers for Life: A Personal Anecdotal History of Kappa Beta Fraternity," Kappa Beta Collection, box 2, folder 15; see also Nahum Lewis, memoirs of a founder of Kappa Beta, in box 1, folder 1, SUNY Albany Special Collections. "B'nai" is more accurately translated as "Sons of."

12. *State College News*, January 14, 1949.

13. "The Story of Chanukah, the Jewish Festival of Lights—a Play Presented by Hillel," *State College News*, December 12, 1947; and "Hillel to Open Jewish Passover with Seder Feast," *State College News*, April 16, 1948. Randy Shilts, who interviewed Harvey Milk's college classmates in 1980, confirms his attendance at meetings of the Intercollegiate Zionist Federation of America and Hillel, in *Mayor of Castro Street*, 13.

14. "Zionist Group Slates Meeting Next Week," *State College News*, February 6, 1948.

15. *State College News*, November 7, 1947, 4.

16. Joseph Persico, '52, interview in "Harvey Milk, '51: From Intramural Athlete to Civil Rights Icon," *UAlbany Magazine*, March 2009.

17. Eade and Schultze, "Common-Stater" column, May 5, 1950, 2.

18. Myskansia candidates' qualifications: *State College News*, April 25, 1950, 6.

19. Interview with Joseph Zanchelli, '51, "Harvey Milk, '51, Honored for His Vision and Courage," *UAlbany Magazine*, October 2009.

20. The predicted princesses were all prominent male students

whose first names, like Harvey's, were turned into women's names of the same initial, e.g., William Englehart became Wilhimena Englehart: Gorskie and Kyle, "Common-Stater," *State College News*, October 27, 1950.

21. See my discussion of these early homosexual witch hunts on college campuses in *The Gay Revolution: The Story of the Struggle* (New York: Simon and Schuster, 2015), xi–xiv and chapter 4.

22. Joseph Persico, interview.

23. Harvey Milk, Letter to the Sports Editor, *State College News*, September 22, 1950.

24. Harvey Milk, "The Spectator," *State College News*, January 6, 1950.

25. Harvey Milk, "No One Asked Me But . . . ," *State College News*, September 29, 1950.

26. Harvey Milk, "Communications," *State College News*, February 16, 1951.

27. "Communications," *State College News*, March 9, 1951.

28. Harvey Milk, "Common-Stater," *State College News*, April 20, 1951. Randy Shilts suggests that the reason Harvey resigned as sports editor in the middle of his senior year was that he'd been arrested for "disorderly conduct" (*The Mayor of Castro Street*, 14), but that reason for his resignation is dubious because very soon after he stopped writing sports columns he began writing opinion columns.

29. Harvey Milk, "Common-Stater," *State College News*, February 23, 1951.

30. "College Fraternity Men Back Restriction Rules," *St. Petersburg Times*, November 30, 1957.

31. Harvey Milk, "In the Right Direction," *State College News*, April 27, 1951.

32. Harvey Milk, "Common-Stater," *State College News*, April 13, 1951, and May 11, 1951.

33. Harvey's transcript from New York State College for Teachers, Albany, in Harvey Milk Archives–Scott Smith Collection (GLC 43), box 2, folder 58, San Francisco Public Library.

Chapter 3. Drifting

1. Harvey Milk, interview with Davidlee Rinker, *Kalendar* (San Francisco), August 17, 1973, in Harvey Milk Archives–Scott Smith Collection (GLC 43), series 2a, box 3, San Francisco Public Library. Harvey did write occasional columns for *State College News* that had a patriotic ring. For example, when Congress was threatening to impeach Harry Truman over his firing of the popular General Douglas MacArthur, Harvey came to Truman's defense, declaring, "A little faith in our president wouldn't hurt the nation": Harvey Milk, "The Common-Stater," April 13, 1951.

2. For a discussion of the military's changing policy in these years, see my book *The Gay Revolution: The Story of the Struggle* (New York: Simon and Schuster, 2015), chapter 3.

3. Allan Bérubé, *Coming Out Under Fire: The History of Gay Men and Women in World War Two* (New York: Free Press, 1990), 116.

4. I am grateful to Walter Meyer of the Lambda Archives of San Diego for first calling my attention to locker clubs in San Diego; see also John Nichols, "The Way It Was: Gay Life in World War II America," *QQ [Queen's Quarterly]: Magazine for Gay Guys*, August 1975.

5. Jack Lait and Lee Mortimer, *U.S.A. Confidential* (New York: Crown, 1952).

6. Randy Shilts writes in *The Mayor of Castro Street: The Life and Times of Harvey Milk* (New York: St. Martin's, 1982), 16, that because so many sailors were being shipped out to Korea from San Diego housing was strained; they often had to sleep on the floor at the YMCA. According to Shilts, Harvey Milk would tempt them to come to his apartment with the line, "Hey, sailor, do you want to sleep on a concrete floor or a bed?"

7. See the Harvey Milk Papers in the Susan Davis Alch Collection (GLC 19), series 1, San Francisco Public Library. I am grateful to Tim Wilson, archivist at the SFPL, for providing me with biographical information about Susan Davis Alch.

8. Ibid., letter of June 21, 1960.

9. Ibid., letter of January 21, 1958.

10. *Miami Herald*, August 10, 1954, sec. 2, 1, and *Miami Herald*, September 2, 1954, sec. 1, 1.

11. See timeline in *The Harvey Milk Interviews: In His Own Words*, ed. Vince Emery (San Francisco: Vince Emery Productions, 2012), 10.

12. Letter: Harvey Milk to Susan Davis (Alch), January 15, 1958, Susan Davis Alch Collection (GLC 19), folder 4, San Francisco Public Library.

13. Shilts, *The Mayor of Castro Street*, 18–20.

14. Letter: Harvey Milk to Susan Davis (Alch), January 15, 1958, Susan Davis Alch Collection (GLC 19), folder 4, San Francisco Public Library.

15. Robert Greenbaum, Woodmere, New York, interview with author, April 5, 2016.

16. Vince Emery, "The Unknown Adventures of Harvey Milk in Dallas," *Dallas Voice*, May 17, 2012.

17. Letter: Harvey Milk to Susan Davis (Alch), January 15, 1958, Susan Davis Alch Collection (GLC 19), folder 4, San Francisco Public Library.

18. Shilts, *The Mayor of Castro Street*, 21.

19. Letter: Harvey Milk to Susan Davis (Alch), January 21, 1958, Susan Davis Alch Collection (GLC 19), folder 4, San Francisco Public Library.

20. Michael Salem, New York, interview with author, April 4, 2016.

21. Letter: Harvey Milk to Susan Davis (Alch), August 1, 1960, Susan Davis Alch Collection (GLC 19), folder 22, San Francisco Public Library.

22. Letter: Harvey Milk to Susan Davis (Alch), December 19, 1958, Susan Davis Alch Collection (GLC 19), folder 16, San Francisco Public Library.

23. Letter: Harvey Milk to Susan Davis (Alch), February 8, 1961, Susan Davis Alch Collection (GLC 19), folder 25, San Francisco Public Library.

24. Letter: Harvey Milk to Susan Davis (Alch), August 27,

1958, Susan Davis Alch Collection (GLC 19), folder 8, San Francisco Public Library.

25. Letter: Harvey Milk to Susan Davis (Alch), July 11, 1960, Susan Davis Alch Collection (GLC 19), folder 21, San Francisco Public Library.

26. Letter: Harvey Milk to Susan Davis (Alch), September 14, 1961, Susan Davis Alch Collection (GLC 19), folder 25, San Francisco Public Library.

27. Letter: Harvey Milk to Joe Campbell, n.d., Harvey Milk–Joe Campbell Collection (GLC 20), folder 46, San Francisco Public Library.

28. Letter: Harvey Milk to Susan Davis, September 14, 1961, Susan Davis Alch Collection (GLC 19), folder 28, San Francisco Public Library.

29. Letter: Harvey Milk to Joe Campbell, December 1, 1961, Harvey Milk–Joe Campbell Collection (GLC 20), folder 28, San Francisco Public Library.

30. Joe's stay in Tennessee was brief. In New York again, he eventually found an arty crowd to hang with and was introduced into The Factory, Andy Warhol's studio, where speed freaks, drag queens, porno actors, and other fringe types helped Warhol make grainy 16mm movies and the pop art that he sold for outrageous sums. In Warhol's 1965 film *My Hustler* Joe played Sugar Plum Fairy, an older male prostitute who pushes a pretty young man into prostitution. But Joe's wild years ended, and he left New York permanently to move to Marin County in northern California. He died there in 2005, his partner of twenty-nine years at his bedside. Joe had become the avatar of domesticity and devotion that Harvey had once begged him to be.

31. Shilts, *The Mayor of Castro Street*, 24. Shilts and Martin Duberman (*Stonewall* [New York: Dutton, 1993], 86–88) both interviewed Craig Rodwell for the stories they tell about the relationship. Rodwell died in 1993.

32. I discuss Craig Rodwell's contributions to the gay movement in my book *The Gay Revolution*, chapters 8, 11, and 12.

33. Shilts, *The Mayor of Castro Street*, 22.

34. Letter: Harvey Milk to Joe Campbell, March 6, 1963, Harvey Milk–Joe Campbell Collection (GLC 20), folder 10, San Francisco Public Library.

35. Letter: Harvey Milk to Joe Campbell, March 8, 1963, Harvey Milk–Joe Campbell Collection (GLC 20), item 14, San Francisco Public Library.

36. Harvey's letter to Joe Campbell from Puerto Rico on March 8, 1963, is written on this stationery.

37. Letter: C. Milner to Joe Campbell, March 8, 1963, Harvey Milk–Joe Campbell Collection (GLC 20), item 15, San Francisco Public Library.

38. Telegram: Harvey Milk to Joe Campbell, March 10, 1963, Harvey Milk–Joe Campbell Collection (GLC 20), item 16, San Francisco Public Library.

39. Lisa J. Huriash, "How Jews Shaped Miami Beach," *Sun Sentinel*, January 13, 1999.

Chapter 4. Will-o'-the-Wisps

1. Dan Nicoletta, interview with Jim van Buskirk, video, *Harvey Milk: A Personal View*, 1998.

2. Randy Shilts, *The Mayor of Castro Street: The Life and Times of Harvey Milk* (New York: St. Martin's, 1982), 30–31.

3. Ibid., 31–32. Harvey Milk's extant address book contains birthdates. Galen's birthdate is listed as October 18, 1946: Harvey Milk Archives–Scott Smith Collection (GLC 35), box 1, folder 1, San Francisco Public Library. In *The Harvey Milk Interviews: In His Own Words*, ed. Vince Emery (San Francisco: Vince Emery Productions, 2012), 342, Emery corrects Randy Shilts's error in *The Mayor of Castro Street:* Shilts implies (30) that the relationship between Harvey and Galen began when Galen was sixteen years old, which would have been almost as soon as Galen arrived in New York.

4. Dan Nicoletta, interview with Jim van Buskirk.

5. Vince Emery, "The Unknown Adventures of Harvey Milk in Dallas," *Dallas Voice*, May 17, 2012.

6. Clive Barnes, "'Futz!' Opens at the De Lys," *New York Times*, June 14, 1968.

7. Eleanor Lester, "'Of Course There Were Some Limits,'" *New York Times*, May 19, 1968.

8. Letter: Harvey Milk to Joe Campbell, December 24, 1968, Harvey Milk–Joe Campbell Collection (GLC 20), San Francisco Public Library.

9. Scott Smith, interview with Randy Shilts, interview #2, November 26, 1980, box 29, Randy Shilts Papers (GLC 43), San Francisco Public Library.

10. Shilts, *The Mayor of Castro Street*, 39.

11. My information about Harvey's termination at Barth comes from the Scott Smith interview #2, cited above; Julie Smith, "The Second Time Around for Milk," *San Francisco Chronicle*, October 23, 1975; and Henry Marx, "Harvey Milk, the Candid Political Activist of San Francisco's Gay Community, Speaks," *Zenger's* (San Francisco State University), November 3, 1976. However, in a later newspaper interview Harvey Milk claimed that he left J. Barth because the company "merged with another firm and his job was eliminated": W. E. Barnes, "An 'Unofficial Supervisor' Gets a Shot at Real Power," *San Francisco Examiner*, November 30, 1977.

12. Marc Cohen, New York, interview with author, September 4, 2016.

13. Vincent Canby, "Screen: 'Alex in Wonderland,'" *New York Times*, December 23, 1970.

14. Letter: Harvey Milk to Joe Campbell, Harvey Milk–Joe Campbell Collection (GLC 20), San Francisco Public Library.

15. The suicide of Jack Lira, Harvey's partner in 1978, is described on p. 193–94. In 1980, when Galen McKinley was thirty-four, he stepped out the window of Tom O'Horgan's eighth-floor Broadway apartment, balanced a moment on the ledge, and jumped.

16. Marc Cohen, interview with author.

17. John Gruen, "Do You Mind Critics Calling You Cheap, Decadent . . . ?" *New York Times*, January 2, 1972.

18. Scott Smith, interview #2 with Randy Shilts, November 26, 1980, in Randy Shilts Papers (GLC 43), box 29, Harvey Milk–Scott Smith Collection, San Francisco Public Library. On the program for *Lenny*, Cohen went by the pseudonym Marker Bloomst. Galen was the production stage manager.

19. Marc Cohen, interview with author.

20. Clive Barnes, "The New York of 'Inner City,'" *New York Times*, December 20, 1971.

21. Scott Smith, interview #2.

22. Marc Cohen, interview with author.

23. Ibid.

24. Scott Smith, interview #2.

Chapter 5. "Who Is This Mr. Yoyo?"

1. Scott Smith, interview #2 with Randy Shilts, November 26, 1980, Randy Shilts Papers (GLC 43), box 29, San Francisco Public Library.

2. Ibid.

3. Timothy Stewart-Winter, "The Castro: Origins to the Age of Milk," *Gay and Lesbian Review* (January/February 2009), 12–15.

4. Harvey Milk, interview with Davidlee Rinker, *Kalendar Magazine*, August 17, 1973.

5. Scott Smith, interview #3 with Randy Shilts, December 1, 1980, Randy Shilts Papers (GLC 43), box 29, San Francisco Public Library.

6. Scott Smith, interview #3.

7. Sharon Saslafsky, San Francisco, interview with author, December 31, 2015; and Anne Kronenberg, "Everybody Needed Milk," in *Out in the Castro: Desire, Promise, Activism*, ed. Winston Leyland (San Francisco: Leyland Publications, 2002).

8. Scott Smith, interview #3.

9. Ibid.

10. Ibid.

11. See the discussion of the Black Cat in my book *The Gay Revolution: The Story of the Struggle* (New York: Simon and Schuster, 2015), 103, 644.

12. Card, Harvey Milk to Scott Smith, Harvey Milk Archives–Scott Smith Collection (GLC 35), box 2, folder 18, San Francisco Public Library.

13. Picture of Scott wearing the chai in Harvey Milk Archives–Scott Smith Collection (GLC 35), box 15, folder 14, picture #001124A, San Francisco Public Library.

14. Photograph of Castro Camera store window in 1973, in *Milk: A Pictorial History of Harvey Milk*, ed. Dustin Lance Black (New York: Newmarket Press, 2009).

15. Bob Ross (n.d.), Tom Randol (November 2, 1980), and Carl Carlson (n.d.), interviews with Randy Shilts, Randy Shilts Papers (GLC 43), box 29, San Francisco Public Library.

16. I discuss Foster and his Democratic National Convention speech in my book *The Gay Revolution*, 254–56.

17. Rick Stokes, interview with author, May 2, 2016, San Francisco.

18. Jim Foster, interview with Randy Shilts, in Randy Shilts Papers (GLC 43), box 29, San Francisco Public Library.

19. Randy Alfred, San Francisco, interview #1 with author, February 8, 2016.

20. Jim Foster, interview with Randy Shilts.

21. Dudley Clendinen and Adam Nagourney, *Out for Good: The Struggle to Build a Gay Rights Movement in America* (New York: Simon and Schuster, 1999), 339.

22. Questionnaire reprinted in *The Harvey Milk Interviews: In His Own Words*, ed. Vince Emery (San Francisco: Vince Emery Productions, 2012), 35–43.

23. Harvey Milk interview with Davidlee Rinker, *Kalendar Magazine*, August 17, 1973.

24. Harvey Milk to *Advocate* editor, August 15, 1973, ONE Subject Files, coll. 2012-001, ONE National Gay and Lesbian Archives, USC, Los Angeles.

25. "S.F. Gay Campaigning for the Straight Vote Too," *Advocate*, October 10, 1973.

26. "Shopkeeper Runs for Supervisor," *San Francisco Examiner*, July 27, 1973.

27. "San Francisco's Strange Alliance," *San Francisco Chronicle*, September 25, 1973.

28. Herb Caen, "File and Forget," *San Francisco Chronicle*, August 16, 1973.

29. Scott Smith interview #3.

30. Jennifer L. Thomas, "Pro-Gays Out for Supervisor" (1973), in Harvey Milk Archives–Scott Smith Collection (GLC 35), clipping file, box 26, folder 1, San Francisco Public Library.

31. Address to the San Francisco NWPC, September 5, 1973, in Harvey Milk Correspondence, ONE subject file, 2012-001, ONE National Gay and Lesbian Archives, USC, Los Angeles.

32. Address to the Joint International Longshoremen and Warehousemen's Union, September 30, 1973, Harvey Milk Archives–Scott Smith Collection (GLC 35), box 9, folder 45, San Francisco Public Library.

33. Mike Wong manuscript memoir, "Harvey," November 1980, in Randy Shilts Papers (GLC 43), box 29, San Francisco Public Library.

34. Ibid.

35. Tory and Bill Hartmann (friends and neighbors of Harvey Milk), interview with Randy Shilts, in Randy Shilts Papers (GLC 43), box 29, San Francisco Public Library.

36. Candidate's Campaign Statement, 1973, Harvey Milk Archives–Scott Smith Collection (GLC 35), box 3, folder 1, San Francisco Public Library.

37. Clarence Johnson, "San Francisco Measure to Limit Candidates' Spending," *San Francisco Chronicle*, February 2, 1995.

38. Ad signed by thirty-eight leaders in the gay community, including Jim Foster, Jo Daly, Rick Stokes, Del Martin, and Phyllis Lyon, *Kalendar*, October 12, 1973.

39. *Foghorn*, University of San Francisco student paper, October 19, 1973.

40. David Talbot, *Season of the Witch: Enchantment, Terror and Deliverance in the City of Love* (New York: Free Press, 2012), 178.

41. Scott Smith, interview #3.

Chapter 6. Learning to Put Up the Chairs

1. Scott Smith interview #3, December 1, 1980, Randy Shilts (GLC 43), box 29, San Francisco Public Library.

2. Timothy Stewart-Winter, "The Castro: Origins to the Age of Milk," *Gay and Lesbian Review* (January/February 2009), 12–15.

3. Dudley Clendinen and Adam Nagourney, *Out for Good: The Struggle to Build a Gay Rights Movement in America* (New York: Simon and Schuster, 1999), 339; and Ron Williams, "I Remember Harvey," *Web Castro: 94114*, April 20, 1997.

4. Scott Smith interview #4, December 15, 1980, Randy Shilts Papers (GLC 43), box 29, San Francisco Public Library.

5. Ibid.; and Dan Nicoletta, letter to his parents and siblings, 1975. I am grateful to Mr. Nicoletta for sharing this letter with me.

6. *An Archive of Hope: Harvey Milk's Speeches and Writings*, ed. Jason Edward Black and Charles E. Morris III (Berkeley: University of California Press), 18.

7. Randy Shilts, *The Mayor of Castro Street: The Life and Times of Harvey Milk* (New York: St. Martin's, 1982), 90.

8. Scott Smith interview #4; and Danny Nicoletta interview in Randy Shilts Papers, October 5, 1980 (GLC 43), box 29, San Francisco Public Library.

9. Sharyn Saslafsky, San Francisco, interview with author, December 31, 2015.

10. Letter, Harvey Milk to City of San Francisco Hall of Justice, February 14, 1974, Harvey Milk Archives–Scott Smith Collection (GLC 43), box 9, folder 55, San Francisco Public Library.

11. Lee Mentley, San Francisco, interview with author, February 22, 2016.

12. Harvey Milk, "Waves from the Left," *Sentinel* (San Francisco), March 28, 1974.

13. GLF Statement of Purpose, printed in *Rat* (underground New Left newspaper), August 12, 1969.

14. Harvey Milk, "Waves from the Left," *Sentinel* (San Francisco), February 14, 1974.

15. Scott Smith interview #4.

16. "Waves from the Left, February 14, 1974."

17. Harvey Milk, draft, January 8, 1974, in Harvey Milk Archives–Scott Smith Collection (GLC 35), box 9, folder 55, San Francisco Public Library. This article appeared in *Vector* (San Francisco) on February 1, 1974.

18. Harvey Milk, "Gay Economic Power," draft, 1974, in Harvey Milk Archives–Scott Smith Collection (GLC 35), box 9, folder 55, San Francisco Public Library.

19. Harvey Milk, "Buy Gay," draft, 1974, in Harvey Milk Archives–Scott Smith Collection (GLC 35), box 9, folder 55, San Francisco Public Library.

20. GLF leader Bob Kohler, quoted in Randy Wicker, "The Wicker Basket," *Gay*, August 24, 1970.

21. Allan Baird, interview with Randy Shilts, December 9, 1980, Randy Shilts Papers (GLC 43), box 29, San Francisco Public Library.

22. Dan Baum, *Citizen Coors: A Grand Family Saga of Business, Politics, and Beer* (New York: William Morrow, 2001), 66.

23. Harvey Milk, "Milk Forum: Teamsters Seek Gay Help," *Bay Area Reporter*, November 27, 1974.

24. Josh Hollands, "How a Battle for Union Rights at Coors Pushed Back Homophobia," *Socialist Review* (February 2014).

25. Harvey Milk, "Milk Forum," clipping, *Bay Area Reporter*, in subject file: Harvey Milk, Coll. 2012-001, ONE National Gay and Lesbian Archives, USC, Los Angeles; and Hollands, "How a Battle for Union Rights Pushed Back Homophobia."

26. Tom O'Horgan quoted in Frank Robinson interview by Randy Shilts, August 14, 1980, Randy Shilts Papers (GLC 43), box 29, San Francisco Public Library.

Chapter 7. Strike Two

1. David Johnston, "One Gay Candidate Runs to Win," *Berkeley Barb*, October 24, 1975.

2. Dan Nicoletta, Grants Pass, Oregon, interview with author, April 15, 2016.

3. "1975 Supervisor's Campaign Finances—Candidate's Cam-

paign Statements," Harvey Milk Archives–Scott Smith Collection (GLC 35), box 3, folder 11, San Francisco Public Library.

4. Lee Mentley, San Francisco, interview with author, February 22, 2016.

5. Mike Wong, "Harvey" (a memoir written at Randy Shilts's request), November 1980, Randy Shilts Papers (GLC 43), box 19, San Francisco Public Library.

6. Mike Wong, email correspondence with author, August 9, 2017.

7. Ibid.

8. Walter Caplan (a close friend of Rivaldo, who died in 2007), San Francisco, interview with author, May 19, 2016.

9. Ibid.

10. Jim Rivaldo, "Remembering How Harvey Milk Paved the Way," *Bay Area Reporter*, June 21, 2001.

11. Jim Rivaldo quoted in *Milk: A Pictorial History*, ed. Dustin Lance Black (New York: Newmarket Press, 2009), 50.

12. Frank Robinson, foreword to *An Archive of Hope: Harvey Milk's Speeches and Writings*, ed. Jason Edward Black and Charles E. Morris III (Berkeley: University of California Press, 2013); and Albert Williams, "Our Town: Milk and Chicago's Frank Robinson," *The Reader* (Chicago), November 27, 2008.

13. Ibid.

14. Del Martin and Phyllis Lyon, interview with Randy Shilts, n.d., Randy Shilts Papers (GLC 43), box 19, San Francisco Public Library.

15. Johnston, "One Gay Candidate Runs to Win."

16. Harvey Milk, campaign letter, February 26, 1975, ONE Subject Files, coll. 2012-001, ONE National Gay and Lesbian Archives, USC, Los Angeles.

17. Johnston, "One Gay Candidate Runs to Win."

18. George Evankovich interview with Randy Shilts, n.d., Randy Shilts Papers (GLC 43), box 19, San Francisco Public Library.

19. *An Archive of Hope: Harvey Milk's Speeches and Writings*, ed. Jason Edward Black and Charles E. Morris III (Berkeley: University of California Press, 2013), 118.

20. Harvey Milk, "Milk Forum: Gay Groupie Syndrome," *Bay Area Reporter*, February 20, 1975.

21. Herb Caen column, *San Francisco Chronicle*, September 10, 1975.

22. Leon Broschura, interview with Randy Shilts, n.d., Randy Shilts Papers (GLC 43), box 19, San Francisco Public Library.

23. Harvey Milk to Scott Smith, note, September 5, 1975, Harvey Milk Archives–Scott Smith Collection (GLC 35), box 2, folder 18, San Francisco Public Library.

24. Lee Mentley, interview with author.

25. Quoted in Shilts, *The Mayor of Castro Street*, 107.

Chapter 8. Milk vs. the Machine

1. David Talbot, *Season of the Witch: Enchantment, Terror, and Deliverance in the City of Love* (New York: Free Press, 2012), 253.

2. Ibid.

3. Dennis Peron, interview with Randy Shilts, Randy Shilts Papers (GLC 43), box 19, San Francisco Public Library.

4. "New Permit Board Overrules Police," *San Francisco Chronicle*, February 3, 1976.

5. Carol Ruth Silver, San Francisco, interview with author, May 5, 2016; Carol Ruth Silver, interview with Mike Weiss, Double Play Collection (SFH 34), box 1, folder 63, San Francisco Public Library; and Mike Wong, "Harvey," November 1980, Randy Shilts Papers (GLC 43), box 29, San Francisco Public Library.

6. Scott Smith interview #4 with Randy Shilts, December 15, 1980, Randy Shilts Papers (GLC 43), box 29, San Francisco Public Library.

7. Wong, "Harvey"; and "Oral History Interview with Leo T. McCarthy" (conducted 1995–96) by Carole Hicke, State Government Oral History Program, California State Archives.

8. "Moscone Warns New Appointee," *San Francisco Chronicle*, February 7, 1976.

9. "Gay Activist Will Run for Assembly Seat," *San Francisco Examiner*, February 7, 1976.

10. "Milk's Right to Run Defended," *San Francisco Examiner*,

February 9, 1976; and "Kopp Takes on 'Unholy Alliance,'" *San Francisco Examiner*, February 10, 1976.

11. George Mendenhall, "Finding the Answers: Harvey Milk vs. the Machine," *Bay Area Reporter*, February 19, 1976.

12. "Statement of Harvey Milk, Candidate for the 16th Assembly District," Harvey Milk Archives–Scott Smith Collection (GLC 35), box 4, folder 8, San Francisco Public Library.

13. Walter Caplan, San Francisco, interview with author, May 19, 2016.

14. Henry Marx, "Harvey Milk, the Candid Political Activist of San Francisco's Gay Community, Speaks," *Zenger's* (San Francisco State University), November 3, 1976; John Ryckman, interview with Randy Shilts, September 23, 1980, Randy Shilts Papers (GLC 43), box 29, San Francisco Public Library.

15. Sasha Gregory-Lewis, "In San Francisco, Milk Gets Canned but Keeps on Running," *Advocate*, April 7, 1976; and Wayne Friday, "World of Wayne: What Makes Harvey Run," *Bay Area Reporter*, April 1, 1976.

16. Quoted in *An Archive of Hope: Harvey Milk's Speeches and Writings*, ed. Jason Edward Black and Charles E. Morris III, introduction notes, p. 25.

17. Gregory-Lewis, "In San Francisco, Milk Gets Canned."

18. Randy Alfred, San Francisco, interview #1 with author, February 8, 2016.

19. Elaine Noble, Santa Rosa Beach, Florida, interview with author, March 26, 2016.

20. See my book *The Gay Revolution*, 707.

21. Jim Jones sermon, Philadelphia, 1976, transcript Q162: Peoples Temple audiotapes, Jonestown Institute, web archive.

22. Anthony Sullivan letter to Jim Jones, March 24, 1976, Peoples Temple Records, MS 3800, box 1, folder 14, California Historical Society.

23. Senator Milton Marks, "Relative to Commending Reverend Jim Jones and People's Temple" (California Senate Rules Committee, 1976).

24. Harvey Milk letter to Jim Jones, March 22, 1976, Peoples

Temple Records, MS 3800, box 1, folder 14, California Historical Society.

25. Dennis Peron interview with Randy Shilts, Randy Shilts Papers (GLC 43), box 19, San Francisco Public Library.

26. Mike Wong, "Harvey"; and Randy Shilts, *The Mayor of Castro Street: The Life and Times of Harvey Milk* (New York: St. Martin's, 1982), 145.

27. Letter, Harvey Milk to Scott Smith, n.d., Harvey Milk Archives–Scott Smith Collection (GLC 35), box 2, folder 18, San Francisco Public Library.

28. Harvey Milk to Scott Smith, card, n.d., Harvey Milk Archives–Scott Smith Collection (GLC 35), box 2, folder 18, San Francisco Public Library.

29. Ron Moscowitz, "The Summing Up: Harvey Milk Blames Two Factors in Defeat," *San Francisco Chronicle*, June 10, 1976.

30. Letter to Harvey Milk from Mr. Joseph X. Polite, promotion director, and Mr. Thomas Manney, executive director of Muslim Temple #26, Harvey Milk Archives–Scott Smith Collection (GLC 35), box 3, folder 42, San Francisco Public Library.

31. Frank Robinson, interview with Randy Shilts, August 14, 1980, Randy Shilts Papers (GLC 43), box 19, San Francisco Public Library.

Chapter 9. Victory!

1. Manifesto quoted in Donna J. Graves and Shayne E. Watson, "Citywide Historic Context Statement for LGBTQ History in San Francisco," prepared for the City and County of San Francisco, October 2015.

2. Rick Stokes, San Francisco, interview with author, May 2, 2016.

3. Flyer: "Harvey Milk Speaks Out—District 5," Randy Shilts Papers (GLC 43), box 29, San Francisco Public Library.

4. Bill Sievert, "Divided They Stand: The Milk–Stokes Split," *Advocate*, July 13, 1977.

5. David Talbot, *Season of the Witch: Enchantment, Terror, and Deliverance in the City of Love* (New York: Free Press, 2012), 265.

6. Tom Greaney (former Alice Club member), San Diego, interview with author, June 2, 2016.

7. Kathleen Connell (former San Francisco lesbian activist), San Diego, interview with author, January 7, 2016.

8. Harvey Milk, "Gay Economic Power," Milk Forum, *Bay Area Reporter*, September 15, 1977; and Ruth Mahaney, San Francisco, interview with author, February 28, 2016.

9. Anne Kronenberg, San Francisco, interview with author, April 29, 2016; Anne Kronenberg, "Everybody Needed Milk," in *Out in the Castro: Desire, Promise, Activism*, ed. Winston Leyland (San Francisco: Leyland Publications, 2002); and Anne Kronenberg, interview with Patricia Loughery, November 28, 2008. I am grateful to Patricia Loughery for sharing a transcript of this interview with me.

10. Harvey saved the newsletters, with Anne Kronenberg's address on the mailing labels: Harvey Milk Archives–Scott Smith Collection (GLC 35), box 9, folder 40, San Francisco Public Library.

11. Lee Mentley, San Francisco, interview with author, February 22, 2016.

12. Anne Kronenberg, interview with author.

13. Mel Lefer, "Memories of Harvey Milk and the Castro," *Bay Area Reporter*, May 19, 2016.

14. John Ryckman, interview with Randy Shilts, September 23, 1980, Randy Shilts Papers (GLC 43), box 20, San Francisco Public Library.

15. Harvey Milk to Jack Lira, January 24, 1977, Harvey Milk Archives–Scott Smith Collection (GLC 35), box 21, folder 2, San Francisco Public Library.

16. Anne Kronenberg; Dan Nicoletta; Nicole Murray Ramirez, interviews with author; and Rink Foto, interview with author, San Francisco, May 2, 2016.

17. *Miami Herald*, June 6, 1977; and David W. Hacker, "Anita Bryant Tells Why She's Against Gay Rights," *National Observer*, March 12, 1977.

18. See my book *The Gay Revolution: The Story of the Struggle* (New York: Simon and Schuster, 2015), part 6: "How Anita Bryant

Advanced Gay and Lesbian Civil Rights," for a more extensive discussion.

19. See ibid., 53–112, for a discussion of the homophile movement.

20. Randy Alfred, San Francisco, interview #2 with author, May 16, 2017; and Tom Ammiano, San Francisco, interview with author, May 6, 2016.

21. Cleve Jones, San Francisco, interviews with author, April 12, 2013, and April 11, 2017.

22. Nicole Murray Ramirez, San Diego, interview with author, January 5, 2016; and Danny Nicoletta, Grants Pass, Oregon, interview with author, April 15, 2016.

23. *Noe Valley Voice* interview, September 1977, report in *The Harvey Milk Interviews: In His Own Words*, ed. Vince Emery (San Francisco: Vince Emery Productions, 2012), 121.

24. Herbert Gold, "A Walk on San Francisco's Gay Side," *New York Times*, "Sunday Punch," November 6, 1977.

25. Draft letter, Harvey Milk to editor of the *New York Times*, "Sunday Punch," in Harvey Milk Archives–Scott Smith Collection (GLC 35), box 5, folder 2, San Francisco Public Library.

26. Robert McEwan (AP), "San Francisco's First Gay Supervisor Sees Self as Symbol," *San Diego Union*, November 18, 1977.

27. Ibid.

28. San Francisco Building and Construction Trades Council newsletter, December 20, 1977, Harvey Milk Archives–Scott Smith Collection (GLC 35), box 5, folder 2, San Francisco Public Library.

29. Anne Kronenberg quoted in *Milk: A Pictorial History of Harvey Milk*, ed. Dustin Lance Black (New York: Newmarket Press, 2009), 80.

30. Anne Kronenberg, interview with author.

31. Harry Britt, "Harvey Milk as I Knew Him," in *Out in the Castro*, 80.

32. Anne Kronenberg, interview with author.

33. Note card: Jim Foster to Harvey Milk, Harvey Milk Archives–Scott Smith Collection (GLC 35), box 5, folder 6, San Francisco Public Library.

34. Mike Wong, "Harvey," November 1980, in Randy Shilts Papers (GLC 43), box 29, San Francisco Public Library.

35. Les Ledbetter, "San Francisco Legislators Meet in Diversity," *New York Times*, January 12, 1977; and Narda Zacchino, "Gay Community Mourns for Man They Called Leader," *Los Angeles Times*, November 28, 1978.

36. Nicole Murray Ramirez (Imperial Court Empress), interview with author.

37. Francis J. Moriarty, "Good Night, Sweet Prince," *Berkeley Barb*, December 7–20, 1978; Nikos Diaman, San Francisco, interview with author, March 23, 2016; and Randy Shilts, "The Life and Death of Harvey Milk," *Christopher Street*, March 1979. Goodstein denied to the editor in chief of *Christopher Street* that he had made the comment Shilts attributed to him in the article: Letter from David Goodstein to Chuck Ortleb, March 14, 1979, in Randy Shilts Papers (GLC 43), box 29, San Francisco Public Library.

38. Quoted in Randy Shilts, *The Mayor of Castro Street: The Life and Times of Harvey Milk* (New York: St. Martin's, 1982), 372.

Chapter 10. Supervisor Milk

1. Letter from Robert Milk to Harvey Milk, January 4, 1978, Harvey Milk Archives–Scott Smith Collection (GLC 35), box 5, folder 6, San Francisco Public Library.

2. Harvey Milk, invitation to Tom O'Horgan and Galen McKinley, Tom O'Horgan Collection, Howard Gotlieb Archival Research Center, Boston University.

3. John Bryan, "S.F. Supervisor Harvey Milk: 'You Can Throw Bricks at City Hall or You Can Take It Over,'" *Berkeley Barb*, January 27, 1978.

4. Ibid.

5. Melissa Griffin, "Hold It: Harvey Milk Was an Occasional SFO Foe," *San Francisco Examiner*, January 16, 2013.

6. Letter from Bill Sunday to Harvey Milk, November 11, 1977, Harvey Milk Archives–Scott Smith Collection (GLC 35), box 5, folder 11, San Francisco Public Library.

7. Letter from Ken Wolff to Harvey Milk, November 11,

1977, Harvey Milk Archives–Scott Smith Collection (GLC 35), box 5, folder 6, San Francisco Public Library.

8. Letter from Sam B. Puckett to Harvey Milk, May 13, 1978, Harvey Milk Archives–Scott Smith Collection (GLC 35), box 5, folder 17, San Francisco Public Library.

9. Anne Kronenberg, San Francisco, interview with author, April 29, 2016.

10. Cleve Jones, San Francisco, interview #2 with author, April 11, 2017.

11. Many of Harvey's supervisorial activities are detailed in the appendix of Vince Emery, *The Harvey Milk Interviews: In His Own Words* (San Francisco: Vince Emery Productions, 2012).

12. Letter from Lillian Guiliane to Harvey Milk, November 12, 1977, Harvey Milk Archives–Scott Smith Collection (GLC 35), box 5, folder 2, San Francisco Public Library.

13. Quoted in Srdja Popovic and Matthew Miller, "Harvey Milk's First Crusade: Dog Poop," *Politico*, February 5, 2015.

14. Quoted in John Cloud, "The Pioneer Harvey Milk," *Time* magazine, June 14, 1999.

15. Dan Nicoletta, Grants Pass, Oregon, interview with author, April 15, 2016; and Ira Kamin, "Letting Their Clowns Out," *California Living Magazine*, in *San Francisco Examiner*, August 20, 1978.

16. Debra Jones, Sacramento, interview with author, February 13, 2016.

17. Dan White campaign pamphlet, in Mike Weiss, Double Play Collection (SFH 34), box 1, folder 34, San Francisco Public Library.

18. Carol Ruth Silver, San Francisco, interview with author, May 5, 2016.

19. Ibid.

20. Quoted in Randy Alfred, "Harvey Milk: We Didn't Need a Martyr," *Berkeley Barb*, December 7, 1978.

21. Bryan, "S.F. Supervisor Harvey Milk."

22. Film documentary, *The Times of Harvey Milk*, produced and directed by Richard Schmiechen and Rob Epstein, 1984.

23. Martin Torgoff, *Can't Find My Way Home: America in the Great Stoned Age, 1945–2000* (New York: Simon and Schuster, 2004), 300.

24. Marc Cohen, New York, interview with author, September 4, 2016.

25. Francis J. Moriarty, "Queen for a Day," *Berkeley Barb*, November 9–22, 1978.

26. Dan Nicoletta in video, *Harvey Milk: A Personal View*, introduced by Jim van Buskirk, James C. Hormel Gay and Lesbian Center, San Francisco, 1999.

27. Mike Wong, "Harvey," November 1980, in Randy Shilts Papers (GLC 43), box 29, San Francisco Public Library.

28. *Milk: A Pictorial History of Harvey Milk*, ed. Dustin Lance Black (New York: Newmarket Press, 2009), 88.

29. Letter, Art Agnos to Harvey Milk, January 4, 1978, Harvey Milk Archives–Scott Smith Collection (GLC 35), box 5, folder 11, San Francisco Public Library.

30. Anne Kronenberg, interview with author; and Wayne Friday, "The Harvey Milk I Knew," December 7, 1978, Harvey Milk Archives–Scott Smith Collection (GLC 35), box 27, folder 3, San Francisco Public Library.

Chapter 11. Leading

1. Quoted above at p. 155–56.

2. The speech was printed in Harvey Milk, "Milk Forum," *Bay Area Reporter*, June 25, 1978.

3. Harvey Milk, "Castro Street—Home," n.d., Harvey Milk Archives–Scott Smith Collection (GLC 35), box 9, folder 55, San Francisco Public Library.

4. Harvey Milk, *Coast to Coast Times*, June 13, 1978, in Harvey Milk Archives–Scott Smith Collection (GLC 35), box 9, folder 55, San Francisco Public Library.

5. Don Sizemore (Briggs's aide and spokesperson for Proposition 6), Sacramento, email correspondence and interview with author, October 19, 2015, and January 5, 2016.

6. Associated Press, "Homosexual Issue on Ballot Signifies

Change in Times," and petition appeal circular: in Save Our Teachers collection (918), Lambda Archives, San Diego; Robert Scheer, "A Times Interview with Senator John Briggs on Homosexuality," *Los Angeles Times*, October 6, 1978; and Peter Calamai, "After Tax Revolts, Morality by Referendum?" *Medicine Hat News* (Alberta, Canada), November 6, 1978.

7. Save Our Teachers collection (918), Lambda Archives, San Diego.

8. Michael D. Lopez, "Evangelist Helps Raise a Hope, a Prayer, and Money for Prop. 6," *San Diego Union*, clipping in Save Our Teachers collection (918), Lambda Archives, San Diego.

9. Harry Britt, "New Group to Fight Briggs," *Gay Vote: News from the San Francisco Gay Democratic Club*, June–July 1978.

10. Sipple had been Joe Campbell's lover after Campbell left Harvey in 1962. Though closeted to his family he'd also been an activist in the San Francisco gay community: see Herb Caen, "In This Corner," *San Francisco Chronicle*, September 24, 1975; and Daryl Lembke, "Hero in Ford Shooting Active Among San Francisco Gays," *Los Angeles Times*, September 25, 1975.

11. Harvey Milk, Gay Freedom Day Speech, reprinted in "Milk Forum," *Bay Area Reporter*, June 25, 1978.

12. David Goodstein, "Opening Space," *Advocate*, June 14, 1978.

13. Randy Shilts, *The Mayor of Castro Street: The Life and Times of Harvey Milk* (New York: St. Martin's, 1982), 222.

14. Paula Lichtenberg, San Francisco, interview with author, February 24, 2016; Gwenn Craig, San Francisco, interview with author, February 26, 2016; John Durham, San Francisco, interview with author, May 7, 2016; and Elaine Herscher, "Witch-Hunt: Everybody's a Suspect," *Mother Jones*, November 1978.

15. Gwenn Craig, interview with author; and Gwenn Craig, interview with Randy Shilts, Randy Shilts Papers (GLC 43), box 29, San Francisco Public Library.

16. John Durham and Nancy Elnor, "NO ON 6 Campaign: A History and Report," June 26, 1979. I am grateful to John Durham for sharing this report with me.

17. Mervin D. Field Survey, "The California Poll," release #990, October 5, 1978.

18. Juana Samayoa, *News Talk*, KBHK-TV, September 26, 1978 (available on YouTube).

19. "John Briggs, The Loner on the Far Right," *San Francisco Examiner*, February 27, 1978; and Larry Liebert, "The Longshot Who Would Be Governor," *San Francisco Chronicle*, June 18, 1977.

20. I'm grateful to Don Sizemore for giving me insights into the senator: Don Sizemore, Sacramento, email correspondence and interview with author, October 19, 2015, and January 5, 2016.

21. Harvey Milk, Notes for Temple Sinai speech, Harvey Milk Archives–Scott Smith Collection (GLC 35), box 9, folder 51, San Francisco Public Library.

22. Correspondence from The Lost Tribe to Harvey Milk, October 23, 1978, Harvey Milk Archives–Scott Smith Collection (GLC 35), box 9, folder 51, San Francisco Public Library.

23. Harvey Milk, "Gay Rights," *Coast to Coast Times*, June 16, 1978.

24. Symposium at Hastings College of Law, September 22, 1978, Harvey Milk Archives–Scott Smith Collection (GLC 35), box 9, folder 51, San Francisco Public Library.

25. John Durham, interview with author.

26. Ibid.

27. Gwenn Craig, interview with author.

28. Lenny Giteck, "An Interview with Harvey Milk," *San Francisco Examiner*, November 29, 1978. The interview had been conducted several weeks before his death.

29. Anne Kronenberg, San Francisco, interview with author, April 29, 2016.

30. Cleve Jones, interview #1 with author, April 12, 2013.

31. Sally Gearhart, Willits, California, interview with author, January 27 and 28, 2013.

32. Quoted in Raul Ramirez, "Verbal, Physical Scuffling Mark Debate on Prop 6," *San Francisco Examiner*, October 12, 1978.

33. Don Sizemore, interview with author.

34. Ibid.

35. Ibid.

36. Raul Ramirez, "Polk Street's Odd Couple," *San Francisco Examiner*, October 1, 1978; and Don Sizemore, interview with author. In his book *The Mayor of Castro Street* (248–49) Randy Shilts's version of Briggs's "solemnity" during his visit to the Polk Street revelries is quite different from the depiction Sizemore presented to me and the *San Francisco Examiner* picture seems to corroborate.

37. Don Sizemore, interview with author.

38. Rachel West, "Prop 6 Dangerous, Reagan Believes," *Los Angeles Times*, September 23, 1978; and Mervin D. Field, "A Major Shift to 'No' on Prop. 6," *San Francisco Chronicle*, October 5, 1978.

39. Gwenn Craig, interview with author; and Gwenn Craig, interview with Randy Shilts.

Chapter 12. Dark Clouds Gathering

1. Brooks Brothers charge account application, Harvey Milk Archives–Scott Smith Collection (GLC 35), box 2, folder 23, San Francisco Public Library.

2. Schedule C, Form 1040, "Profit or (Loss) from Business or Profession," 1977, Harvey Milk Archives–Scott Smith Collection (GLC 35), box 2, folder 27, San Francisco Public Library.

3. Corey Michael, "A Last Interview with Our Supervisor" (conducted November 12, 1978), *Noe Valley Voice*, December 1978.

4. Tom Randol, interview with Randy Shilts, November 2, 1980, Randy Shilts Papers (GLC 43), box 29, San Francisco Public Library; and Anne Kronenberg, San Francisco, interview with author, April 29, 2016.

5. Bea Pixa, "Harvey Milk: A Wider Constituency," *San Francisco Examiner*, March 11, 1979; Scott Smith, interview with Mike Weiss, June 10, 1980, Double Play Collection (SFH 34), box 1, folder 66, San Francisco Public Library; and Dan Nicoletta, interview with Michael Flanagan, podcast (on YouTube), February 15, 2009.

6. Hate mail in box 6, folder 6, Harvey Milk Archives–Scott Smith Collection (GLC 35), San Francisco Public Library; and Anne Kronenberg, interview with author.

7. Quoted in Jesse Hamlin, "Quotes from Harvey Milk and

Friends," *San Francisco Chronicle*, November 23, 2008; and Wayne Friday, "The Harvey Milk I Knew," clipping, Harvey Milk Archives–Scott Smith Collection (GLC 35), box 27, folder 3, San Francisco Public Library.

8. Anne Kronenberg, interview with author.

9. Glenn McElhinney, Palo Alto, interview with author, February 23, 2016; and Celeste Newbrough, Berkeley, interview with author, February 27, 2016.

10. Harvey Milk, "Keynote Speech at Gay Conference 5," report in *An Archive of Hope: Harvey Milk's Speeches and Writings*, ed. Jason Edward Black and Charles E. Morris III (Berkeley: University of California Press, 2013), 203.

11. Bob Lynn (founder of the San Diego Democratic Club), San Diego, interview with author, January 12, 2016.

12. FBI Report, "Allegations of Political Corruption, City and Country of San Francisco," September 26, 1978, file #SF 183-432-1, in Randy Shilts Papers (GLC 43), box 29, folder 4, San Francisco Public Library.

13. Cartoon: Seegull, "San Francisco Seen," October 20, 1978. I am grateful to Glenn McElhinney for sharing a copy of this cartoon with me.

14. FBI report; Walter Caplan, San Francisco, interview with author, May 19, 2016; and Matthew S. Bajko, "FBI Releases New Files on Milk, Moscone, and White," *Bay Area Reporter*, August 11, 2011.

15. Dan Nicoletta, Grants Pass, Oregon, interview with author, April 15, 2016; Anne Kronenberg, interview with author; Chris Perry, interview with Randy Shilts, and Danny Nicoletta, interview with Randy Shilts (October 5, 1980), Randy Shilts Papers (GLC 43), box 29, San Francisco Public Library.

16. Milk's supervisorial activities: *The Harvey Milk Interviews: In His Own Words*, ed. Vince Emery (San Francisco: Vince Emery Productions, 2012), 335–36.

17. Anne Kronenberg, interview with author.

18. Bradley Campbell, "Harvey Milk and the Boy from Minnesota," *City Paper* (Minneapolis), January 14, 2009.

19. Emery, *The Harvey Milk Interviews*, 19.

20. Anne Kronenberg, interview with author; Wayne Friday, interview with Randy Shilts, August 13, 1980, Randy Shilts Papers (GLC 43), box 29, San Francisco Public Library; and Randy Shilts, *The Mayor of Castro Street: The Life and Times of Harvey Milk* (New York: St. Martin's, 1982), 233.

21. Nikos Diaman (Toad Hall patron on August 28, 1978), San Francisco, interview with author, March 23, 2016.

22. Letter from Patricia [Didi] de la Cruz to Harvey Milk, September 25, 1978, Harvey Milk Archives–Scott Smith Collection (GLC 35), box 1, folder 25, San Francisco Public Library.

23. Michael Salem (Harvey Milk's cousin), New York, interview with author, April 4, 2016; and Sherrie Feinberg, email correspondence with author, May 21, 2016.

24. Invitation and RSVP note, Harvey Milk Archives–Scott Smith Collection (GLC 35), box 6, folder 2, San Francisco Public Library.

25. Ron Lezell, San Francisco, interview with author, March 17, 2016; and Rabbi Allen Bennett, eulogy at Temple Emanu-El, in "A Community Mourns in Wake of Slayings," *San Francisco Jewish Bulletin*, December 1, 1978.

26. Condolence letters to Harvey Milk from Jonestown residents in Harvey Milk Archives–Scott Smith Collection (GLC 35), box 1, folder 36, San Francisco Public Library.

27. Documentary: "Jonestown: The Life and Death of the Peoples Temple," *The American Experience*, PBS, 2006.

28. Michael Kilduff and Phil Tracy, "Inside the Peoples Temple," *New West Magazine*, August 1, 1977.

29. Harvey Milk letter to Jim Jones, August 1, 1977, Peoples Temple Records, MS 3800, box 1, folder 21, California Historical Society.

30. Assemblyman Willie Brown letter to Honorable Prime Minister Forbes Burnham, Guyana, November 22, 1977, Peoples Temple Records, MS 3800, box 1, folder 23, California Historical Society.

31. Supervisor-Elect Harvey Milk letter to Joseph Califano,

NOTES TO PAGES 201–11

Secretary of Health, Education, and Welfare, December 20, 1977, Peoples Temple Records, MS 3800, box 1, folder 21, California Historical Society.

32. "Jonestown: The Life and Death of the Peoples Temple."

Chapter 13. "If a bullet should enter my brain . . ."

1. Doug Franks, interview with Randy Shilts, January 23, 1981, Randy Shilts Papers (GLC 43), box 29, San Francisco Public Library.

2. Ibid.

3. Armistead Maupin, "Harvey Milk's Last Love," *Towleroad*, February 20, 2009; and Steve Beery, "Harvey Milk's Last Month, and Last Boyfriend" (c. 1993?), report, *Mr X*, November 26, 2008.

4. Art Bierman, interview with Mike Weiss, April 16, 1982, in Double Play Collection (SFH 34), box 1, folder 4, San Francisco Public Library; and Quentin Kopp, interview with Mike Weiss, February 25, 1982, box 1, folder 42, ibid.

5. Lee Dolson, interview with Mike Weiss, May 4, 1982, box 1, folder 18, ibid.

6. Ray Brown (Board of Realtors), interview with Mike Weiss, May 17, 1982, box 1, folder 10, ibid.

7. Harvey Milk form letter to "Dear Friend," May 3, 1978, Randy Shilts Papers (GLC 43), box 29, San Francisco Public Library.

8. Duffy Jennings, "Several Jurors Weep in Court," *San Francisco Chronicle*, May 22, 1979.

9. Chris Perry, interview with Randy Shilts, Randy Shilts Papers (GLC 43), box 29, San Francisco Public Library; Wayne Friday, "Politics and People: Looking at an Alleged Killer," *Bay Area Reporter*, December 21, 1978; Helen Fama, *While I Still Have All My Marbles: Memoir of a Women's Advocate* (San Francisco: Fama, 2012); and Doug Franks, interview with Randy Shilts.

10. Les Ledbetter, "Bill on Homosexual Rights Advances in San Francisco," *New York Times*, May 22, 1978.

11. Richard Rapaport, "Jonestown and City Hall Slayings Eerily Linked in Time and Memory," *San Francisco Chronicle*, November 16, 2013.

12. Debra Jones, Sacramento, interview with author, February 13, 2016.

13. Letter, Harvey Milk to Tom O'Horgan, November 25, 1978, Howard Gotlieb Archival Research Center, Boston University.

14. Recollection of Robert Milk, in Randy Shilts, "The Life and Death of Harvey Milk," *Christopher Street*, March 1979, 25–43.

15. Transcript of testimony of Cyr Copertini, report in Kenneth W. Slater, *The Trial of Dan White* (El Cerrito, Calif.: Market and Systems Interface, 1991).

16. Cleve Jones, San Francisco, interview #2 with author, April 11, 2016.

17. Duffy Jennings, "The Trial of Dan White," *San Francisco Chronicle*, November 29, 1978; and Vince Emery, email correspondence with author, August 16, 2017.

18. Transcript of testimony of Cyr Copertini; and Corey Busch, interview with Mike Weiss, in Double Play Collection (SFH 34), January 6, 1982, box 1, folder 13, San Francisco Public Library.

19. Cleve Jones, San Francisco, interview #1 with author, April 12, 2013; and Cleve Jones, *When We Rise: My Life in the Movement* (New York: Hachette, 2016).

Chapter 14. Aftermath

1. Carol Ruth Silver, San Francisco, interview with author, May 5, 2016; and "Dan White's Last Confession" (from a taped 1985 interview), in *San Jose Mercury News*, September 18, 1998. White claimed in this taped interview that he was also gunning for Willie Brown, who was "the mastermind of the whole thing," but Brown says in his autobiography that White had seen him that morning as he was leaving Moscone's office and White was on his way in: Willie L. Brown Jr., *Basic Brown: My Life and Our Times* (New York: Simon and Schuster, 2008), 130.

2. Trial Testimony of Inspector Frank J. Falzon, in Kenneth Slater, *The Trial of Dan White* (El Cerrito, Calif.: Market and Systems Interface, 1991).

3. Dan White's taped confession: *Double Play Companion DVD*,

in Mike Weiss, *Double Play: The Hidden Passions Behind the Double Assassination of George Moscone and Harvey Milk*, rev. ed. (San Francisco: Vince Emery Productions, 2010).

4. Cleve Jones, San Francisco, interviews with author, April 12, 2013, and April 11, 2017.

5. Randy Alfred, San Francisco, interview #2 with author, May 16, 2017.

6. "Eyewitness News," San Francisco channel 5, November 28, 1978, CBS5.com.

7. Gwenn Craig, San Francisco, interview with author, February 26, 2016.

8. Debra Jones, Sacramento, interview with author, February 13, 2016.

9. Tom Ammiano, interview in *The Times of Harvey Milk*, film documentary produced and directed by Richard Schmiechen and Rob Epstein, 1984.

10. The line "We are a gay and lesbian people" was later changed to "We are gay and straight together."

11. Walter Caplan, San Francisco, interview with author, May 19, 2016.

12. Daniel Chesir, San Francisco, interview with author, March 19, 2016.

13. Ron Lezell, San Francisco, interview with author, March 17, 2016; and Rob Tat, San Francisco, interview with author, March 19, 2016.

14. Rabbi Allen Bennett, San Francisco, interview with author, March 22, 2016; and "A Community Mourns in Wake of Slayings," *San Francisco Jewish Bulletin*, December 1, 1978.

15. Will of Harvey Bernard Milk, clause 6, March 23, 1976, Probate Department, County of San Francisco, Superior Court of California.

16. Tom Randol, interview with Randy Shilts, November 2, 1980, Randy Shilts Papers (GLC 43), box 29, San Francisco Public Library.

17. Dan Nicoletta, Grants Pass, Oregon, interview with author, April 15, 2016; Marc Cohen, New York, interview with author, Sep-

tember 4, 2016; and Dan Nicoletta, "Harvey Milk and the Castro of the 70s," eastvillageboys.com, January 21, 2009.

18. David Talbot, *Season of the Witch: Enchantment, Terror, and Deliverance in the City of Love* (New York: Free Press, 2012), 343; and Cleve Jones, *When We Rise: My Life in the Movement* (New York: Hachette, 2016), 163.

19. I discuss jury selection, the prosecution, and the defense at greater length in my book *The Gay Revolution: The Story of the Struggle* (New York: Simon and Schuster, 2015), 405–7.

20. Daniel White's taped confession, November 27, 1978, 12:05, "People's Exhibit 54 in the trial of Daniel White." The most extensive discussion of Dan White and the double murder is in Weiss, *Double Play.*

21. "The Shocked Jurors Defend Their Verdict," *San Francisco Chronicle*, May 23, 1979.

22. Cleve Jones, interview #1 with author, April 12, 2013; Sally Gearhart, interview with author, Willits, California, January 28, 2013; Richard Saltus and Peter H. King, "Gay Plea: We Must Keep Cool Tonight," *San Francisco Examiner*, May 22, 1979; Katy Butler, "A Bloody Protest at City Hall," *San Francisco Chronicle*, May 22, 1979; Mike McWhinney, "Violence Erupts from White Jury Decision," *San Francisco Progress;* Katy Butler, "Anatomy of Gay Riot," *San Francisco Chronicle*, May 23, 1979; and Warren Hinckle, "How Cops Waded into Castro Street," *San Francisco Chronicle*, May 23, 1979.

23. "Britt's 'Gay Anger' at Dan White's Verdict," *San Francisco Examiner*, May 22, 1979.

Epilogue: Harvey Milk's Legacy

1. Susan Stryker, Saint Harvey exhibit curator, GLBT History Museum, San Francisco, interview with author, May 3, 2016.

2. Quoted in Randy Shilts, *The Mayor of Castro Street: The Life and Times of Harvey Milk* (New York: St. Martin's, 1982), 281.

3. Andrew J. Epstein, "Richard Kirk Schmiechen, Queer Filmmaker," *Artdaddy*, June 3, 2008.

4. Scott Anderson, "A City Grieves Good Men Slain," *Advocate*, January 11, 1979.

5. Anne Kronenberg, San Francisco, interview with author, April 29, 2016; and Anderson, "A City Grieves Good Men Slain."

6. Joyce Hunter, New York, interview with author, March 11, 2013.

7. "SF Board Goes International," *SF Progress*, May 3, 1978.

8. Patrick Buchanan, "Nature Exacts Retribution" (syndicated column), *Roswell (N.M.) Daily Record*, May 24, 1983, 4.

INDEX